LIFE IS
SHORT and
SO AM I

LIFE IS SHORT and SO AM I

My Life Inside, Outside, and Under the Wrestling Ring

Dylan "Hornswoggle" Postl

WITH ROSS OWEN WILLIAMS AND IAN DOUGLASS

Editor for the press: Michael Holmes
Cover design: David A. Gee
Cover photos: © Jill McKee
Back cover photo: © WWE
All photos, unless otherwise noted, are from Dylan Postl's private collection.

To the best of his abilities, the author has related experiences, places, people, and organizations from his memories of them. In order to protect the privacy of others, he has, in some instances, changed the names of certain people and details of events and places.

LIBRARY AND ARCHIVES CANADA CATALOGUING IN PUBLICATION

Title: Life is short and so am I : my life inside, outside, and under the wresting ring / Dylan Postl with Ross Owen Williams and Ian Douglass.

Other titles: Life is short and so am I .

Names: Postl, Dylan, 1986– author. | Williams, Ross, author. | Douglass, Ian, 1979– author.

Identifiers: Canadiana (print) 20190124733
Canadiana (ebook) 20190124741

ISBN 9781770414846 (softcover)
ISBN 9781773054049 (PDF)
ISBN 9781773054032 (ePUB)

Subjects: LCSH: Postl, Dylan, 1986– | LCSH: Wrestlers—United States—Biography. | LCGFT: Autobiographies.

Classification: LCC GV1186.P68 A3 2019
DDC 796.812092—DC23

PRINTED AND BOUND IN CANADA

PRINTING: FRIESENS   5 4 3 2 1

CONTENTS

FOREWORD

BY KOFI KINGSTON

Let me preface this by saying that Dylan has agreed not to read this foreword until his book publishes. I don't know why anyone would actually request that I do this to them. Dylan . . . *you fool.*

Now clearly, many of you reading this are wrestling fans. That means that you know the author of this book as "Hornswoggle" — a man of seemingly endless gimmicks. What you may not know is that this is an art-imitating-life situation, because in real life, actual Dylan Postl has endless aliases. Allow me to elaborate by highlighting three of many.

Alias 1: "Doo-Doo" Dylan

This title was initially earned when Dylan and I were on a drive from New Orleans to Baton Rouge. Twelve minutes into the ride, he started to flip out, demanding that I pull over and find a bathroom because his stomach was "tore up."

When he finally returned to the car, he had a glazed-over look in his eyes. When I asked if everything was okay, he just stared forward in silence for what seemed like forever. Finally, voice quivering, he said that the bathroom resembled a murder scene, but instead of blood . . . it was poop.

On the floors.

On the walls.

On the ceiling.

Everywhere.

I could see from the tears welling up in his eyes that he was neither lying nor exaggerating. Looking closer, I noticed that he was half smiling. Not because he was joking, but because he was kind of proud! A true savage. But he did at least manage to avoid getting any poop on his clothes before getting into the car, so as far as I was concerned, we were cool. We drove on.

He then proceeded to inform me that he "gifts" himself the option of three self-poops a year. I take him at his word because . . . I mean, I don't want to be responsible for keeping the tally. The honor system will just have to do.

Alias 2: Big Nick from New Joisey ("Joisey" said with the accent of a squeaky-voiced 1930s gangster from *Boardwalk Empire*)

I won't go into too much detail about this one because it will be talked about later in this book, but I will say that this could be the single worst, half-hearted, quarter-assed, and consequently comical attempt at an accent in human history. The "Big Nick" moniker is all that remains of the greatest character to *never* happen.

Alias 3: The Soda Free-Loada

Curt Hawkins, Swoggle, and I traveled together often (known

amongst ourselves as "Team Two and a Half Men"). One day, we inevitably decided to stop for food, but Swoggle had just eaten and didn't want anything. Hawkins and I proceeded to order while Swoggle repeatedly insisted he wasn't hungry and didn't want to order "a diddle-damn thing" (direct quote). But he finally broke down and ordered a cola.

When the bill came, the waitress gave Swoggle a check for somewhere around $1.37. His eyes got wide as anger and pure, utter disgust built steadily upon his face. His eyebrows furrowed and his bottom lip started to fold downward toward the floor. Steam actually started to rise from his scalp. (The waitress was completely oblivious to all of this, by the way.)

Dylan then started to shake his head, left to right, slowly at first, but quickly building to a closed-eyed, rapid, and aggressive full-body Eric Cartman–esque shudder, culminating in a high-pitched shriek to the gods, causing the entire restaurant to stare with legitimate concern. The tantrum finished with him violently shoving the tab across the table to me and Hawkins before he stormed out and back to the car.

Later, we came to find out that in his hometown of Applebee, Wisconsin, it is known as FACT (and in some areas, as law) that he is NEVER to EVER actually PAY for soda, under ANY circumstances. Even though we were nowhere near his hometown, Dylan couldn't believe this rule was not intergalactic common knowledge.

It's important to note that in his everyday persona, Dylan is not at all an entitled person. Actually, quite the opposite, which is what makes the tale of the Soda Free-Loada that much funnier . . . it's also important to note that I may or may not have enhanced some or all of the details for the sake of a more humorous scenario. Either way, this is how we choose to remember this story.

There are so many more stories like these that I just do not have the time for in this foreword, but Dylan and I traveled together for years, and tales like these were commonplace. As time went on, each weekend, they became fully expected.

I am seven and eight years older than my siblings. I always think about how jealous I am of the bond my little brother and sister had because, being a year apart, they did everything together. They grew up together. They went to school together. They hung out and partied together. I never had that special kind of bonding experience with a sibling . . . until I met Dylan.

My friendship with Dylan filled that void. I consider him wholeheartedly as my brother. The Krillin to my Goku, he is one of the only people that I can actually tolerate sharing a hotel room with on the road. He was (and still is!) my *Royal Rumble* moment consultant. He's one of the few people I looked to for advice and experience as I was preparing for fatherhood.

Most importantly, and this is easily my absolute favorite of Dylan's qualities, he's always been completely honest. This book certainly reflects that to the fullest, as it is an unapologetically honest account of his life story. Interestingly enough, for all the years that we traveled together and got to know each other, I don't think we ever discussed the intimate details of his journey. I thoroughly enjoyed reading about them. His story is compelling, emotional, and very entertaining. I know you all will love and appreciate it as much as I did.

— KOFI SARKODIE-MENSAH, AKA KOFI KINGSTON

FOREWORD

BY CURT HAWKINS

As I'm sitting down to write this, I can't help but laugh to myself.

Dylan Postl and I have next to nothing in common. He's a vertically challenged fellow from small-town Wisconsin and I'm a 6'1" fast-talking New Yorker. We grew up in completely different worlds. Our friendship makes absolutely no sense on paper. But our common bond is what brought us together; we both have an almost disturbing level of love for professional wrestling.

Professional wrestling is a form of entertainment unlike any other on this planet, something that I saw for the first time as a very small child and became completely fascinated by. And Dylan did too. (I can't believe they had cable in Oshkosh in the nineties.) We became friends almost immediately. Together we got to do what we love for a living and travel the world. Riding up and down the roads of America, telling stories, making memories, and always completely busting each other's balls. There's an old saying in pro wrestling that you do most of your integral learning in "bars & the cars." I've found this to be true, but through my experiences it's also where the most invaluable friendships are forged as well.

Dylan and I have always been very honest with each other. I know he's always going to tell me what he thinks whether it's something I want to hear or not. That aspect of our relationship is something that I'll always cherish. I'm so proud of Dylan. This guy has never had it easy, but he never made excuses for himself, either. He just continued to defy the odds. Dylan (although it pains me to say it) is an incredible performer inside of a professional wrestling ring. But, that's not the best version of Dylan. The best version of Dylan can be seen when he's home with his son Landon, being a father. Dylan is an absolute mega dad. He's done all he can to build the best life for his son and that's an inspiration.

Dylan, I love ya, pal.

— BRIAN MYERS, AKA CURT HAWKINS

MAY 23RD, 2006

The Rabobank Arena, Bakersfield, California
"My name is Finlay . . . and I love to fight."

The voice of Dave "Fit" Finlay boomed over the sound system, followed by his intimidating Celtic-themed entrance music. Of the several thousand people in the arena who heard it, I was the only one who couldn't see the barrel-chested, gap-toothed, fighting Irishman approaching the ring.

Finlay climbed through the ropes and stomped across the mat, each footstep reverberating beneath the ring, where I sat alone, dressed as a leprechaun, in the darkness that I've been afraid of as far back as I can remember.

This was to be my debut with World Wrestling Entertainment, a company I'd dreamed about being part of since before I learned to walk. To say I was nervous would be an understatement. As Finlay's opponent, Paul Burchill, made his way to the ring, I tried to distract myself from my nerves by reflecting on everything that had led me to this moment. I thought of the multiple surgeries I had to endure as a kid, and how I'd play RBI *Baseball* on my old NES while trapped in a full body cast at the hospital. I thought of the house fire that destroyed my childhood home, and the yellow rubber ducky sitting on the bathtub that somehow survived the blaze. I thought of my brother and my mom, who both left my life so early, and of my grandpa, who believed in me when no one else did. Most of all, I thought of my dad and how I wanted to show him that the son he raised was going to amount to something.

As the match began above me, the butterflies in my stomach turned into elephants. My heart was pounding in my chest. What if I messed up? What if it went the same way as when we'd first rehearsed the spot earlier in the day — when the first impression I'd made on the most powerful man in the wrestling industry wasn't good at all? Everything I'd worked for all came down to what I did in the sixty seconds after that green light came on. If I blew it, my run in the big leagues would be as short as me.

I kept myself focused on the task at hand. It was simple. I just had to crawl out from under the ring, give WWE owner Vince McMahon the "Tasmanian Devil" he wanted, and everything would be fine. Then there would hopefully be a second week, and further weeks beyond that. Who knew how long it would last?

Sitting in the dark under that ring in Bakersfield, I had no idea that it was the first of what would end up being more than 500 weeks with the company. I couldn't know I'd visit volcanoes in Ecuador and get chased by roosters in Guadalajara. I couldn't know I'd appear in feature films and meet my childhood heroes. And I certainly couldn't know I'd surprise everyone with exciting matches at big WWE events or that I'd climb a ladder in the middle of the ring at Ford Field, looking around at 80,000 screaming fans and thinking, "How did a midget from Oshkosh, Wisconsin, make it to *WrestleMania*?"

I heard the referee's hand strike the mat three times. The bell rang and Finlay's music started up again. This was it.

The green light came on. The ring apron was lifted up.

I took a deep breath, then scurried out from the darkness and into the spotlight.

CHAPTER I

THE COFFEE TABLE

I'm fine with the word midget. A lot of little people consider that term insulting, and some get really worked up when they hear it. Others steer clear of it for fear of causing offense, like the time wrestling commentator Michael Cole accidentally used it and Vince McMahon went off on him, yelling, "You can never say that — ever! It's so demeaning."

When there's a need to make reference to my diminutive stature, most regular-sized people get stuck. As the moment approaches, they'll start to look like a deer in the headlights. Some people will say midget and then backtrack, tie themselves up in knots, and stumble over their words. Others will use "people like you," which I don't mind. I far prefer that to option three, where they'll pause, look awkward, and eventually go with "I don't really know how to say it . . ." The level of panic it can create can be quite hilarious. Usually though, I won't let it get that far — I'll jump in and say, "Midget is fine" and they'll breathe a sigh of relief.

Honestly, I've never once had a problem with the word. I always say the word midget makes me money. You used to see "midget wrestling" all the time on posters for shows, and it would help draw a crowd. I never feel like I'm being ridiculed or marginalized by the word and, as you'll see in this book, I use it liberally myself. It's just a word and it can only be offensive if the person using it means it as an insult — and even then, it's not the word that offends, it's the attitude.

Some people only see a little person when they look at me. Others see me for who I am. Being small is *part* of who I am, but only part. I don't consider it my defining characteristic and never have. I can't change it, so it's not worth getting upset about.

My parents learned I was going to be undersized midway through the pregnancy. The news came as a shock — there was no history of dwarfism on either side of the family. My mom already had two children from a previous marriage and they were both normal-sized. Dad was thirty-four and Mom was twenty-six — neither could be considered an older parent with a higher risk of having a baby with complications. The delivery itself was as straightforward as childbirth ever is and, in Oshkosh, Wisconsin, on May 29, 1986, I was born Dylan Mark Postl, with my middle name being chosen for my dad's brother, who had died of cardiomyopathy when he was eighteen.

There are different kinds of dwarfism. I have achondroplasia, which is the most common and presents the fewest health issues. I have a normal-sized torso with an oversized skull and short, bowed arms and legs. My condition is far more noticeable when I'm standing up but, when I'm sitting, I'm about the same height as a normal person. Because of the size of my head and arms, you'd still notice I was different but it's not as obvious when I'm off my feet.

In the first few years of my life, there was no difference between me and other kids in terms of many developmental milestones, such as starting to speak, but it did take me longer to learn how to walk because I was top heavy and born with scoliosis — a curvature of the spine, which is common in little people. When I was six, I underwent corrective surgery for that. What was supposed to be a relatively straightforward procedure didn't go to plan because the surgeon had never operated on a little person before. He had assumed my insides would be the same as a normal-sized person but, once he'd opened me up, he found everything was "completely different in there." He attempted to put a rod in my back to straighten my spine but it didn't work and, worse still, pinched a nerve, which paralyzed me from the waist down. Fortunately, shortly after the surgery I regained full use of my lower half, but that had to have been terrifying for my parents. I still have some complications from this though. My feet always feel like they are different temperatures; my right foot is always much colder than my left. There will also be three or four times each year when I'll have a day or two where it'll feel like I'm constantly being electrocuted in my feet. It's not much fun but things could have been a lot worse.

Although I was only partially paralyzed for a short time, I was still bedridden for a couple of months, confined to a full-body cast that went from under my armpits to just above my groin. Even when I was released from the hospital, the cast came with me and I had to wear it until it was time for the surgeons to try again.

I don't remember much about my first surgery, but I do have several memories of the second. You may think that going into a major surgery at the age of seven would be terrifying but my parents told me everything would be fine. That was all I needed to hear and, at that age, I didn't think too hard about potential complications. I just knew that it was something that needed to happen to fix my back.

The second surgery went much more smoothly. The new surgeon removed one of my ribs and fused it into my back along with a metal rod. When I came around afterward, I found I was sporting the familiar full-body cast. I was laid up in hospital again, unable to go home, so my parents came in to visit as much as they could, and my dad's parents, Grandpa and Grandma Postl, were regular visitors who went out of their way to make sure I knew how much they cared. The other side of the family was a different story. My mom's parents never once visited me any of the times I was in the hospital. It felt like they were embarrassed.

I needed as much support as I could get since I couldn't do anything for myself — I wasn't even able to get to the bathroom, which meant bedpans and bottles. And whenever I couldn't manage to pee, which was often, I had to get catheters. I remember that they were bright red and hurt like hell. The moment I'd see one being brought toward me, I'd start crying. My family was always there to hold my hand, but I would bawl my eyes out. Dad was always so sad for me because I had to have catheters so frequently, sometimes a couple of times in a single day. Even the nurses hated doing it because they felt so bad for me. On top of the daily catheterization, I had to have regular blood tests, too. I guess that's where my fear of needles comes from.

The nurses were great though — they did everything they could to make the best of a bad situation and always made sure I had my stuffed animal and my blanket. I actually had *two* blankets and they used to put one in the freezer. Whenever the one I had got too warm and uncomfortable, they'd switch it with the one in the freezer. To this day, I can't sleep when I get too warm. Toward the end of my stay in hospital, we had water fights, which aren't as fun when you can't really move but better than doing nothing. The nurses would spray me with huge syringes filled with water, and I'd splash them right back with my water bottle.

There was only so much the nurses could do to keep me occupied so, to help with the boredom, Dad brought in a Nintendo Entertainment System and we played a ton of RBI *Baseball*. I'd spend all day looking forward to seeing Dad in the evening and playing that NES into the night. Those visits were everything to me. RBI *Baseball* was the only thing we'd play. It carried on being our thing after I got back home and remained something we'd do together for many years. No matter what other video game systems I would get through the years, we'd always keep the NES and RBI *Baseball*. Some of my favorite childhood memories come from that, especially how fired up Dad would get whenever I'd bunt and get an easy base.

Even after I'd been discharged, the full-body cast had to stay on. Being trapped in that cast twenty-four hours a day was uncomfortable at best and, over summer, I would become so overheated that I'd itch all over and have to use a fork to try to scratch myself. Whenever I managed to get that fork to an itch, it was a great feeling — but better still was the brief period every few months when I would get cut out of the cast. As much as I looked forward to the outcome, the process of getting the cast off was terrifying: The doctor had to use an electric saw to cut into the plaster. In reality, the saw wasn't very big but, in my young mind, this grown man was using a chainsaw on me. I was always scared he was going to saw into my chest. There was a horrendous noise as the blade cut, plaster went everywhere, and I'd cry my eyes out. It was worth it though — when they pulled the cast apart and I could feel air on my chest, it was the best feeling in the world. They'd put me in a fresh cast shortly thereafter, but I always looked forward to those few minutes of freedom every few months.

One of the main problems with being in the cast was that I found it impossible to stand upright, so if I wanted to get anywhere at home, I'd have to roll from room to room. Everyone laughed at first but, after a while, the novelty wore off and it just became an everyday part of life. I'd learned to walk before my first surgery but a couple of years in the body cast had set me back a lot. My physical therapy sessions didn't seem to be helping at all and I started to wonder if I'd ever be able to walk again.

One day, at home, I decided I'd had enough of rolling or being carried everywhere. While my parents were in their bedroom, I pulled myself up against the wall in the hallway and started taking little kicking steps, with my arms out in front of me for balance. I must have looked like Tommy from *Rugrats*. My mom came out of the bedroom, saw me, and gasped, "Oh my God!" All I could say was "Hi Mom." She was already crying as she shouted for my dad to come out and see. They tried to get me to walk to them but I told them to grab me and hold my hands because I didn't know if I'd hurt myself if I fell. Gradually though, I got the hang of walking. Just being able to get from room to room standing upright felt like a miracle.

Another weight was lifted when I was permanently freed from the cast, even though I was moved straight into a back brace that I had to wear ninety percent of the time. It was made of hard plastic, with Velcro and straps for fastening. It was a challenge to get on and off because it was so tight and if you bent the plastic too much, it would break. Dad would always be the one to help me with it and, a few times, the brace would slip out of his grasp, pinch my skin, and hurt like hell, causing yet more tears. He felt so bad whenever that happened. That plastic brace presented problems for other people, too. Whenever I'd spend time at Grandpa and Grandma Postl's house, which I loved doing, I would lean on the coffee table in their living room and the bottom of the brace would get caught and scratch it up. My grandparents didn't care about the scuffing, but once I was out of the brace, Dad made sure to have the table refinished so that it was presentable again.

Those weren't the only surgeries I had to endure as a child — I found out that I had a tumor on my eardrum when I was eleven. It was affecting my hearing, so it had to be removed. Just like with my first back surgery, the doctor wasn't prepared for the job. Shortly after he'd put me under and opened me up, he hit an artery. Once that was under control, the doctor decided he wasn't the right man for the job, closed me back up, and called someone else. Three months later, just after I turned twelve, another surgeon removed the tumor successfully, though the surgery left a scab on my eardrum that is still there today. It affects my hearing in that ear and gets infected at least once every six months.

I was always confused as to why the doctors weren't more prepared for what they found. Maybe everything looked normal enough on the scans and X-rays, but it seemed to me that the people who were performing my first back and ear surgeries cut me open and then said, "Hold on, why is this here?" I've joked a few times to Dad that if that sort of thing happened now, the malpractice lawsuits would have made us millionaires. Dad just says that everyone was doing the best they could and all anyone wanted was for me to get better.

Looking back, I went through physical hell in my preteen years — I don't know many people who have a single major surgery before they become a teenager, let alone four. On top of that, you've got all the associated complications that come with my stature but, honestly, I didn't feel that different from any other kid. My teachers treated me the same as everyone else, and that was the way I wanted it. My dad echoed that behavior — but Mom had her own ways of dealing with my condition.

CHAPTER 2

THE RUBBER DUCKY

I didn't grow up as the only little person in town. When I was a kid, my mom took me to meet the other person in Oshkosh who was affected by dwarfism. He was an older guy, nice enough if slightly weird. But the main memory I have of that day isn't of the little person — it's of how confused I was. Why was my mom making me meet this little old guy? Was she trying to tell me, "Dylan, this is your future"? Was she trying to show me how different I was from all the normal-sized people? I didn't get it. As far as I was concerned, I was just a kid. It didn't feel like Mom saw me the same way.

I first realized my Mom's need for the spotlight when I returned to school after my second back surgery. I didn't want to make a big deal of it, but Mom made it into "Dylan's Comeback to Elementary School," like it was some sort of major event. She had me do an announcement over the school's public-address system to say I was back and then paraded me in my wheelchair from classroom to classroom, getting everyone to clap as I handed out a piece of gum to each kid. I just wanted to be like any other kid, but Mom went out of her way to see that things changed for me. Before long, the school had a shorter toilet, shorter drinking fountain, and a shorter swing — just for me. Every classroom I was in had a shorter desk, a chair with a foam backrest and footrest. Even at the age of six, I remember thinking, "Why are they doing all this?"

You might think these were the actions of a protective mother, who was making sure her kid was looked after. There might have been an element of that, but in time I came to realize — whether she knew it or not — that it was mostly about getting attention for herself. Being the "mother of the little kid" gave her an identity. She didn't care how, she just cared that everyone knew her. It felt like she would use me to get sympathy for what she must have been going through as the mom of the midget. The reality is, however, I never viewed myself as different from any of the other kids.

Although I was my dad's first child, I was Mom's third. She already had two kids, Tera and Clint, from a previous marriage. She and their biological dad had divorced not long after Clint was born, and my dad had come into the picture shortly thereafter and raised both kids as his own. By the time I was born, Clint was seven and Tera was nine. I never looked on them as anything other than my full brother and sister, and they felt the same about me. By then, Mom was their only living biological parent — her ex-husband had died by suicide when Clint was just three.

I shared a bedroom with Clint and, while there was the big age gap, we were very close. Whenever Mom wasn't around, he'd cook meals for me and make sure I got to and from school. Clint was the one who first introduced me to wrestling by giving me some of his wwf action figures. He drew the line at letting me use his toy wrestling ring though, so my dad built me a wooden replica to stop me complaining.

As well as being the person behind my lifelong love of wrestling, Clint was also responsible for my lifelong fear of the dark. We slept in bunk beds: he had the top bunk and I had the bottom one. Whenever cars would go past our house, their headlights illuminated the ceiling of our second-floor bedroom. Clint told me they were ghosts, and I was young enough to believe him. He didn't help matters by swinging his head down over the edge of the top bunk and scaring the shit out of me when I was trying to go to sleep. He was also a sleepwalker, so I'd never know if he'd be in his bed or not and that scared me, too. My parents sometimes found him standing around in the kitchen or the laundry room. On one occasion, when I was half-asleep, he fell clean out of the bed. I saw a body drop and land with a huge thud on the floor right next to me. It was a hell of a bump but, somehow, he wasn't hurt at all. I was scared to death though — I pulled the covers over my head, closed my eyes tight, and tried to go back to sleep.

My family was very big on traveling, and every summer we would go on a trip. One year we went out to Montana, and the next year we went to Disney World. My Disney fanaticism started when I was very young. We went to Disney for the first time in 1992. I

Clint looking after his little brother.

remember going on Space Mountain, which scared both Dad and I half to death. I didn't like that or the Star Wars ride at MGM, but I thought the overall experience was amazing. I loved meeting the characters and seeing the castle — the whole thing felt so magical to me. We went to Universal Studios as well and that was awesome, too. The only bad part of that whole vacation was that I was in a wheelchair after one of my back surgeries. That sucked but it wasn't the real problem — I didn't like how much of a big deal my mom made about it, rushing me to the front of lines and telling everyone, "You need to let him in *right now.*" I liked not having to wait, but I didn't think Mom needed to be so obnoxious about it.

A lot of kids are into one thing for a brief time and then they move on, but it wasn't that way with me. When I liked something, I got *obsessed* with it. I liked Disney, I liked *The Muppets* (especially *Muppet Babies*), I liked the Teenage Mutant Ninja Turtles, and, above all else, I liked wrestling. Actually, I *loved* wrestling. Everything about it. And that hasn't changed.

My first memories of wrestling are playing with the action figures Clint gave me and watching WWF *Superstars of Wrestling* and WWF *Wrestling Challenge* on TV. Even though I couldn't walk, I knew that one day I wanted to be a pro-wrestler just like my hero, the Ultimate Warrior. Over the years, I became a fan of high-flyers like the 1-2-3 Kid, character wrestlers like Doink the Clown, and big guys like Diesel. But, at the very beginning, it was all about the Warrior for me. Whenever I went over to Grandpa Postl's house, we would rent wrestling tapes from the local video store. We might as well have bought *WrestleMania* VI for the number of times we rented it — seeing the Warrior beat Hulk Hogan for the WWF Championship never got old. Almost every birthday, I'd get the same cake with the Ultimate Warrior on it. One year, for a change, my parents got me a Hulk Hogan cake and I was really disappointed. Back then, it was Warrior or nothing.

A Short Story: Hasbro

The first Hasbro wrestling figures I remember getting from Clint were the Ultimate Warrior, André the Giant, and Hulk Hogan. Clint and I had the same Hogan figure — the gorilla press slam model — but we could tell which one was mine, because mine was missing the ring finger on his left hand. Those figures were just the start for me. In time, I'd get the bear-hug Hogan (which I hated because you couldn't do any moves with it apart from the bear-hug) and the mail-in Hogan with the suplex action. Every time I had to go to one of the Minneapolis hospitals for a checkup, we'd go to the Mall of America. The first time we went there, I must have bought at least twenty figures. Collecting and playing with those toys was my release but even if I liked the wrestler, it didn't mean I would be a fan of his action figure.

Even though the Ultimate Warrior was my hero, I didn't like his first figure, which had the bulky upper body on tiny legs to make a springing action. The second Warrior, with the white trunks and gorilla press action, was much better. The Undertaker's figure was cool because his hand was molded in a way that you could use it to do a chokeslam. Even though I thought the figure of Bret Hart looked more like Elvis with the stupid snarl on his face, it was fun to play with because you could do a lot with it. My least favorite figure of all time was Giant Gonzáles. He had the action where if you pushed him down on his feet, his arms would go up and down. I also didn't like the Legion of Doom figures, because their shoulder pads didn't come off, so they weren't ready to wrestle, only to do their entrance. It took WWE years to bring out a 1-2-3 Kid figure, so I pretended one of my

Ninja Turtle figures was Kid after he changed his gear from blue to red and silver.

Hasbro stopped making the figures in the mid-'90s and Jakks took over as the manufacturer. I remember the first few, like Bret, Diesel, and Goldust, were disappointing because their limbs would get so loose so quickly. After those first few though, some of the figures were great. I would call up Walmart and Target and Toys "R" Us to ask, "Hey, have you got the Jakks Series Whatever Bone Crunching Action Rockabilly figure?" (That's a joke, they never made a Rockabilly figure and rightly so.) The people at the store must have found that so annoying, especially with how often I'd call back.

The first major trauma I remember — other than the surgeries — happened on what was an otherwise regular day. Mom had pushed me down the block in my wheelchair to get my hair cut. As the barber was finishing with me, the phone rang. The call was from one of our neighbors. I have a vivid memory of Mom saying, "You're kidding me!" before hurrying me back into my wheelchair and rushing home. There were fire trucks everywhere, and our house was black, with smoke billowing all around it. We found out later that something had gone wrong with the wiring in the attic and started a fire that spread quickly. The only things that survived unscathed were our chocolate Labrador, Maggie; a big clock my grandparents had given us for Christmas; and a rubber duck. I still remember that bright yellow rubber ducky sitting on the edge of our downstairs bathtub, looking out over what was left of our house. I was happy our dog had escaped unharmed, but I was devastated about the damage to my wrestling figures.

While the house was being rebuilt, we moved into a condo. Once we'd settled in, Dad surprised me by giving me back all my wrestling figures, all professionally cleaned. Dad was careful with money, but he knew how much my toys meant to me and wanted to make sure I got them back as soon as possible. All he ever wanted was for all of us kids to have every opportunity to enjoy our childhood. The Christmas after our house burned down, we got a pool table that could convert into a ping-pong or air hockey table. Clint and I played pool almost every night after dinner, and we each had our own specific cue. It was easy to tell the difference because mine got broken early on. He and I had some great times playing pool.

Unfortunately, my parents weren't having many great times by that point. Since I was so young, I'd never noticed them arguing much, but things seemed tense after we'd moved back into the house. One night, the sound of my parents arguing downstairs about their financial situation woke me up. I clearly heard Dad yelling, "This has got to stop! I'm cutting up the cards!" It wasn't long after that that they began divorce proceedings, with Mom getting custody of me while Dad moved into a tiny apartment. I didn't ever really talk to Tera and Clint about the divorce, but it had to have been upsetting and confusing for them both. They'd been born with the surname Binder, then switched to my mom's maiden name, Werner, after Mom divorced their biological father. When she married my dad, Clint and Tera's surname changed again, to Postl, and when *they* got divorced, it went back to Werner. Even though they weren't biologically his, Dad had raised them for so long that it was a real kick in the teeth for him. Clint was fully on Team Mom, but Tera was split between the two and would spend time with them both.

I didn't realize it at the time because I was just a kid, but Mom started trying to turn me against Dad. He knew that she would attempt to brainwash me after the divorce but, to his credit, he never spoke ill of her, realizing that I needed to come to my own conclusions. He put his head down, kept his mouth shut, and did his best to provide.

While Dad started working more than ever to cover child support and his own bills, Mom was out, either spending or dating. I assume the men she dated all had money, because she wasn't earning much from selling calendars, pillows, and stuffed bears at craft shows. A lot of the spending went on gifts for me. Mom and whoever her boyfriend was at the time would tell me I deserved everything I got because of how hard my life was. I was a kid getting gifts so I wasn't about to argue with them. When I saw my dad, I would always excitedly tell him about these presents. Of course, he saw them for what they were — attempts to buy my love — but never said a bad thing about any of it. He was working so hard just to make ends meet and pay child support, so watching these random guys give his son gifts that he himself couldn't afford must have been so tough for him.

Even though I was in my mom's custody, she wasn't around anywhere near as much as she should have been. On the rare occasions she was at home rather than out with some guy, she just seemed off. I know now that it was because of the alcohol use but, at the time, all I knew was my mom was different after the divorce. A lot of the time, she didn't even come get me from school, sending Clint or Tera instead. Every day when I came out of school, I had no idea who was picking me up. Sometimes, I didn't even get to school in the first place. Whenever Mom was going away with a guy for the weekend, I was pulled out of school to fit in with her schedule.

None of this sat well with Clint and Tera, who were always telling Mom she needed to stop dumping her responsibilities on them. One night, after Clint had to look after me because Mom had been drinking, they got into a huge fight that turned physical. I was upstairs in bed as they fought on the landing, grabbing onto each other by the clothes and yelling. They were right up against the bannister and I was so scared. Not just because of the shouting, but because if that bannister had broken, they would have both died from the fall. I didn't get it — I couldn't understand why they were yelling and why Clint was so mad that he was grabbing her. "You need to stop this bullshit," Clint screamed. "You're our mom, for God's sake. Start acting like it." After that, he let go and stormed out of the house, which was something that happened a lot.

Meanwhile, the more my dad saw how much Mom was letting me down, the more frustrated he became. The final straw was when he got a call from my school at 6 p.m. one day, telling him that I'd been found sitting out by myself on the curb and crying because Mom hadn't shown up. There was no reason for it; she wasn't working or caught up with anything. I think she'd just got drunk and forgotten she needed to pick up her child. I was so confused — I didn't understand how she could abandon me. Dad rushed straight over. The moment he got there, he promised me, "Dylan, I won't let this happen ever again." As soon as we got back to his place, he called his lawyer and started proceedings to get custody of me. It was the best thing he ever did for me.

I don't know whether it actually took weeks or months but, to me, it felt like I immediately went from living with Mom to living with Dad. Mom only had me at weekends and, even though she'd spent so long neglecting me, she wasn't happy with that arrangement. It was like I was a possession and she was demanding her fair share. I don't know why she did that, because she didn't seem interested in parenting me, often just leaving me with Clint and Tera while she did other things. Whenever she *did* spend time with me, I didn't want to be around her and that made her even more upset and angry.

Things went in a downward spiral until, one weekend, I decided I just wanted to go back to my dad's. I called him and asked him to come get me. Mom found out and told me I wasn't going. I grabbed my duffel bag, stuffed all of my wrestling figures inside, and went to the door. Mom attempted to make me feel guilty, asking, "How could you do this to me?" as I was trying to put on my shoes. She kept at it as I was in tears, begging her to tie my shoes because I didn't know how. "No," she told me. "You're leaving me, so you're on your own." Even though I was young, that was where my feelings for my mom completely changed. At that moment, I stopped caring about her. As soon as I saw my dad's headlights in the driveway, I threw the door open and ran out of the house. Mom came running out after me, yelling and screaming, telling Dad he had no right to take me away from her. After giving me a hug, the first thing my dad did was tie my shoes.

CHAPTER 3

THE POOL CUE

As soon as Dad was granted custody of me, I began to see more clearly who my mother truly was. She told me she called every day, sometimes twice, but that my dad wasn't letting her speak to me. In response, Dad let me answer the phone every single time it rang. Even if I was in the bathroom, he wouldn't answer it. I quickly realized Mom wasn't calling anywhere near as much as she said she was. Later, he bought caller ID so we could see the number before picking up, and it was rarely Mom's. Even after I told her I knew she wasn't calling because Dad let me answer the phone, she still insisted he was blocking her calls.

Whenever she did call, she would speak to me for less than a minute before asking for my dad. Again, to show he wasn't withholding anything from me, he would put her on speakerphone. Dad would try to warn her several times to stop yelling and swearing and, when she didn't, he'd hang up. If she called back, he would ask if she wanted to speak to me and, after another thirty seconds at most, she'd ask me to pass the phone back to Dad again, so she could yell at him some more. Dad knew her slurring and temper were alcohol related, but when I asked what was wrong with Mom, he'd simply say that she "has a problem," or "Your mom's got stuff going on." Even then, he was still trying to preserve my relationship with her as best he could. He could have very easily destroyed it, but he knew I had to come to my own conclusions. The older I get, the more I'm impressed with how well he handled the whole situation, never once saying a bad word about her despite having so many reasons to do so.

On top of fixing roads and sewers and plowing snow in the winter with the Oshkosh Street Department, Dad was picking up Saturday shifts driving a semi-trailer truck for Lang Oil so he could make a little extra money. Seeing him put himself through so much to make sure my life was as comfortable as possible taught me a lot about what it is to be an adult and a parent.

His work schedule made things difficult during the weekends he had me, so he would sometimes ask my older friend Mike Wilharms, who was thirteen, to come over and hang out with me while he went to work. One day, not long after Dad had left, the phone rang. It was Mom calling to invite me over to see her new shar-pei puppy. "I'll make milkshakes and we can have lunch," she said, laying it on thick. "I don't ever see you anymore. Don't you love me?" Feeling guilty, I talked Mike into riding across town with me. To put into perspective how bad of an idea this was, it wasn't just down the block, it was a two-mile ride that took us down the second busiest street in town and across the road. To top it all off, since I'd only re-learned to walk a couple of years before, I was still using training wheels on my bike. I don't think Mom thought of any of that. In her mind, if I couldn't ride my bike, I should have walked. The whole thing was just to prove she still had control over me.

When Dad got home, he started asking questions about our day. We told him we'd just hung out and played Super Nintendo. "Were you over at your mom's house, Dylan?" he asked. I told him no, but Mike started to crack because he knew how much my dad trusted him. Dad kept asking the same questions and, eventually, we admitted that we'd gone over to see her. It turned out that one of our neighbors had seen me and Mike leaving and tipped my dad off. He was furious at Mom for putting me and Mike in that situation, as well as scared that we'd been on a cross-town bike ride, even if we did somehow make it there and back in one piece.

The only time I remember my dad answering the phone was when he saw on caller ID that it was Tera. After he'd picked up and said hello, I vividly remember hearing him calmly say, "I think you should be the one to tell him."

He handed me the phone and I heard Tera's voice, heavy with emotion. "Dylan, your brother committed suicide."

I didn't understand. At nine years old, I had no idea what suicide was, so Tera explained it to me. When she and her boyfriend had pulled into the garage of Mom's house, Clint had been hanging there. He was only sixteen.

After I got off the phone and the news sank in, I started crying and couldn't stop. Dad held me for what seemed like forever. "It's okay, Dylan," he said. "This isn't your fault. This is no one's fault." Moments like that show me how great a man my dad is. He'd just lost a boy he'd raised, a boy who'd always known him as Dad, and yet he put his own feelings to the side to comfort *me*. The news must have crushed him, but he put me first and never wanted me to blame anyone, not me, not even my mom, for what happened to Clint.

The funeral was a horrible experience. I remember them playing "Comfortably Numb," because Clint was a huge Pink Floyd fan. Tera managed to compose herself enough to give a speech, but I couldn't stop bawling. My mom was even worse than me but it wasn't her I wanted for comfort — I wanted my dad, who hadn't been allowed to attend. Even though Dad's relationship with Clint had become difficult after the divorce, he'd asked my mom if he could come to the funeral. I don't know what Mom told him, but I remember being so happy to see him turn up, then running over and hugging him in the doorway of the funeral home before asking him to come sit with me. "I can't," he told me. When I asked why, he said, "I'm sorry but I just can't." Instead, I sat with Josh Binder, whose dad was distantly related to Clint and Tera's late father. Sitting there at my brother's funeral is the first memory I have of my life-long friendship with Binder.

All the way through the service, I couldn't stop thinking that Clint needed to be buried with the cue he used whenever we played pool, but I'd left it at Mom's house. I got more and more upset until I started frantically yelling, "Clint needs his pool cue! It needs to go with him!" Tera's boyfriend eventually managed to calm me down by saying he would go back to the house to find it. The burial was the next day and I don't know if Clint's cue ended up in his casket, but whenever I went to my mom's house after that, only the broken cue remained — not that there was any need for it. I didn't play much pool after my brother died. Tera had grown up with Clint, so she was far more hurt by his death than I was. Even though she had

With Clint and Tera at my grandparents' house.

been raised by my dad since she was four, their relationship became strained and I would only see Tera at my mom's house, so she and I drifted apart, too.

My dad had moved on with his life since the divorce proceedings had begun. He'd been a longtime member of the South Side Ice Yacht Club in Oshkosh, an ice boating club known for its great fish fries, and met Dorothy Vanoudenhoven there. Dorothy was a third-grade teacher from Hortonville. Even though my parents were separated, my mom had a major problem with her. She immediately began trying to turn me against this wonderful, decent woman. Mom would use the fact that Dorothy had two children from a previous marriage, telling me that this woman would always prefer her own kids to me and never treat me the way I deserved. It didn't help that I would fight over anything and everything with Tim, who was two years older than me, and Ben, who was a year younger. It also didn't help that whenever we fought, I would call my mom for support and give her the chance to say, "You see? This is why you should be with me." When she told me Dorothy, Tim, and Ben were bad people, she was saying exactly what I wanted to hear — and she knew it.

Looking back, I can see that Mom was intimidated because she knew what a screwup she was in comparison to Dorothy. Rather than doing something about her own inadequacies and issues, she tried to demean Dorothy to make herself look and feel better. Dorothy knew all of this was happening but she never once said a bad word about my mother.

Eventually, and out of the blue, without saying a word to her own son, Mom moved to Florida. That was when I finally realized that she didn't want to be in my life. She would call every few months and accuse my dad of screening calls or throwing away the letters she said she was writing to me every day. Dad made sure I brought the mail in after that, so I could see there wasn't any truth to her new claim but, by then, I knew who she was. After a while, when I was ten, Mom stopped calling altogether.

I've not had any real interaction with her in more than twenty years. When I was a teenager, I bumped into her a few times at the movie theater or Target when she was in the area, but I didn't speak with her. She turned up to one of the WWE shows in Oshkosh where my friends and family were in the first row. They later told me that she was in the third row and had rushed the barricade when I did my spot, making a typically big scene. I'll give her this though — she never reached out to me for money. That's something, at least.

I'm fine with things the way they are, and I don't feel any need to reach out. There are times I can remember that she did something that had a lasting impact on me, like when I was recovering from my second back surgery and she arranged for Dan Marino, the quarterback for the Miami Dolphins, to send me a personalized autograph, wishing me well. I was a big Dan fan, so that meant a lot to me. But unfortunately, for every time I can remember her being there for me, I can remember countless moments when she wasn't. She was never a parent to me in the way Dad has always been. I truly believe that my life would have turned out entirely differently if I'd stayed with her. I doubt I would have accomplished any of the things I've done and I would have grown up with a very "woe is me" attitude — playing a situation for sympathy or attention seemed second nature to her but it's never been for me.

Even though my mom was out of the picture, family stress continued to be a staple in my life when Dorothy, Tim, Ben, Dad, and I all moved in together. Ben and I shared a room and that guaranteed there was going to be constant trouble. If either of us stepped on the other person's side of the room, we'd fight. If we played with each other's toys, we'd fight. Almost every interaction we had ended in a fight. I'd tell him that he and his mom didn't deserve to be there, and he'd come back at me by saying that me and my dad were the outsiders because his family outnumbered mine. One night, he got to me so much that I charged across the room and tried to spear him as if I was Goldberg. Even though Ben was a year younger, he was a lot bigger than me, so all he had to do was hold an arm out to stop me. He put his hand on the top of my head and held me at arm's length while I flailed at him with zero chance of connecting on any of my punches. It was comical. As angry as I was, it's a good thing he caught me that time because if I'd missed him, I would have gone right by and out of the second-story window.

Over the years, Dad and Dorothy called the three of us together on a number of occasions and told us, "We want to be together, but you guys are going to make us separate if nothing changes. We've got to be a family." I didn't care. As I got older, I only got more defiant.

I wasn't shy about telling Dad, "She's not my mom." Looking back, I'm so embarrassed about how much of an asshole I was. However, whenever Dorothy would hear me say that, she'd tell me, "No, Dylan, I'm not your mom. But I do love you and I'm here to help you." She was so patient with me, but Dad would get frustrated with how I was treating her. My biological mom hadn't done any of the things a mother should and Dorothy was doing everything she could to fill that gap, but there I was, behaving like a dickhead teenager.

As I got older, I had my difficulties with school, but not in the way you might assume. My size was never an issue and I wasn't bullied. I think others were comfortable around me because I was always the first one to make fun of myself and my stature. I won people over at parties by mimicking Wee Man from *Jackass*, one of my favorite shows as a teenager, and kicking myself in the head, sometimes crushing a soda can against my forehead with my foot. Classes weren't a problem, either. All of the teachers treated me like any other student — and I didn't want it any other way.

The biggest issue was that I just didn't like homework. I didn't bother doing it a lot of the time, nor would I study for tests, so I'd end up getting bad grades and being grounded. Dorothy and Dad would then make sure I completed my homework, but I still wouldn't turn it in, even though I'd done it. For whatever reason, I thought it was cool to not turn in my homework. I have no idea what I was thinking. I don't remember it being an act of rebellion. I wasn't inherently dumb, and I think I could have been a good student. I just wouldn't do what I was asked for reasons I don't recall and I probably didn't even know at the time.

I was never held back because I would always finish the year strong, but I seemed to spend most of each school year grounded. Once the first quarter grades came out and my report card was filled with Ds and Fs, that was the end of my freedom until the next summer. Being grounded meant I would get only half an hour of TV time each day, I wouldn't be able to see my friends as much, and I couldn't go to sleepovers. What I really couldn't cope with, however, was when my parents took away my wrestling figures. Even when I was fourteen or fifteen, they were still my most cherished possessions. At that point, I wasn't just playing, I was booking, laying out the matches, working out details of storylines in my head, and writing down everything I did, so having my figures taken away was devastating. It still didn't make me turn in my homework though. I may not have been dumb, but my behavior was definitely stupid. At the time, I didn't like either of my parents for coming down hard on me, but everything they did, they did for my own good — even the time I got grounded and Dad ripped up the tickets he'd bought me to go to *Over the Edge '98* in Milwaukee, causing me to miss a classic match between Steve Austin and Dude Love.

The one class I loved was gym, despite it sometimes being a challenge. There were certain things my body wouldn't let me do, such as pull-ups and climbing rope, and I was given extra time to complete the course during runs. Looking back, one thing I would have loved to have done is climb the rope. It's funny how most normal-sized people wouldn't consider being able to climb a rope a wish list item but I was always mad that I could never do it.

Even though my stature stopped me from joining every activity, I gave my all at everything I could do. I never wanted to let my physical situation prevent me from trying something. This attitude went beyond class. After my surgeries, the doctors had all been all very clear with me that I shouldn't get involved in any contact sports. According to them, I couldn't even bounce on a trampoline because jarring my body the wrong way could result in the rod being knocked out of my back and me being paralyzed. But, honestly, I never felt like I couldn't do anything I wanted to do in terms of sports.

I tried amateur wrestling in seventh grade but that didn't last long. I couldn't do a lot because of my small limbs, and it wasn't anything like the wrestling I wanted to do. To me, it just looked like two guys hugging each other. The main reason I'd joined was that I hoped Binder and I would be able to stay behind after practice and use the mats to wrestle WWE-style. When it became clear that wasn't an option, I quit. I enjoyed playing basketball in middle school, and at home with my dad, but softball was the sport I liked best, even if I was always second to last in the batting order. I played in the summer league for a few years and was on a team run by a company with another team in the same league. We were the team that had the kid with the thick glasses and the one with the limp — clearly the B-team. We were still pretty good though, and for three years running, the final came down to us against our owner's A-team. They won easily the first two years, but the third came down to the wire.

The pitcher on the other team was a guy named Randy and he had such an attitude — he was convinced he was God's gift to softball. He hated pitching to me because my strike zone is way smaller. Everyone would move in when I was up to bat because I couldn't hit worth a crap, but it didn't matter because Randy could never strike me out. I'd just let him keep throwing until I got a walk. It got to the point where he refused to pitch and told the umpire to let me go to second base. When that idea was rejected, Randy used some strong language and things got heated. Being the little asshole I was, I pointed to the fence like I was Babe Ruth. If it'd been a cartoon, there would have been steam coming out of Randy's ears. I held the pose until I heard my dad, behind me in the crowd of parents, say "Stop that" under his breath. Randy pitched. For a change, he got a strike, then another one. I knew I had to swing at the final ball. I wish I could say I sent the ball flying over exactly where I'd been pointing, but I missed, and he struck me out. He was so happy with himself that day — until our team won the game. He finally got me, but his team lost the championship.

Until I was fourteen, the only other little person I'd encountered in my life was the older guy in Oshkosh my mom had taken me to meet. All my friends were normal-sized, so when my dad suggested I might like to go to a little person convention that was being held in Illinois, I wasn't particularly interested. I'd never cared to find out much about my condition. My attitude was that I couldn't change it, so I shouldn't worry about it. Dad and I had never really spoken a great deal about my condition and he wasn't trying to force me into going to this convention, but he wanted me to at least consider it. "Keep an open mind," he told me. "Who knows what you'll get out of it." I still wasn't convinced. In the end, he gave me the push I needed by booking us into a hotel and saying we were going on a trip. That sounded good to me, so I didn't ask any questions. When we got to the hotel in Peoria, I noticed a few little people milling around the lobby and began to realize Dad had tricked me. He knew it would do me good and I didn't mind once I was there.

After that regional event in Peoria, I decided to go to Minneapolis for the Little People of America National Convention in 2001. It was overwhelming. There were thousands upon thousands of little people and their families and so many things to do. There was weightlifting, track, basketball, even bocce ball (which is like lawn bowling) — every sport and activity you could imagine, exclusively for little people. I didn't participate, but I enjoyed the dances they held every night. I made friends with some of the other kids there and kept in touch with them online after the convention. I went to five more national conventions over the years, as well as several more regional events, and the funny thing is that I never really thought much about my size *until* I started going to them. Going there didn't change my world or give me a sudden, unexpected feeling of peace or belonging, but I did learn a few things along the way.

One of the things that took me by surprise was I realized I could find girls with a similar condition attractive. I hadn't considered that before. I also became more aware of activity surrounding little people. For example, I heard about a lot of medical cases in the early 2000s which could best be described as bone stretching on people with achondroplasia. Surgeons would literally break the little person's bones, stretch them out, then add screws and rods to give them maybe three extra inches in height. It didn't make sense to me — the little person would have to learn to walk again and they'd still have the obnoxiously large head and ample backside that comes with the condition, so I didn't know why anyone would put themselves through that for such a marginal change. A couple of extra inches wouldn't solve the *real* issue, whatever it might be.

The biggest thing I took away from these conventions was how lucky I was. It might sound strange to hear that from someone with achondroplasia, but even with the surgeries I'd been through, I was generally a happy, healthy kid. Some of the other little people looked like tiny ceramic dolls, barely two feet tall. The people with that type of dwarfism won't be able to reproduce, they have a significantly reduced life expectancy, and they experience a lot more pain and health issues than I'll ever deal with. When I realized people with other types of dwarfism had it so much worse than me but were still doing their best to be happy, I realized I didn't have any reason to complain whatsoever. I also encountered other little people at these conventions who were so bitter about their condition they'd made life into an "us against the world" situation, and that made me feel lucky that I've never thought that way. I've always felt we're all the same, all people.

CHAPTER 4

THE GREEN DODGE NEON

By the time I became a teenager, I'd decided to start wrestling. My friend Josh Binder would come over and, along with my step-brothers — who I got along with better by this point — we'd film ourselves wrestling in my and Ben's bedroom. Soon enough, it moved out into our backyard, where we'd put down sleeping bags and blankets as our ring.

We all came up with characters that weren't even slightly original — mine involved me entering the "arena" with two cans of pop and whoever was commentating would say they were beer, then I'd bash them together à la "Stone Cold" Steve Austin, drink one, then channel the Sandman and smash the can against my forehead. Always the side of the can — the bottom would have hurt. As for the wrestling matches, it was just a bunch of fake punches and kicks and about a million DDTs, where we'd trap our opponent in a front facelock and fall backwards, driving his head into the "mat." When we found out there were some other guys doing a similar thing down the street, we joined up with them and started taping "shows" from my buddy Wesley's yard. We upgraded to a ring made of mattresses with PVC pipes for the corners and thin rope hung around it all. We even made our own kendo sticks — we'd go to Maynards or Walmart and spend three bucks to buy eight dowels and some electrical tape. When we'd bind them all together, those dowels made the exact same noise as the kendo sticks during the hardcore wrestling matches on TV. Through trial and error, we found the perfect size of dowel to get. If they were too small, our kendo sticks would shatter immediately, and if they were too thick, there wouldn't be any noise when you were hit — but it would hurt like hell.

We even got ourselves on local access TV. We had a friend who worked for a TV station edit our videos, then give us a 2 a.m. slot. Every Saturday, anyone who was flipping through the channels and stumbled upon our show could see us wrestle for twenty minutes. For us, being wrestlers on TV was the coolest thing imaginable. Soon after that, we found out about another, bigger, backyard group over on a busy corner in Appleton that ran a couple of times during the summer. They'd get at least a hundred people at their events and, sometimes, even two or three hundred. Their ring was made of railroad ties and pieces of wood, with carpet padding and a tarp. Taking bumps on it hurt a lot, but it was the closest thing to a real ring we'd ever been in.

Unsurprisingly, there weren't any other local midget backyard wrestlers I could work with, so I started competing as the Hardcore Wonder, which meant I could work against regular-sized guys and make up for what I couldn't do with garbage wrestling, doing stupid things like getting smashed in the head with fluorescent light tubes. Another thing I could do just as well as any regular-sized wrestler was bleed. In my mind, cutting yourself in a match or "doing a bladejob" was the coolest thing a hardcore wrestler could do.

Before I bladed for the first time, I knew I'd need to thin my blood to make it look gorier, but I took it a little too far. Over the course of the day, I took fourteen aspirin. Meanwhile, I'd found a box cutter and removed one of the razor blades. Usually a wrestler will cut the blade down, wrap it up to make it safe, and then hide it in their wrist tape or gear, or leave it with the referee until it's needed, but I didn't know that. I just gave the unprotected razor blade to one of the fans before the show and told him to hand it to me when I went over. I was working with Binder that day and, after I took a shot to the head with a mailbox, I fell to the floor and crawled toward to the fan who had my blade. I ran that razor all the way across the top of my head, making sure I kept it in my hairline so that Dad wouldn't see what I'd done, and it wouldn't leave a visible scar. I didn't know much, but I knew not to cut my forehead. It felt fine but, immediately, I felt warm liquid streaming down my face. I looked up at Binder and he said, "Oh my God, you're bleeding too much." With two minutes, the white T-shirt, black shorts, and yellow and grey skateboard shoes I was wearing were covered in crimson. The ruined shirt didn't worry me but I knew my only pair of shoes being drenched in blood was going to be a problem. We carried on the match for another five minutes; by the end, whenever I'd breathe out, blood would spray everywhere.

Even though I did my best to hide what I'd done from my dad, he found out soon enough. When I was on the phone to Binder the next day, discussing our match, Ben picked up the other line to make a call and heard me talking about how much blood I'd lost. He went right to my dad and told him what he'd heard. The next time I saw Dad, he asked me what had happened to my head. I told him I fell badly when I was wrestling, but he wasn't buying it. He repeated his question until I admitted that I'd cut myself. He waited awhile before then asking, "So, how many aspirin did you take?" He wasn't happy at all. "Do you realize what could have happened?" he asked. "With that much blood loss, you could have wound up in the hospital." In the end, I wasn't allowed to go back for the next show we'd planned. As far as I know, I'm the only wrestler in history to be grounded for blading.

Somewhere along the way, our backyard antics came to the attention of the owner of a local independent promotion called All-Star Championship Wrestling, or ACW. He and his buddies packed a couple of cases of beer inside a cooler and came to see us wrestle. Afterward, he invited us to check out one of his shows and see if we wanted to pay to join his training school. After we'd looked into it, a few of us decided to take him up on that offer and started putting down $100 a month to train. Binder and I were joined by Seth Wittkowske and Corey Berndt as we started training under Shane Hills and Jason Hedrick, who went by J-Cash.

I'm certain my dad hated it when I started training with Shane and J-Cash. It wasn't so much the physical side of it — that just made him nervous. Even though the doctors had said I shouldn't participate in contact sports, Dad never told me not to wrestle because he knew that would have made me resent him (plus, he knew I'd go ahead and do it anyway). What bothered him the most was the money. The cost of the training plus the cost of fuel to get there and then to shows was taking up almost all the money I made from my part time job. The money didn't matter to me because I was dead set on learning how to wrestle properly.

My hope was that one day I'd be able to work for WWE as a small performer, not a midget wrestler. I'd grown up idolizing comparatively smaller guys like X-Pac and Jeff Hardy and I added Rey Mysterio to my list of idols after he joined in 2002. In my mind, I was going to be like Rey, a guy who would use high-risk, death-defying moves to make up for his lack of height and allow him to compete with the big guys. I figured that, since Rey was only seven or eight inches taller than me, my lack of height wouldn't be a big deal, completely overlooking the fact that Rey was, by far, the shortest guy on the WWE roster.

Keeping with my lifelong attitude of not wanting to be treated differently, I insisted that the trainers not take it easy on me and I made sure I did everything the other guys did. They taught me how to give and take moves the same way any other wrestler would, and

My "roots" — the backyard in Appleton, Wisconsin.

never let me chicken out on any bumps — soon I was falling like a pro. It was great for Shane and J-Cash because any time one of the normal-sized guys was having trouble with something, they could point at me and say, "If he can do it, so can you."

There weren't many moves where my stature got in the way. I couldn't trust my legs to go up properly on vertical suplexes, and I had trouble with hip tosses because I couldn't jump that high. That didn't matter when I was with Shane, because he was a big, thick 300-pounder who could throw me across the ring with ease. He was used to working with guys at the top end of the 100s and into two bills; it must have been like play wrestling with a child whenever he got hold of me.

At the end of every session, we'd take a press slam off the top rope. That's a long way down, and even more intimidating when you're my size, so I never enjoyed it, but Binder took that bump better than anyone. He would fly across the ring effortlessly and land perfectly. I preferred doing the tilt-a-whirl headscissors since I was skinny enough that anyone could get me up for the move and whip me around. Binder and I could even do the lucha spot where I'd go up and around his back, then into a headscissor take-down. I learned how to do Rey's 619, but modified so I would swing through the bottom and middle ropes. As incredible (and incredibly stupid) as it sounds, during all of this, it never occurred to me that doing any of these moves might damage my surgically reconstructed back. Not once.

What did scare me was the thought of getting chopped. That scared everyone. Whenever we messed up at training, we had to stand there and let someone else chop us. I thought it was stupid because if someone was screwing up a bump, getting chopped hard in the chest wasn't going to help them learn to land better.

While Shane and J-Cash were the main trainers, someone else who was regularly involved in our training was Ken Anderson. Even though Ken hadn't worked in any of the major promotions yet, he was already an excellent instructor, although whenever things didn't go exactly as he'd planned, he would get pissed off. Ken seemed to single Binder out a lot and none of us could understand why. He just went a little harder on Binder than he did on everyone else. He was great to me though and I loved training with him. Ken was a fun-loving smartass who could come across as cocky, but he could back it up — he was just as good in the ring as he was on the micro-phone. There were always rumors circulating that he was on WWE's radar, so we all considered training with him an honor.

Binder and me with Ken just before he headed off to WWE.

The rumors turned out to be true and he was signed by WWE in 2005. At the last ACW show before he left to report to Ohio Valley Wrestling, then one of WWE's developmental territories, he bled all over the place and did a somersault dive off the top of a rickety cage. I couldn't believe he took those kinds of risks when he was just about to start in the WWE system.

After only a couple of months of training, I started getting used on ACW shows. As much as I wanted to think it was because I was making ultra-fast progress in training, it was just because they wanted to get a midget on the card as soon as possible. J-Cash gave me the name "Shortstack" and used me as a heel manager for his character. The crowd would laugh more than they would boo because being told to sit down and shut up by a midget is more amusing than it is intimidating. I had to be careful about taking bumps, too, since the average person in the crowd might not feel good about cheering a normal-sized guy beating the piss out of a little person, no matter how much of a jerk I was.

Once Shane and J-Cash thought I was ready to work matches of my own, I started appearing in tag and singles bouts on ACW shows and, as time went on, other promotions in the area. As I was still a rookie, it would have been easy for some of the other wrestlers to take a few liberties, but everyone I worked with took great care of me and, since there'd never been a midget wrestler in the Green Bay area before, people were jumping at the chance to wrestle me. Although I worked hard in the ring, a lot of people I met on shows seemed surprised and, sometimes, disappointed that I didn't work like a midget. They told me that no one wanted to see me actually wrestle, so working like a midget would be easier on my body and give me a longer career. Even though their advice was well intended, I still couldn't get past the mentality that I wasn't a midget, I was a small cruiserweight — and Rey Mysterio never pulled people's pants down or bit them on the ass.

Starting to work shows meant I was traveling a lot. Fortunately, I already had my driver's license and a car Grandpa had bought me, a green Dodge Neon. Driving is something many people assume little people have difficulties with but I've never had a problem. My dad taught me how to drive in his van when I was fifteen and I passed my test on the second attempt when I was sixteen. Just like school, I was held to the same standards as everyone else. The first examiner failed me without a second thought because I screwed up the parallel parking, not because I'm a midget.

I met a lot of awesome wrestlers on the indie circuit, including future WWE *Champion AJ Styles.*

In comedy films, you'll see midgets sitting on a big book or using blocks on the pedals but the reality is nothing like that, at least not for someone with achondroplasia. I need to use extenders on the pedals because of my short legs, but since my torso is the same as most normal-sized people, I don't need to sit on anything to see over the steering wheel. I do need to pull the driver's seat as far forward as it will go though, and I put a cushion behind me, in order to be able to reach the wheel. The biggest issue for me when driving is that if I get in a crash and the airbag goes off, it's probably going to cause more injuries than it'll prevent. Because I'm sitting much closer to the wheel than a normal-sized person, the airbag will hit me sooner and harder, and I worry the whiplash back into the headrest will break my neck. That did (and does) worry me, so when I started driving we looked into the possibility of getting the airbag disengaged, but no one would even consider that due to the insurance issues and legal risk that would go along with it. As a teenager, as well as an independent wrestler who needed to get to shows, I wasn't going to let any of that get in my way.

That's an attitude I've had as far back as I can remember and still have today. There really isn't much that being about a foot smaller than your average shorter man prohibits me from doing. I can get car rentals without any issues, although some of the people at the desk give me "the look" when I'm picking up the keys. You learn to ignore it. I constantly get asked if I have to shop in the kid's section at clothing stores, which I don't, but buying certain items of clothing can be difficult — my short legs mean I can't buy pants off the shelf, for example, but I'm fine with an adult medium shirt and I just roll the sleeves up if it's a long-sleeve shirt. There are even some benefits to my size — since I wear a size five or six shoe, I can buy the same style I want but in the kids' size and it'll save me about forty dollars per pair. The only other thing I absolutely can't do (theoretically) is ride the bigger rollercoasters that have height restrictions because I'm just a couple of inches too short (sometimes I get sneaked on anyway). For the most part though, I've found that any challenges my size presents can be overcome with hard work or an alternate approach.

As a teenager, however, one area in which overcoming my stature was a huge challenge was dating. I did get to take a girl to homecoming, but I know that was only because I was going with a group she wanted to be with. She didn't even dance with me that night. Things like that didn't make me feel sad or resentful, they just made me angry at myself, wondering, "What's wrong with me?" I couldn't comprehend that, as nice as everyone was to me, teenage girls just weren't able to see past the dwarf thing. No one wanted to be known as the girlfriend of the midget. The closest I got to dating was when a group of people from school all went to hang out at the park and sometimes I'd end up messing around with a girl a little. Whenever I'd ask the girl out on an actual date, she'd back off. Whenever I'd tell a girl that I liked her, the reply would always be "I like you, too, you're a really good friend." It was tough being held at arm's length all the time. I didn't necessarily think I'd be alone my whole life, but I had no idea how or when I'd find someone.

As it happened, I met that first someone in the locker room at a wrestling show. I met Anne Kulow when I was working for South Shore Wrestling in Milwaukee. At twenty-six, she was eight years older and eighteen inches taller than me, a good-looking girl who would be a valet for some of the wrestlers. We instantly took a liking to each other, especially since we were both fans of Ring of Honor. Whenever we were on shows together, we'd end up hanging out and talking for hours. After one show, we got extremely drunk and ended up kissing. It wasn't anything like the "You're nice but . . ." situations. Anne took me for me. We were so in love, and it all happened so quickly.

Me and Anne — just another day at the office.

Dad was happy I'd met someone, but he still wasn't happy about my financial situation. Even though I was wrestling on shows in front of paying customers, it wasn't making me any money. We were given the choice between being paid twenty bucks a night or getting a videotape of the previous show. I'd always take the tape so that I could see what I'd done. If anything, my finances were getting worse because now I was driving to Green Bay, Luxembourg, Manitowoc, and all around Milwaukee, and I wasn't making a dime. Grandpa was behind me all the way, telling me, "You've got to do what makes you happy." He even came along to see me at a few of these events. Dad was less encouraging but he didn't stop me doing what I wanted to do. He was willing to let me fall on my face — literally and figuratively — in pursuing my dreams.

At least I was making some money from other jobs. Toward the end of high school, I'd been working at Dairy Queen to make a little extra cash. I never liked being put on dish duty because I had to use a stool to get up to a sink so big that I could have taken a bath in it. I also didn't enjoy going home with ice cream all over my clothes and sticky shoes but it was a decent enough job and the pay was good. I was getting $7.25 an hour, which was way above minimum wage at the time and more than other people my age were getting for doing the same job. I didn't understand why I was being paid that much, but I wasn't about to start asking questions. When new management came in, they reduced my pay to $5.25, before letting me go a couple of weeks later, claiming they had too many people on staff. I got a job as a cashier at Target instead.

I loved working at Target. I always used to tell people that when I was done with wrestling, I'd go back to Target in a heartbeat. The people were great, the job was fun, and I got to see Grandpa a couple of times a week there. He would come in just to buy toilet paper so he could go through my checkout. I'd love getting an extra moment with my grandpa, even if it was just a smile or a wink. Because of his Target expeditions, he ended up with toilet paper everywhere around his house. My managers usually gave me days off for my indie wrestling bookings. If they didn't, I called in sick. It was a terrible attitude and led to me losing money in two ways — not only was I not earning money from my shift at Target, I was spending more to get to the indie show than I was making on it (if I was making anything at all). My attendance record probably didn't help when I interviewed for a job there as the assets protection manager. The job went to a guy named Josh Weimer, whom I instantly resented. After a while, I realized the store simply couldn't have hired a midget to be an undercover assets protection worker since we little people do tend to stand out in a crowd and people would notice me watching them. I still didn't like Weimer though and remember being pissed off one day when I walked into the break room to find he was the only person there. I grabbed my food and sat far away from him. As I ate, I noticed *Monday Night Raw* was on the TV. "Are you watching this?" I asked. He told me he was. "Do you like wrestling?" I asked. He told me he did. That was the start of our lifelong friendship.

CHAPTER 5

THE DOG COLLAR

Now that Weimer and I talked about wrestling constantly, it wasn't long before everyone at Target had heard about my in-ring activities and some of them even came along to support me. At one show in Appleton, in front of a crowd containing about thirty of my co-workers, I won my first wrestling title, the ACW-NWA Wisconsin X-Division Championship. The Target crew gave me such a great response that night that I felt like the Ultimate Warrior at *WrestleMania* VI. The reality was that ACW only made me champion because they thought having a midget with a title belt on their posters might get them more attention. Even after I realized that, I was still so happy because I was a wrestling *champion*, something I'd always dreamed of but never thought I'd be. The belt itself was hideous, with plastic plates and a red and yellow X made from electrical tape right in the center, but I didn't care how bad it looked — it was *my* title.

Another first I remember vividly is the first time I was in the ring with other little people. For the first six months of my career, I'd only wrestled against regular-sized people but Wisconsin Organized Wrestling, or wow, booked me in a midget tag match. I was tagging with Toad against Short Sleeve Sampson and Meatball who, despite being a midget, weighed 300 pounds. Wrestling a big little guy like Meatball was a different experience than working with other midgets. He didn't bump a lot and that angered me at the time because I thought he was being difficult. But, given his size, it wouldn't have made sense for him to be bumping all over the ring.

One of his big moves was an elbow drop off the ropes. When you're a midget, that's a difficult move to pull off — you don't have a lot of elbow to drop. When a normal-sized guy drops an elbow, they land on the mat with their elbow and forearm on the other side of your head and barely touch you. When a midget does it, he lands on you with all of his weight — and there was a lot of weight behind Meatball's elbow. Another big spot of his was doing Rikishi's stink face, where he'd back you into the corner and shove his ass in your face. I only took that once and that was twice too many.

That first midget match was held on a regular wrestling card which featured little people as a novelty but, later on, I did some work for companies who promoted all-midget wrestling, including Micro Championship Wrestling. The one show I did for them was at a strip club and the thing I loved the most about that night was that because they couldn't do the same comedy midget match over and over, we had to wrestle — so I got to do a bunch of moves I usually wouldn't or couldn't do. As much as I wanted to work a proper match on regular shows, it wouldn't look believable if I gave a suplex to a regular-sized guy, but I could do anything I wanted to with a midget and it would work. We were wrestling in a twelve-foot ring that was only about six inches off the ground since that was all they could fit in the club. Everything was so small that I could hit the ropes like a normal-sized wrestler in a big ring, but the bumps hurt like hell because the ring had no give.

Weimer came with me for that show but, because the club was twenty-one and up, he couldn't get in. I thought that was hilarious, especially since his eighteen-year-old midget buddy ended up winning the Micro Wrestling title in front of a couple hundred people and got to watch hot women strip all night long while he had to stay at the hotel. He didn't mind too much though because the room had a hot tub. He watched March Madness college basketball while I was off working in a strip club, so it ended up being a great night for us both.

As I got more bookings, I worked a lot with Binder around the local wrestling circuit. We joked that we were Wisconsin's version of CM Punk and Colt Cabana because we wrestled each other so much. I loved the physicality of our matches. Most wrestlers held back on me because they didn't want to hurt the little guy, but Binder knew I was tougher than most people realized. My matches with him made me feel like a genuine wrestler rather than a midget in a ring.

I trusted him completely, but accidents still happen: Binder gave me my first concussion — and he wasn't even in the match! I was wrestling a guy called TC Washington, who was short but not quite a midget wrestler, and we were doing a fan distraction finish with Anne as the plant. She started distracting me, asking for an autograph and waiting for Binder to hit the ring. It seemed like he was taking forever and I kept having to ask her, "Is he here yet?" The problem was that Binder was coming through the audience and not only was he having trouble getting through the fans, but security wouldn't let him through because they didn't realize he was part of

The first person to knock me out? My best friend, Binder.

the show. Eventually, he got into the ring, I turned around and he almost took my head off with an unintentionally ultra-stiff clothesline. It knocked me out cold, so I don't remember it at all but I was told my legs went fully over my head.

I was a little stiff with Binder here and there, in particular on one show we did for Brew City Wrestling in Milwaukee. The plan for our dog collar match was for him to get busted open when I used the chain to pull him face-first into the ring post. After he hit, he dropped to the floor for a moment, made the cut, and then looked up at me to ask, "How am I doing?" I couldn't see a single drop of blood, so I told him, "Not very good." He told me to hit him, so I punched him as hard as I could, right in the face. He shook it off and looked back at me. "Okay, now how about you do it where I cut and with the chain?" he asked, sarcastically. I did, and his eyes started to glaze over, but he *still* wasn't bleeding. "Again," he demanded, so I nailed him right in the forehead with the chain. His eyes rolled back in his head and he fell back, out cold. At least he was bleeding by then. When he came to, he was pleased to find out he had a good flow going, but that didn't last long. We did a spot where Anne, who was Binder's manager for the match, threw baby powder at me. I ducked, and she got Binder instead. The moment that baby powder hit Binder's face, it stopped the bleeding. "Come on, get it going again!" Binder urged, so I started punching him over and over. No matter how much I tried to make him bleed, all I was doing was making his forehead stickier. When we got to the back, his forehead was bright purple. He took one look in the mirror and said, "Well, this'll be great for work on Monday."

When it came to training and getting to shows to perform, my work ethic was great. It was pretty decent when it came to my job at Target. It wasn't as good when it came to my education but, after years of Dad and Dorothy constantly telling me that I was a smart kid and could get through school if I just applied myself, I pulled it together and did well enough to graduate. I'm sure a lot of that was because, whether I would admit it or not at the time, I didn't want to let my parents down.

Graduation day was memorable, and not just because I got my diploma when for a long time it looked like I might not. I was with all the other Ps in a row where everyone who'd just been on stage passed behind us on their way back to their seats. My buddy Binder was one of the first to get his diploma and, as he walked behind me, I braced myself knowing he was going to mess with me in some way.

Sure enough, I heard a loud "whack." But I felt nothing. Then the kid with special needs sitting next to me let out an ear-splitting screech and grabbed his shoulder, where Binder — thinking it was me — had just punched him as hard as he could. Binder turned beet red, stammered, "I thought he was you," and rushed back to his seat. It was worth graduating just for the look on Binder's face when he realized he'd assaulted a guy with disabilities.

After high school, Dad made me a deal. Either I could go to college and he'd pay, or I could get a full-time job or two part-time jobs and stay with him, rent-free, while I built up some savings. I chose the college option. I was accepted at the University of Wisconsin at Fox Valley, where I started taking courses in radio broadcasting and radiology. Apart from the word radio, those two things have nothing in common. I'd grown up making mix tapes and listening to the radio all the time, so I liked the idea of being a DJ. In high school, one of our assignments was to write a letter to someone in the profession we wanted to pursue. I wrote to a DJ at the local radio station and he wrote me back a very encouraging letter. As for radiology, we took a career aptitude test in school and my result said I should look into being an X-ray technician. My grandpa and dad both told me there was a lot of money in that field and *that* was all I needed to hear.

I treated college the same way I treated high school, maybe even worse. Out of the six classes I took in the first semester, I failed four. One of those courses was choir. I think I'm the only person in history to fail choir as a college course. It wasn't because I couldn't sing, because I can (or, at least, I could back then), I failed because I missed the end of semester concert to take a wrestling booking. Two weeks after the second semester started, I decided college wasn't for me and walked out in the middle of a class. I was getting more and more wrestling bookings, plus I was working at Target, so I figured that was the equivalent of two jobs.

My dad didn't agree. While he was fine with the Target job, he wasn't willing to accept that wrestling counted as a job (which, given that I was making thirty dollars at most for a match at that point, was probably fair). Dad told me I needed to either get a second part-time job, or I needed to pay rent — it was his way of getting me to take my life seriously. When I got to the end of the month and had no money, he hoped I'd realize I needed to grow up and that wrestling wasn't going to pay the bills. To keep him happy, I got another part-time job in the call center for Eastbay, a sports apparel company. That didn't last long because I had a terrible attitude. My shift started at 7:30 a.m. when no one would be calling in, so I'd just sit there, watching the clock. Within an hour, since I was doing nothing, I'd start asking if I could go home. Usually I'd be out of there by 8:15 a.m. I got fired pretty quickly and, as soon as Dad found out, he told me I needed to start paying rent.

Instead of talking it through with Dad and working out a compromise, I decided to move out. Even though I'd only been with Anne for a couple of months, I started gradually moving in with her and her mom, taking more and more of my stuff over each time I went, and spending more time there than I did at home. The worst thing is that I didn't even tell my dad what I was doing. By the time holiday season rolled around, I considered Anne's place home. When I visited Dad on Christmas Day, I stayed for an hour and spent about twenty dollars on all my family's gifts. In my mind, I was an adult and I'd moved on. In reality, I was acting like a kid convinced he knew it all. Meanwhile, Anne and her mom didn't get *anything* for each other but gave me a ton of gifts. It made me feel so special that they wanted to make sure I felt like part of their family — and made me feel more self-righteous in my decision to walk away from my own family. After that, I didn't talk to my dad for months. It's the biggest regret of my life. He'd done so much for me and didn't deserve for his son to act like such an asshole.

When I finally did get in touch, it was by email. In February, I emailed Dad on his birthday because I couldn't be bothered to call. He just wrote back, "Thanks, Dylan. I really love you. If you want to talk sometime, please give me a call. I miss you." That broke me up. Anne was at work, but when I showed the message to her mom, she urged me to talk to my dad. I did, and during a highly emotional call, we hashed everything out. It was only then I realized how much I missed him. I still stayed with Anne and her mom, and I kept wrestling, but at least Dad and I started talking more again and rebuilding the relationship I'd nearly wrecked.

While my relationship with Dad was getting back on track, my wrestling career didn't seem to be going anywhere. I'd travel, I'd perform, sometimes the crowds would be in the hundreds, other times they'd be double digits — or less. For the show I was told I'd be dropping the ACW-NWA Wisconsin X-Division Championship, we drew a grand total of nine people. I tried so hard to argue my way out of losing the championship that night, pointing out that I could drop it on any other show, so more people would get their money's worth from seeing a title change. Looking back, I can't believe I made such a fuss about dropping a fake championship but, at the time, I was so bummed out about doing it in front of such a small audience. It didn't make any sense to me that we would waste a title change on a house of less than a hundred bucks. That night and our single digit audience definitely made me wonder if I was making the right career decisions. I had bills to pay and was hardly making any money, so I started thinking maybe my dad had been right all along and the wrestling thing just wasn't going to work out. Maybe I did need to grow up. But before I'd had too long to think about my future, I picked up a message on my phone that changed everything.

"Hey Dylan," the voice said, "this is Ken Anderson."

CHAPTER 6

THE GREEN NURSE PANTS

I was convinced it was one of my friends playing a joke on me — a rib, in wrestling terms — but I called back. I quickly realized it actually *was* Ken. He explained that WWE had been asking if anyone knew a local midget they could use in a backstage comedy segment with Candice Michelle, Gene Snitsky, and Goldust on *Raw*. Just as I'd started thinking my wrestling career was never going to amount to anything more than a run in the indies, I was being offered the chance to be on WWE TV. Naturally, I jumped at the opportunity.

Ken told me to come to the show in Milwaukee that night, so I grabbed my gear, and Anne and I headed off to the arena. I was nervous when we got there but Ken was one of the first people I saw so that helped put me at ease. After sitting around for what felt like forever, I decided to explore. Eventually, the unknown midget wandered out into the huge, empty arena and noticed Arn Anderson, Pat Patterson, and Viscera sitting ringside, having a meeting. The

49

midget then proceeded to plop himself down in an empty chair next to Viscera, interrupting the meeting by cheerfully saying, "Hey guys, how's it going?" WWE officials Arn and Pat simply stared while the 6'9" Viscera heaved his 500-pound frame out of his seat and boomed, "Why don't you come with me for a second . . ."

You might think meeting a genuinely huge guy like Viscera for the first time would be extra intimidating for a guy of my stature — but you'd be wrong. It's actually the opposite. A normal-sized person will meet some people who are a little bigger and some who are a little smaller. A giant like Vis is something different for them, and that can be overwhelming at first. However, for me, it's every-day life. I got used to being the smallest person in the room from a very young age, so meeting this behemoth up close for the first time didn't faze me at all. To me, everyone taller than six feet looks pretty much the same, height-wise. The Undertaker might tower over most wrestlers but he's no more or less physically imposing to a guy like me than Sheamus or Mark Henry. There's only so far back my neck can go when I'm looking up.

Once we were away from the ring, Vis calmly and politely smart-ened me up: extra talent shouldn't be wandering around at ringside and interjecting themselves into meetings they haven't been invited to. He advised me to just keep to myself — one of the unofficial rules of being a new extra in the locker room. Without realizing it, I'd already broken another unofficial rule by bringing Anne to the show: you don't bring people with you when you're an extra and you certainly don't ask for them to get a free ticket to the show, too, which was something else I'd done (and, to WWE's credit, something they'd agreed to without question).

After Vis had smartened me up, I went backstage and continued breaking the rules. Who knew if I'd ever get to go backstage again, so I tried to get as many photos with WWE superstars as I could! I'd managed to get photos with four or five people before WWE's head of security, Jimmy Tillis, came over and sharply told me to stop both-ering the talent or I'd be asked to leave.

I went back to sitting patiently with Ken, which was when he casually mentioned that I wasn't even the only little person they'd had backstage that day. Earlier on, before I'd got there, management had given another midget a tryout for a newly created role — a leprechaun sidekick for Irish brawler Finlay. As I was still processing that piece of information, I was called to film my segment — a weird sexual innuendo sketch involving a large chunk of cheese, a jar of peanut butter, and me as the punchline.

At some point during filming, Vince McMahon wandered past and saw the new midget shooting a segment with the hot girl, the foot fetishist, and the walking Academy Award. Without missing a beat, Vince came over to say hello, shook my hand, asked how I was, then kept on walking — just another day at the office for the boss.

It definitely wasn't just another day at the office for me. I was so excited that the moment we finished filming, I got on MySpace and told all of my friends to make sure to watch *Raw* that night. I was convinced this was my big break, even if it was in some bizarre backstage comedy sketch.

But that night, *Raw* started, *Raw* finished, and my segment was nowhere in sight. I was crushed. (I learned later on that segments get cut from WWE shows all the time, especially when they're not important to the overall direction of the show.) I still got paid $500 for the night and the sketch did end up on WWE.com later, but that wasn't much of a consolation for not being on the biggest weekly show in the industry. There was, however, a silver lining to my trip to Milwaukee. I'd been given a chance to be backstage at a WWE event and found out they were looking to hire a midget — that was something I wasn't going to let pass me by. I'd never met Dave "Fit" Finlay before and his reputation preceded him as a double-tough brawler you didn't want to mess with. But I didn't know if the opportunity would ever present itself again, so I went up to him, introduced myself, and asked if I could come back the next day for the *SmackDown* tapings to try out to be his leprechaun. I was over the moon when he said yes and told me to go talk to Tony Garea, who was in charge of extra talent at the time. When I told Tony that Fit wanted me to try out for him, he told me to come back the next night and they'd pay me another $500.

Anne and I drove home that night on a complete high. She was happy that I'd been able to get two of her favorites, Trish Stratus and Mickie James, to take a picture with her, and now I was going to get a chance to try out for a spot in WWE, as well as being paid $1,000 for going to wrestling shows two nights in a row. That was more than I was getting paid in a month at Target. Immediately, I started thinking how many video games and wrestling figures I could buy.

The next day, I drove out to Green Bay for the *SmackDown* tapings and hung out backstage, waiting for Finlay to tell me it was time to go do our interviews. When the moment finally came, I was given a script and was asked to do my lines in an Irish accent, which, given the role was a leprechaun, I probably should have seen coming. I've never been able to do any accent, least of all a convincing Irish brogue. We tried over and over, but I couldn't do it. I got really flustered and kept apologizing but Fit stayed perfectly calm. Eventually, after it became clear it just wasn't going to work, Finlay said, "That'll be fine for now." I asked him how he thought I did. "It was okay," he said, unconvincingly. "We'll let you know." I already knew. I was so angry with myself. Even so, I gave Fit a DVD I'd made of some of my work — just in case.

As I was getting ready to leave, I saw Rey Mysterio walking about with his mask off. Rey had been one of the wrestlers I'd grown up idolizing and, since I didn't have anything to lose, I asked if I could take a picture with him. Without hesitation, Rey said, "Sure, let me go grab my mask and get someone to take it for us." As we went out into the hallway, the first person he ran into was Jimmy Tillis. Jimmy took one look at me and hissed, "You again . . ." But Rey insisted Jimmy take the picture. Through gritted teeth, Jimmy did and then handed me back my camera, telling me, "You're lucky I don't break this goddamn thing right now." Over those first two days, I think I made the worst impression possible when it came to backstage etiquette.

When I got home, convinced I'd blown my one chance to get a spot with WWE, I settled back into my life of wrestling for independent promotions on weekends and working at Target during the week to try to make a dent in the sizable credit card bills I'd run up. It definitely wasn't the life I'd dreamed of but, since I'd screwed up my tryout, it was the life I had.

Six or seven weeks later, I woke up to find several missed calls on my phone. Most of them were from a withheld number but a couple were from Ken so, sitting there in bed, I tried calling him back. I couldn't get hold of him but, when I gave up trying, the phone rang — another withheld number. I was convinced it was going to be a debt collector, so I didn't answer. Moments later, the phone rang again. The withheld number. Again, I didn't answer it. A few minutes later, it rang again and Anne, still mostly asleep, told me to just answer it. Getting ready for the debt collector to demand money I didn't have, I picked up and held the phone to my ear.

"Dylan, this is Tommy Dreamer. It's a good thing you picked up. If you hadn't, we were going to hire the other midget . . ."

Tommy, who'd been a performer for both ECW and WWE, was now working in the WWE office and involved in recruiting new talent. I listened in a daze as he told me they were going to go with me as Finlay's sidekick, I was going to be making $56,000 a year, and I needed to get myself a leprechaun outfit by Sunday. He told me Howard Finkel, the legendary ring announcer, would be calling me with my travel details, then left me to wonder if I was still dreaming or if this was one of my friends ribbing me. My tryout had been the shits. I couldn't figure out why they'd gone with me. I found out later that Ken had fought hard for me with Tommy, Fit, and John Laurinaitis, who was the head of talent relations. Ken had explained to them that I wasn't just a little guy, I was a wrestler. I could work, take bumps, had a great attitude, and was definitely the guy they needed to hire. They respected his opinion enough that it got me a job and I'm forever grateful to Ken for sticking his neck out for me.

The first person I called was Grandpa who, with the laugh that only came out when he was truly happy, congratulated me. Grandpa had always sworn to my dad that I'd make something of myself in the wrestling business. I never had to guess about my grandfather's pride in me — he was always my number-one supporter. Whether it was getting through my surgeries, playing softball, graduating, or even making no money as an independent wrestler, he'd always tell anyone who would listen how proud he was of everything I did. I'm sure part of his pride was because I had an extra thing to overcome given my achondroplasia, but he never once spoke to me about my height or my condition.

I knew I had to let Dad know next, but I was worried about making that call. We weren't as close as we'd been before I left home, and I knew he still had strong reservations about me wrestling. I tried to put off the call but Anne, rightly, forced me to get on with it. When I let him know that I'd just been offered a contract with WWE, he told me, "Dylan, I'm your dad so I will always look out for you, but I've never doubted how much you want this. All I want is for you to be happy and now you're going to get to live your dream."

I called Binder and Weimer next and they were both blown away. I'm sure it must have been hard for Binder to hear that his friend had just got signed by WWE for being a midget, while he was working his ass off on the indie scene for next to nothing. If it *did* bother him, he didn't let it show — he was supportive and enthusiastic.

Everything became very real when my phone rang again about an hour later and I heard the unmistakable voice of the "Fink" telling me I was going to be flying out to Phoenix, Arizona, on May 21, for the *Judgment Day* pay-per-view. I thanked Howard, told him I'd be there, and hung up with so many questions swirling through my head. How would Target react when I told them I was leaving? Where was I going to get a leprechaun outfit? How could I travel around the country — and maybe the world — by myself?

And, above all else, how had this happened? Deep down, I'd always known the odds of me ever getting a spot with WWE were microscopic, yet here we were and the contract was on its way.

The first order of business was arranging my outfit. I called a bunch of costume shops in the area and no one could help me until I spoke to a lady who said she thought she could put something together. Still surprised at being offered the contract, I forgot to mention my height to her so, when I got to her shop, she got a surprise of her own.

She had a selection of full-sized items — a fluffy white shirt, a green vest and an overcoat — that she was prepared to let me hire for $200 a week, but she told me I'd have to find the pants and shoes by myself. She also said that I wouldn't be able to tailor it and would have to pin it every time I wore it. I called Tommy to explain what she'd said, and he just told me to bring in the receipts and WWE would pay me back. Just to be certain, I reiterated that she'd said we couldn't tailor it. Again, Tommy told me to go ahead. "But Tommy, she said . . ." I heard how annoying I sounded and didn't want to make Tommy sick of dealing with me after only one day, so I told him I'd take care of it.

A trip to a Payless shoe store got me a pair of white and green shoes, and I found a pair of green nurse's pants at the Uniform Outlet which I cut off to complete my look. Even though the rest of the costume was going to cost me (or WWE) $200 a week, that one pair of eleven dollar scrubs was the only pair of pants I ever wore as part of my leprechaun outfit. They lasted me for years.

Outfit arranged, I moved on to the next task — quitting my job. I called Target and told them that I was starting with WWE on Sunday. "So, you're back on Monday then?" they asked. I tried again, explaining I wasn't coming back and I'd been offered a contract. For some reason, they couldn't grasp what I was saying so I kept trying until they eventually said, "Oh, so you're *leaving* leaving!" I don't think they had too many people say they were quitting their job to go touring with World Wrestling Entertainment.

When I got to Phoenix, I was disappointed to find out that Vince McMahon had decided I wasn't going to make my debut that night in Finlay's match against Chris Benoit. Vince's reasoning was that more people would see my first appearance if I made it on *SmackDown*, a network television show, instead of on the *Judgment Day* pay-per-view. It made sense, but I just wanted to get on screen as soon as possible. Another thing that upset me that day was when the producers started talking about how they needed to make my outfit dirtier since my character was supposed to live under the ring. I told them that the costume was a rental so they couldn't get it dirty. That was when I quickly learned that you don't say "no" in wrestling — I was simply told, "Well, that's what we're going to do," and that was the end of that discussion. John Laurinaitis told me to buy the outfit from the costume woman and they'd pay me back. Even when I said the woman had been clear it was only a rental, John told me, "Whatever they want, we'll cover it."

I was sent to Richie Posner in props, also known as the "magic department," where Richie used oil to make my outfit suitably dirty. Among many things, Richie had worked on all the costumes for Al Snow's European title run, played an usher for Goldust, a doctor in several random backstage scenes, and was involved in several other higher profile visual effects. He could make anything out of anything and get whatever you needed on short notice, and that wasn't the only magic that happened there — he loved to do magic tricks, especially if there were any kids around. After he'd made my clean costume disappear and replaced it with a dirt-covered outfit, I went back to show the producers, who then asked me to bleach my hair and eyebrows. I had to do that for years, every couple of weeks. How I have any hair left at all now is beyond me.

I hung around backstage for the next couple of days and, by the time we got to Bakersfield, California, on Tuesday for the *SmackDown* taping, I couldn't wait to get started. I soon found myself standing around with Finlay, John Laurinaitis, and Vince McMahon, discussing Finlay's upcoming match with Paul Burchill, a great wrestler who was always in a positive mood. Being around Vince was intimidating to say the least — I knew he could fire me on the spot if he heard anything he didn't like. It didn't help that during this planning session, Laurinaitis reminded me that my run as Finlay's leprechaun was only going to be a short-term thing. Still, even if I only worked there for one day, I'd get to say I'd worked for WWE.

Vince explained I'd be under the ring during the match and, after the finish, Finlay would roll out to the floor, lift the apron, and a beam of green light would come from under the ring, at which point I'd come storming out. "You'll be like a Tasmanian devil," Vince told me. "You'll act like a frantic, wild animal, and you'll roll in the ring, and you'll jump on Paul. Finlay will pull you off, pick you up, and throw you back down on him, then he'll shove you out and kick you back underneath the ring." I was told that I should be expressive, and should yell and scream and grunt, but I wasn't ever specifically told I shouldn't talk. The fact that I didn't came back to bite me in the ass for years.

We ran a rehearsal — WWE always rehearses on the afternoon of a show, but they don't go through everything. Matches and entrances are left up to the people involved, unless there is anything either new, complicated, or vitally important, but all of the talking segments and the more creative elements for the show are run through to make sure they go smoothly.

We got ready to start the rehearsal, so Paul and Fit climbed into the ring while I lifted the ring apron and dived underneath. I knew I'd see a big green light sitting there, but I was surprised to see a mat, a monitor, and a headset, too. Nick Daw, one of WWE's technicians, crawled under with me and demonstrated how to use the headset and monitor, then we were set to go. My heart was racing and I was determined to make a great first impression on Vince and his team. I could hear what was happening on the mat above — Finlay walked over to the ropes, left the ring, and lifted up the apron. The green light came on. I rushed toward the outside, ran straight into the metal beam at the edge of the ring, knocked myself silly, and fell over backward.

"Stop!" screamed Vince. "Stop! Stop! Stop! The moment he lifts the apron and the light goes on, you have to be out!"

We tried it again. This time, the green light didn't come on. Worried I'd get screamed at again, I stayed under the ring.

"Goddammit! Where are you?!"

I creeped out from under the ring. "I was waiting for the light."

"Where was the light, goddammit?!" he yelled at the production crew. At least it wasn't me being shouted at this time.

(And, yes, Vince likes to say goddammit *a lot*, especially when he's trying to make a point.)

On the third attempt, I heard Finlay roll out and the light came on, so I shot out from under the ring — to more shouting from Vince. "No! Wait for him to lift the apron!" By now, I was convinced this would be my first and last day under contract to WWE.

We tried it a fourth time and finally it all clicked. Finlay rolled out, the light came on, the apron came up, I came out and went crazy. Finlay threw me into the ring and slammed me on Paul Burchill. Then Fit forced me outside the ring, ushered me back underneath, and the light went out.

"That was perfect!" Vince shouted. "Perfect!"

I lay under the ring, feeling only relief in the silence that followed. It was broken by Vince's voice booming, "Where are you?" I shouted back that I was under the ring. "Well, come out here, I'm talking to you!"

Thinking I'd just messed up again, I crawled out to find Vince grinning. "Do that again later."

During the show that night, when the arena was dark and the audience of thousands was focused on a video being played on the screen, I went out to the ring with a black hoodie and sweats over my leprechaun outfit, surrounded by a group of local helpers and security. As they pretended to adjust the ring apron, I slid underneath. The anticipation — and nerves — grew as I heard Finlay's music play, then Paul's, then the sounds of the match going on above me. The ref counted three, Finlay's music came back on, and I heard him leaving the ring. This was it — showtime. Fit lifted up the apron, yelled at me to get out there, and I scurried out just like the Tasmanian devil Vince wanted. Finlay picked me up and threw me in the ring, where I grabbed his shillelagh (the traditional Irish wooden club Fit brought to the ring with him) and started to hit Paul with it. Finlay slid back in the ring, picked me up, and threw me down hard on poor Paul, before dragging me out of the ring and kicking me back underneath. It couldn't have gone better.

Lying under that ring, I was as happy as can be. The audience had reacted well to my sudden appearance and I knew it had looked good. I put the headset on and started watching the monitor when Vince's voice came through — "Dylan? Good job." Hearing that made me feel great.

As the arena went dark for a video before the main event, I wasn't sure if I should sneak out and go to the back or just stay where I was, so I use the headset to speak to Kevin Dunn, the main producer of all WWE TV, and asked when I could leave. He told me to just wait and they'd get me out of there when they could. The main event started, and I was still under the ring. As the match went on, I found I could sit up comfortably and even stand bent over. Provided I didn't sit directly under any of the beams, I wouldn't get hit by anything happening above me. After a while, I began to wonder if I was going to be kept there until everyone had left the arena, so I checked in again with Kevin. Once again, I was told to wait. The bell rang, the main event ended, and I still wasn't being told anything. Finally, as people were filing out of the arena, the message came through for me to slide out and run to the back.

After I got back home from my first week with WWE, I stopped by to see the lady who had rented me my outfit and, rather than explaining that her costume was now covered in oil and dirt, I told her I'd ripped the jacket. She just said to give her $150 and I could keep the clothes. I paid, wondering how the math behind that deal made any sense given the $200 rental charge, then asked her if she had any more outfits, at which point she politely asked me to leave.

The next week, I did a similar spot during Finlay's match, got back under the ring, and put the headset back on. Kevin's voice came through soon enough. "All right, Vince, when are we going to get the little guy out of there?"

"Goddammit, Kevin — he has a name!" came the reply. He continued, "Dylan, I'm sorry about last week — we forgot you were under there. This is all still new to us, but we'll be sure to sneak you out of there soon." It felt good to know that Vince was looking out for me. Over the next few weeks, he'd always check to make sure I had something comfortable to lie down on and there was always water or Gatorade with me under the ring.

One of the unexpected benefits of my role in the company was that I got to see and hear so much about how a wrestling show is produced. From where I was under the ring, I could hear the commentators faintly but, on the headset, I could hear what Vince and Kevin were instructing them to say, as well as when they told people to cue replays and other technical aspects involved with running live or taped TV shows. I never heard either Vince or Kevin lose their temper with the commentators though, something that I'd heard happened regularly — they evidently could push a button and communicate privately when they wanted to talk to (or yell at) one specific person.

Because *SmackDown* was taped at the time, there were times when I heard Vince order the finish of a match to be redone. At times, they'd have one of the wrestlers go back to the ring and say something on the microphone to get the other guy out there, then they'd go right to the same finish. Other times, the two wrestlers would simply come out with no explanation to the audience and start running through the end of their match again.

I would also hear a few comments about talent here and there. Sometimes it would be about their look, either pointing out that someone needed to get in better shape or that their gear wasn't particularly flattering. Other times, it would be about their ring work, usually either wanting people to tighten up on their strikes to make them look more believable or to work a hold properly so it looked like they were trying to wear down their opponent rather than just sitting and resting while barely touching their opponent. I took everything on board as best I could and I think it helped me understand both the wrestling and the entertainment industries so much better. The knowledge I picked up from my time under the ring still helps me to this day.

CHAPTER 7

THE TRAVELING CIRCUS

For my first month with WWE, I was only working the TV tapings but, at the end of that month, Howard Finkel called to let me know management wanted me on the live events, too. As I was going to be going on the road full-time, Howard explained that my weekly schedule meant I would fly out on Saturday mornings, work shows on Saturday and Sunday nights, take a night off on Monday (because WWE didn't want to run a live event against *Raw*), then tape *SmackDown* on Tuesdays before flying back home on Wednesday mornings. I was so happy to hear they were interested in using me more that I didn't think about the financial ramifications of this — going on the road and working the house shows meant I would have a chance to make a lot more money.

I was told I would be traveling with Shawn Daivari, which suited me fine because I knew him from the indie circuit. Riding with Daivari meant that I was also riding with his regular travel companions, Mark Henry and the Great Khali. Our van must have seemed ridiculous to anyone who looked inside — a regular-sized guy driving, a seven-foot giant in the passenger seat, a huge strong-man in the middle row. and a midget surrounded by all the bags in the back. We were like a traveling circus.

Everyone got along well most of the time, but Khali would sometimes try to get a rise out of Mark using the handful of English words he knew, then he'd sit back and laugh his giant laugh. Now and then, he'd push it too far. There was one time in particular where we all thought Mark was asleep and Khali started trash-talking him. When Khali said something about him being stupid, Mark shot up out of his seat, furious. Khali quickly started back peddling in his broken English — "No, man — I no call *you* stupid . . ."

Despite being a giant, Khali knew that he didn't want to piss Henry off — Mark is inhumanly strong. I saw him roll up a frying pan with his bare hands in rehearsal once. He was understandably proud of himself whenever he'd do that. I've also seen Mark rip a phone book in half and crush an apple with one hand. Khali was scary strong him-self but, of the four of us, it was Daivari who worked the hardest in the gym. I'd never gone to gyms with any regularity and I had to make that adjustment when I was on the road. Mark didn't go much and whenever Khali went, he'd walk around, take a bunch of phone calls, lift a few weights, take a bunch more calls, lift again, and then say, "I'm done, brother." He'd only do about twenty minutes total, all arms and chest, never anything with his legs. There was a reason he wore the long baggy pants when he wrestled: he has very long, skinny legs and a short, thick torso, and that makes it difficult for him to get around. I felt bad for him at times because I could see how hard it was for him to move. It was almost the opposite of me, where I've got short legs that get tired quickly.

Khali could be something of a diva. When he first came over to the WWE developmental system, management put people on what was called "Khali duty," where another of the boys would have to take care of him and his wife all week. I think that led to him feeling like he was entitled, which could be annoying. The worst part about traveling with Khali though was that he'd smoke in the car all the time. Despite that, I got on well with him and we had some fun when we were out in public. Whenever we'd go to a bar, I'd hold Khali's pinkie finger on the way in and he'd tell everyone I was his son. Then he'd lift me onto a stool or sit me on the bar and we'd hang out. A lot of people didn't have any idea how to take us. Bartenders wouldn't card me as often when I was with Khali but I'd get it a lot at other times. Up until I was around twenty-five, I'd get carded at every bar I'd go into, although in many places, the people who challenged my age looked like they didn't want to because they were afraid of offending me.

When it came to restaurants, Khali wasn't as much fun because he didn't like to eat anywhere other than Denny's. He was comfortable there because he knew he'd always be able to get something he wanted. He would order so much food that he'd take up all the space at the table with his plates. We'd usually have to get two booths, Mark and me at one, Khali and Daivari at the other. Khali would almost always have the same thing — four chicken breasts, eight eggs, and toast. It was like watching an elephant eat — although he had pretty good table manners for a giant.

One time, when he had to go outside to take a call, he asked me to order for him. Without thinking about it, I ordered him a burger. He was upset when the food came, telling me, "I no eat this, man." I didn't understand what his problem was until Daivari smartened me up to the fact that cows are the most sacred animals in Hinduism, so offering him a burger was asking him to commit sacrilege. He got his chicken, eggs, and toast in the end.

There were some benefits of traveling with Khali — one of his friends worked at Sony's film studio and, because Khali had worked on *The Longest Yard* with Adam Sandler, he asked us if we wanted to stop by and see Adam's office. It was just another day for Khali but it was my first time being inside the world of a major celebrity and I was blown away. There was cool memorabilia everywhere, a bunch of arcade games, even a completely separate room just for his dog. Before we left, I was given a DVD of every Adam Sandler movie ever released.

The WWE locker room seemed to warm to me pretty quickly and I never had any problems with being hazed to any great extent. Sure, I was subjected to my share of ribs just liked everyone else, but no one messed with me too much. Just like in high school, I didn't take myself too seriously and always cracked jokes about my stature. Also, it didn't hurt that everyone knew Finlay was looking out for me. He's genuinely one of the toughest and most respected men in the business and people know not to mess with him. I clicked with Fit right away. They'd been trying out other midgets for the role for three months before they decided to go with me. Knowing that I'd been picked after so many tryouts was an amazing feeling. I really think that if I hadn't got the gig, I probably wouldn't have continued wrestling for very long.

The more time I spent with Fit, the more I discovered that as well as being one of the toughest men in the industry, he's also one of the smartest. He's done so much and worked in so many places that the amount of knowledge and the depth of his understanding of wrestling is incredible.

For our first couple of months together, we'd go through the same routine. I'd jump in the ring and Fit would slam me on people or I'd sit on their belly like he did when he pinned them. I couldn't believe that in such a short space of time, I'd gone from being Shortstack the indie midget to someone who was getting weekly exposure on network TV. I may have been being seen by more people but no one knew what to call me other than Finlay's leprechaun or Finlay's midget. Then, on commentary one week, Michael Cole repeatedly referred to me as Little Bastard. When I heard that, I thought, "That can't be what they're going to call me." But when my official WWE contract came through, sure enough, there it was — WWE made it clear in the terms that they owned the names Little Bastard and L'il Bastard. It was surreal seeing that name in an official WWE program and on promotional photos. I thought it was great, although I did wonder how they'd get action figures called Little Bastard on the shelves at Toys "R" Us if things went well.

Working on live events was fun, but I wasn't as comfortable as when I worked the TV tapings. At the house shows, there was no pad under the ring for me, no monitor or headset, and if they couldn't black out the building enough for me to get to the ring between matches, I'd need to get in position before the fans were let in and stay under the ring until they'd all left. That meant I'd need to be in place ninety minutes before some shows started and could end up staying under there for almost five hours, so I had to train myself to not need to pee for a long period of time. I found I could fall asleep as the fans were coming into the building but I'd always wake up at the beginning of the show — especially if there were fireworks involved. The first few times the fireworks woke me up, I'd jump out of my skin and momentarily wonder where the hell I was. Soon enough, it became second nature to wake up when they played the first video of the night — that intro video became my alarm clock.

After a while, I started being able to visualize the matches just by the noises I'd hear. I would be able to tell when people locked up, when people were shot into the ropes, when they'd hit an elbow and take a bump. And not just in Finlay's matches either — I heard the matches so many times it felt like I was watching them.

Soon after I started, Finlay won the U.S. title from Bobby Lashley with my help. This led to my first appearance on the WWE pay-per-view *The Great American Bash* in 2006. Finlay and Bobby were supposed to have a rematch for the title but Bobby was taken out with elevated liver enzymes. William Regal took his place and he and Fit had a hard-hitting match that I was involved with. I chased Regal around the outside of the ring with the shillelagh, bit his fingers when he put them over the edge of the ring, and, to set up the end of the match, unlaced his boot when he was straddling the ring apron. The only problem was that, when we got to that spot, the knot in his laces had become too tight and I couldn't undo it. We were live on PPV, I was taking what felt like forever to do my job and

Regal was looking down at me, asking what was going on. I ended up clawing at his laces until I cut my index finger. We finally got the boot off, Finlay and Regal went to the finish, and I sat under the ring, holding my bleeding finger and worrying that a blunder like this so early in my run could cost me my job. As it turned out, everyone understood things don't always go to plan.

Finlay and I carried on working with Bobby when he came back, as well as getting into things with two of the company's biggest stars in Booker T and Dave Bautista, who wrestled as Batista. Finlay would usually tag with Booker, although they fought one time where I had to chase Booker's valet, his real-life wife Sharmell, around ringside with a mouse. Booker was doing a King gimmick at that point and I loved him in that role. He would get completely in the zone when playing that character and make everyone laugh. At live events, he and Sharmell would mess with Tony Chimel, the ring announcer, demanding Chimel say "All hail King Booker" every eight seconds. Each night, Booker would take longer and longer to get to the ring to the point where, one show, his music played a full three times and still Tony was held to the eight-second rule.

A Short Story: Booker T Needs His Red Bull

Backstage, there would always be a big bucket filled with ice, bottles of water and Gatorade, and Booker's two cans of Red Bull. At every live event and every TV show, without fail, Booker T would have two cans of Red Bull. He'd either bring them himself or have a runner get them. He'd drink the first when he was getting changed into his gear and the second just before his match, when he was jumping rope and stretching.

On one show, just before he warmed up, he went to the bucket for his pre-match Bull. After digging around, he turned to the room, eyes bulging out of his head, and yelled, "Who the hell be taking my Red Bull?" Sharmell told him not to get worked up, but there was no calming him down.

Michael Hayes, one of the producers, asked around and, after a minute or two, came over to Booker, holding one of the Gymini twins by the ear like a naughty child. The Gymini twin said he thought it was there for anyone to take and Booker absolutely went off on him, saying there was always water and always Gatorade but never more than two Red Bulls, so why would the one remaining Red Bull that night be for the Gymini guy who only just joined the company? I couldn't believe this was all over a can of Red Bull. It happened another time when we were on an overseas tour and Booker flipped out again.

Sharmell could calm him down most of the time, but when there was a Red Bull involved, all bets were off.

As the year went on, I got to appear on a few more PPVs, including an event that meant a lot to me.

Growing up, the *Survivor Series* had been one of my favorite annual events, second only to the *Royal Rumble*. I loved the way they would put together random teams just for that one night, and I would go to the local video store just to see the covers of the boxes showing who the captains were and who they'd picked for their team. *Survivor Series '93* is one of the first events I remember distinctly, with Lex Luger's team against Yokozuna's team. Even though, looking back, the event wasn't great, as a seven-year-old, I loved it. I was less impressed the following year when Jerry Lawler and his "King's Court" of three little people took on Doink the Clown and *his* team of three little people. I wasn't insulted by it because I felt they were making fun of midgets, I was just embarrassed by it because it wasn't funny at all. Even as a kid, I thought it was dumb.

After that, there wasn't another little person on the *Survivor Series* for twelve years until I crawled out from under the ring in the second-to-last match at *Survivor Series 2006*. Finlay threw me at Bobby Lashley, who ducked, and the company's top star, John Cena, caught me. Moments later, the Big Show kicked Cena, sending me flying. The spot wasn't much, but appearing on one of WWE's most established special events was still an incredible feeling.

I appeared on the *Armageddon* pay-per-view in December, playing a brief role in the main event where Finlay was teaming with Booker to take on Batista and Cena. My job was to climb into the ring when the referee was distracted, then try to kick Cena. He would move and instead of connecting with him, I'd employ the old midget party trick and kick myself in the head. It all went well but what very few people realized is how close I came to missing my moment in that match.

Even though I was only going to be part of the closing ten minutes of the show, that was one of the nights where I was told to get under the ring before the first match. That meant a several hour wait under there which, by itself, wasn't an issue. The problem was that the opening match of the PPV was an Inferno match between Kane and Montel Vontavious Porter where there were burners placed around the outside of the ring. The propane tanks fueling them were underneath the ring with me and Nick Daw, who was in charge of controlling the flames. As we waited for the show to start, Nick told me that I needed to be careful to not hit any of the pipes and that once the match was over, they were going to slide the burners under the ring — and that they'd be extremely hot.

As I was watching the match on the monitor and the underneath of the ring became hotter and hotter, I noticed a strange smell. There must have been a leak in one of the pipes, as the smell got increasingly worse and started to make me feel dizzy and sick. I told Nick that I had to get out of there, but he insisted I stay where I was.

Before the match finished, I'd thrown up in a bucket and almost passed out. Fortunately, there were several matches before I was needed to make my appearance so I had enough time to drink some water and recover.

It would have been one thing to find a midget gassed into unconsciousness under the ring but it was another thing entirely when Finlay found a sleeping midget under the ring at a live event on an overseas tour.

A combination of international travel and a few too many drinks the previous night had run me down and, because it was a live event and not TV, I didn't have a monitor to watch. I'd fallen asleep under the ring at other shows but I'd always woken up during the evening's introduction video. On this night, however, I slept through the whole show, even when they introduced all six people in the main event — Finlay, who was the only man under 280 pounds, the Undertaker, Kane, Batista, the Great Khali, and Big Daddy V (Viscera's new character). In spite of the near ton of weight stomping around just above my head, I was out like a light.

When the time came for my spot, Fit lifted the apron for me and waited — nothing happened. "Dylan!" he shouted. Still nothing. Then he looked under the ring and saw me lying there, facedown. Later, he told me that he thought I was dead. He reached in and shook me until I started to come around. "What are you doing?" he asked. All I could come back with was "I'm sleeping!" Laughing his ass off, he grabbed me, dragged me out, and threw me in the ring.

As I got to my feet and dusted off the cobwebs, I suddenly remembered what my spot was and realized how much trouble I was in. The Undertaker was lying in the ring, waiting. My spot was to bump into him, then he would do his zombie sit up, grab me by the throat, get to his knees, and chokeslam me. I could tell how much trouble I was in from the look in his eyes. All I could do was keep saying, "I'm sorry, I'm sorry, I'm sorry . . ." He heaved me up, me still begging forgiveness, and planted me down (carefully) on the mat. As he rolled me out of the ring, I was still apologizing.

As each of the wrestlers came backstage after the match, they found out why I'd been late for my spot and couldn't stop laughing. The Undertaker was the last one to make it to the back and fixed me with a terrifying glare. "Where were you?" he asked. All I could manage was another "I'm sorry." Finlay jumped in and told me to tell him why I was late. I shook my head and kept apologizing. 'Taker kept glaring at me and said, "Son, I think you should tell me why." I finally told him that I'd fallen asleep. Finlay let out a huge laugh as 'Taker's eyes widened in disbelief. I waited for him to pass sentence — but he just shook his head and walked away.

I turned back to Fit and asked how I could fix it. Fit told me 'Taker liked Jack Daniel's, so I gave one of the show runners some money and asked him to pick me up a bottle when they went out to get the supplies for the tour buses. The next day, I climbed up into the babyface bus (they had one bus for the heels and another for the good guys) and approached 'Taker, who always sat in the center at the very back so he could see everyone. With my head hanging, I walked the length of the bus and placed the bottle of Jack on the table in front of the godfather of the locker room. "You didn't have to do that," he said. "I was just giving you shit — I can't believe you fell asleep under the goddamn ring." He laughed, I breathed a sigh of relief, and he told me to sit down and that I was riding with them that night. We shared that bottle with the other guys on board, even though I should have been riding with the heels. Fit came over to check on me and they made him stay, too. He hated it, partly because he was so committed to being a heel that he felt out of place anywhere other than the heel bus, and partly because I wouldn't stop prodding him, asking, "How're you liking being a babyface?" Even though Fit hated it, I loved it. A lot of the time, the heel bus would end up being for the people who wanted to sleep or play cards quietly. The baby-face bus was for partying. I'd sometimes arrange to be "kidnapped" so I could to join in with their evening on the road.

On some of the international tours, both buses could turn into party zones. There'd be a cooler or two in each, stocked with beer and wine laid on by the company (if you wanted hard liquor, you had to get it yourself). I was on the heel bus one night when we pulled in to a rest stop. We realized we were nearly out of beer so, as the least obvious suspect, I was sent over to the babyface bus to steal some of theirs. I sneaked across the parking lot, crept through the side door of their bus, put several cans in my pockets, grabbed another few, and turned around to find myself face to stomach with the Undertaker. "What are you doing, son?" Before I could answer, someone else saw me and shouted, "The midget's stealing beers!" At the same time, Armando Estrada — another heel — had made it into the front of the babyface bus and grabbed a whole cooler full of beers. I ran out of the side door and sprinted as fast as I could (which isn't very fast) after Armando, across the parking lot, with the babyfaces chasing us both. The heels emptied out of our bus and tried to block the entrances to the vehicle. It turned into chaos — a game of capture the flag but with beer. The only two people who weren't involved were Undertaker on the babyface bus and Finlay on the heel bus. They just watched as everyone else, even guys who didn't drink, wrestled in the parking lot. Beers were thrown, some were caught, most were dropped, Armando was now shirtless for some reason, and before he could get back on our bus, he tripped over a curb and landed right on his face. That was one of the best nights I ever had with the boys. Being thousands of miles away from home for weeks at a time is tough but it's the camaraderie among the wrestlers that gets us all through it.

CHAPTER 8

THE LADDER

Through the first half of 2007, Fit and I found ourselves working on-and-off with the Boogeyman. Marty Wright was an older guy who'd started wrestling comparatively later in life but had joined Ohio Valley Wrestling, which was a developmental territory for WWE at the time, and had been given an awesome gimmick. It wasn't long before he was called up to *SmackDown* and even though he wasn't the best in the ring, the combination of great face paint, a cool entrance with pyro, and a stick that billowed smoke made audiences love him. Up until that point, all of the people I'd seen Fit working with were good to great pro-wrestlers, and it was only now, when he had to work with someone who wasn't at that standard, I realized just how talented Fit really is. He figured out how to magnify Boogey's strengths while hiding his weaknesses, and they ended up having some pretty decent matches. Fit would control the pace, then make sure he was wherever Boogey needed him to be when it was time to bump around for his comeback.

Outside the ring, Marty seemed borderline insane. He'd drift between Marty and the Boogeyman throughout the day, even when the cameras were off. When he was traveling to shows, he'd wear a nice suit with a fedora — and a black nylon face mask. He didn't want people to see his face without the Boogeyman paint on, so instead he walked around looking like Rorschach from the *Watchmen*. When he got in the ring, part of his gimmick was that he'd eat worms. Finlay and I couldn't figure out why he didn't just put them in his mouth and let them drool out from there but, no, he would chew and swallow them, then chug a whole bottle of Pepto-Bismol the minute he got to the back.

The worms did, at least, give me some literal ammunition in my attempts to mess with Tony Chimel. I'd become close with Tony during the previous year, and it was all in fun. Some of the worms that got away from Boogey would end up underneath the ring; I'd pick them up and fling them at Chimel. He didn't know what was happening for the longest time because I wouldn't have to lift the ring apron up more than a couple of inches to do it — I could see through the material to line up my target. Now and then, I'd miss and hit one of the fans behind him. When that happened, I'd have to stop for a while, so the crowd didn't figure out what was going on but, for the most part, my aim was pretty good.

Another rib I liked to play on Chimel came when he was ring announcing at live events using a wired microphone. Whenever he'd take a wrestler's ring jacket to the back, I'd get my hands on the microphone cable and slowly pull it away from him so he didn't notice it creeping away under the ring. The first few times, watching him search for his microphone and trying not to show his concern was hilarious. When he got smart to what I was doing, he would watch the mic carefully to make sure it wasn't moving and step on the cord whenever I started to pull on it. His microphone wasn't the only thing that wasn't safe around me. He would use a wrench to hit the ring bell at the beginning and end of the matches. As he stood in the ring, introducing the people in the next match, I would scoot out the moment the lights went down, grab the wrench, and take it back under the ring with me. After a while, he started keeping a second wrench as a backup, so I would take that, too. Then other times I'd take the ring bell instead. I never let any of this ruin a show, and I'd always give him his stuff back in time, but I would hold on to it until he started to get worried.

Chimel is one of the hardest working guys in WWE and everyone knows it. All the wrestlers bust his balls, but it's a sign of how much they respect him. Even though he's not a WWE superstar, they treat him as one of the boys. He's been shoved around in the ring, put through tables, and, on at least one occasion, had a 400-pound Samoan's ass shoved in his face, but he never once complained. He was a great ring announcer who understood how to do his job well without overestimating his importance. That wasn't all he did for the company — he was also on the ring crew, setting things up before the show, and breaking them down afterward, and that meant he'd be the first one to get to the arena and the last one to leave every night. He's a production manager now and I can't think of a better guy for the job.

A Short Story: The Backpack

Over my first couple of years with WWE, I kept myself occupied under the ring by playing my PlayStation Portable. That was just one of the things I'd bring with me on the road, in what Chimel called my "backpack of entertainment." In there, I kept my laptop, a mini-DVD player, a bunch of movies and PSP games, my phone, and my wallet . . . that backpack weighed more than my gear bag.

When I was still in my first year with the company, we were at a live event in Indiana where our locker room was a long way from the entrance curtain. When I got back after my spot on the show, my backpack was gone. I knew it wasn't a rib from one of the boys because everyone was in Gorilla (the backstage area right behind the entrance ramp) watching the show on the monitor. I tried not to sell how much I was freaking out because I didn't want the boys to feel bad for me, but I mentioned it to Fit so he could report the theft to the arena.

On the drive to the next town the following morning, I asked Ken Kennedy to stop at a Best Buy so I could replace all of my electronics. Ken wouldn't do it — no matter how much I begged him, he just said, "No, we need to get to the arena." When we got there, there was a brand-new backpack on the table in the middle of the locker room. Inside was a new DVD player, PSP with games, two seasons of *Heroes*, and $300 cash. Ken was smiling to himself, so I asked what was going on. "You deserve it" is all he'd say. Dave Bautista walked into the room after that and asked what all the stuff was. I told him, "I don't know, someone got me all this stuff, but I can't accept it." Dave stared me down and said, "Yes, you can and yes, you will — because *I'm* not taking it back."

It turned out that when they found out what had happened, Dave and Ken had gone around and collected donations to replace my stolen belongings. I sent Dave and Ken thank-you cards the next week and included a $100 gift card in each — which they both refused to accept. I was blown away by how nice everyone was to me in that situation, especially since I hadn't been in the locker room for long.

Soon after the program between Finlay and Boogey started, someone else was added into the mix. Since Finlay had a midget, the idea was to even things up by introducing the Little Boogeyman. You couldn't have done that with most of the other wrestlers on the roster, but given the bizarre nature of his gimmick in the first place, it made perfect sense that the Boogeyman would have a Mini-Me. The guy they got in to play Little Boogey had wrestled a little but his main work was as a motivational speaker. He would come to shows wearing suits and a fedora as well, although he didn't wear nylon on his face. He was a nice enough guy but he never fit into the locker room — he didn't seem particularly interested in being there. WWE shows were just a paycheck to him and he only worked the TV tapings because he had motivational speaking engagements on weekends.

Little people as motivational speakers can be hit and miss. I've heard of a lot of people with achondroplasia or other forms of dwarfism going out there and using their condition as a crutch, almost hiding a lack of content by playing the "poor me, I'm little" card. It doesn't make me angry, but I think it's too easy a subject to fall back on. There's got to be more to a motivational speech than simply, "I've overcome being born little." I've done a few motivational talks at my old high school, and I'm sure my condition played the main part in being invited to do so. But I've focused those talks on not accepting "no" — when people tell you that you can't do something, if you really want to do it, you'll find a way and prove them wrong. There are plenty of obstacles I've encountered that have had nothing to do with my height, so I talked about those rather than pigeonholing myself in the little person bracket.

I never saw or heard any of Little Boogey's speeches, and I didn't talk to him about them, so I can't say what he was like in action. I can talk about what he was like in the ring though — and he was scared to death of Finlay. Whenever we did a match where Fit had to interact with him physically, he'd keep asking if we were sure it was going to work, then begging Fit to take care of him. Even though

Little Boogey was worried, I was excited because it meant I would get to wrestle a little and show everyone in the back that I could do more than chase people around the ring. It was also helpful that Little Boogey was quite a bit older than me, so he was always blown up. I was skinny, young Dylan at that point, so I could run rings around him until he was sucking wind.

The hardest bump I ever saw him take was under the ring. By this point, I was the crafty under-the-ring veteran who knew how to get around but I didn't think to smarten him up about not standing beneath the beams. One of the boys in the ring took a big bump and the beam he landed on hit Little Boogey right in the back of the head, knocking him flat on his face. He just stared up at me with a comical look on his face and said, "I wasn't expecting that." It was hard not to laugh.

In the only singles match we had, I figured that since Little Boogey was going to do something with the worms, I should have some trick to come back with. I went to Fit and asked him what he thought about me doing the mist gimmick (where a wrestler sprays green mist from his mouth into the face of his opponent). Fit loved the idea, so I went off to see what Richie Posner had in his bag of magic tricks. Richie mixed up some water and green food coloring and put it in a condom that he tied off. The idea was that the ref would have one in each pocket and, when the time came, he'd pass one to me. I'd put it in my mouth and burst it with my back teeth, spray the mist, then when I could, spit the condom out. Richie told me to make sure I brushed my teeth as soon as I got to the back, explaining that the food coloring would stain unless I took care of it quickly.

When we got in the ring that night, the mist spot looked great, although I nearly spit the condom out as I was spraying Little Boogey and had to catch it with my teeth. I won the match with a frog splash off the top rope (the commentators called it a tadpole splash) and the crowd loved it. I was so elated about how it had gone that when I got to the back, I completely forgot Richie's advice. By the time I remembered and went to brush my teeth, the green dye seemed to have soaked itself into the enamel. I ended up having to brush for more than an hour to get it off and, even then, my teeth still had a green tinge for days. Despite that, I loved getting to do the mist — I did it one other time that year, at the *Survivor Series* against Ranjin Singh, but I wish I'd done it more. It could have been a great gimmick for me.

While that was the only singles match I had with Little Boogey, we worked a few times in tag matches with Fit and Boogey, the first of which was at the *No Way Out* pay-per-view in February. This was the event where I got to speak for the first time on WWE TV. In a segment we shot backstage where Finlay was trying to motivate me, I explained why I was worried about the match. When I told him "little people are scary," he gave me a supportive hug and then threw me in a dumpster. That was the only time I spoke on screen in years and I don't know why it was for that night only.

After Finlay and I won the match later that night, I figured that since we were the heels, the WWE would use the next few weeks to build up a rematch at *WrestleMania*, then the babyfaces would go over on the biggest show of the year. It turned out that WWE had other plans. Boogey ended up in a backstage skit where Donald Trump, the future president, asked Boogey to go make him a sandwich, and Finlay ended up in the Money in the Bank ladder match. I think we got the better end of that deal.

I was so excited to find out we were going to be doing Money in the Bank. It had only been done twice before at that point and I loved the gimmick that whoever climbed the ladder and grabbed the briefcase from above the ring earned a title shot that they could cash in, any place, any time. It had already given both Edge and Rob Van Dam a final push toward the top of the card and had created several very memorable *WrestleMania* moments. Finlay had been in the match the year before, just after I'd been brought in as an extra for the sketch that didn't make it onto *Raw*. At first, I hadn't liked that Finlay was in Money in the Bank back then because I didn't think it was the right sort of match for him and Ric Flair. In my mind, a ladder match was supposed to be a spot-fest with people flying everywhere and taking crazy bumps, but both Fit and Ric did an incredible job and ended up making that match so much better.

A Short Story: The Nature Boy and the Wildman

Within wrestling, Ric is as legendary for partying as he is for wrestling. He'll walk into any bar and own the place within seconds. After a couple of drinks, he starts to *know* he owns the place and the more he drinks, the more "Nature Boy" he gets. Whenever I've been out with him, he's kept his clothes on. But, then again, I always left before he did . . .

He calls me Wildman. He'll say that whenever he sees me and if he's with a woman, he'll start saying, "You should see the thing on this guy — it hangs to the floor." I'll say that's not true at all, but Ric will cut me off and say, "He's lying, you should have some fun with him sometime, he would rock your world." I'm pretty sure he's got me confused with Cowboy Lang, who was infamous in wrestling for what he had in his holster. Or maybe Ric thinks all little people make up for their lack of height elsewhere. Whatever it is, I don't care — being called Wildman by Ric Flair is pretty awesome.

Joining Finlay in the *'Mania 23* Money in the Bank match were a combination of established stars — namely former winner Edge, King Booker, Matt and Jeff Hardy, and Randy Orton — as well as a few guys who were rising through the ranks. They included CM

Punk, who had started in WWE's version of ECW about a month after I first appeared, and my former trainer, Ken Anderson. He was now known as Mr. Kennedy and it was clear that the office had plans for him. Ken had a great look, he could talk, he could wrestle, and he was getting over with fans with his obnoxious heel gimmick. On top of that, Vince McMahon himself was a big supporter of his work.

As part of the buildup for the match, Ken and Fit were scheduled for a match on the final *SmackDown* before *WrestleMania* and they wanted to involve a ladder as a nod to where things were headed. I suggested that I do one of Ken's signature moves, a flip dive he called the Kenton Bomb, off a stepladder and onto Ken. They loved the idea so during the match, when Fit was distracting the ref, I set up a tiny three-step ladder, climbed up, did my best Jeff Hardy pose (Jeff used the same move), and dived onto Ken.

When Finlay initially qualified for that match in early March, there was a change to our act — and it involved my name. After almost nine months of being referred to as Little Bastard, someone in the office must have finally pointed out that it wasn't exactly family friendly.

I found out about this from Anne. She used to work the nightshift at Target a lot and, during her breaks, she would check out the wrestling news online. On her way home one morning, just as I was getting up, she called and let me know that WWE.com had changed my name and I was now going to be Hornswoggle.

That was news to me. Nobody from the office called to let me know. In fact, nothing was mentioned to me at all and the first I knew about it officially was during Finlay's Money in the Bank qualifying match on *SmackDown*, when Finlay went up to Michael Cole on commentary, grabbed him by the shirt, and shouted, "His name isn't Little Bastard, it's Hornswoggle." I still had no idea what the word meant until I got backstage and one of the writers told me it meant to swindle or cheat. I thought it made sense and was definitely a better name to have if I ever hoped to see my action figure on the shelves of Toys "R" Us which, given the increasingly positive reactions I was getting from the younger members of the audience at shows, was starting to look like it wasn't out of the question.

WrestleMania week arrived. As I landed in Detroit, I couldn't believe I was there — when I was younger, I'd thought I might get to go one day as a fan, but never as a member of the WWE roster. The whole week was just one neverending oh-my-God moment. The company put everyone up in an beautiful hotel in Detroit and hired the ballroom so they could set up two rings. They would do this every year for *'Mania* and create a schedule so people could come and work on their match in advance of the big event. Most matches would get a couple of sessions, each lasting a few hours.

Two days before the show, everyone involved in the Money in the Bank match got together, along with the agent for the match, John Laurinaitis, and we started throwing some ideas around. Before that meeting, I considered pitching the idea of taking finish moves from everyone in the match. At the very least, I wanted to take the Twist of Fate and the Swanton Bomb from the Hardys, the Go to Sleep from CM Punk, and anything that Ken wanted to do. Fortunately, before I opened my mouth, I realized I couldn't be the focus of the match and would be lucky if I got one memorable spot.

As we discussed the match, it looked like there was going to be a moment where everyone was going to be down on the mat or on the floor. That it seemed like an ideal place for me to do something. Fit asked me if I had any ideas. Instead of blurting out "I want to take everyone's finisher!" I simply said I'd do whatever they wanted. The next question was whether I wanted to take a bump off the ladder. I didn't even need to think about that for a second. I was all in.

The idea was for Ken to catch me trying to climb up the ladder, grab me from underneath, and powerbomb me, driving me back-first onto the mat. We gave it a go in the ring in the ballroom but kept screwing it up. Over and over, we tried it but we just couldn't get it right. I say "we," but really it was "me." To this day I still can't properly take a powerbomb. Even knowing there was a crash pad beneath me, I kept looking over my right shoulder and twisting my body. I couldn't take a bump like that or I'd seriously hurt myself. Frustrated, Ken and I got out of the ring and everyone started talking through other parts of the match again.

As they talked, I had an idea. I knew I couldn't take everyone's finish but I figured I might be able to take Ken's — and not just off the ropes as usual. It needed to be big because it was *WrestleMania*, so I thought we could do it off the ladder. I called Ken over and told him what I was thinking, then we both got back in the ring and each climbed a separate ladder. No one was paying attention to us until Ken hauled me off my ladder and up across his shoulders. At that point, Finlay noticed what we were doing and said, "Oh, this is going to be good." Everyone stopped to watch as Ken leapt off the ladder into a somersault with me still across his shoulders. We hit the crash pad so hard that it knocked the wind out of me but, judging from the reaction of the boys, it had looked good, so I got up and asked Fit if we could do that. He looked at Laurinaitis and they both nodded. I had my *WrestleMania* spot.

The next night, I sat among the WWE superstars watching Dusty Rhodes, Mr. Perfect, Jerry Lawler, Jim Ross, Mr. Fuji, the Sheik, the Wild Samoans, and Nick Bockwinkel get inducted into the Hall of Fame. More than once, I found myself looking around and thinking, "How did I end up here?"

Sunday was the big night. There were more than 80,000 fans at Ford Field in Detroit. I'd never been part of anything that huge. Before the pre-show match, the house lights were brought down and a video played on the screens as I marched to the ring surrounded by a group of stagehands, all of us wearing black hoodies and sweatpants. It was the longest aisle I'd ever walked down. I got so distracted looking around in awe of the size of the crowd that I slowed down and the guys behind kept bumping into me. When we eventually got to ringside, I slid under the ring and pulled off the sweatpants and hoodie — I already had my gear on underneath. As the pre-show match started, I got more and more excited. The adrenaline was pumping for sure.

Money in the Bank was the opening match of the pay-per-view, so I didn't have to wait long for my spot. Toward the end of the match, everyone else was down on the outside while Fit was setting up a ladder in the ring. This was my moment. I scurried out and climbed into the ring, where Finlay was now on his knees, holding onto one of the two ladders that were set up. The idea was that he was too hurt to climb, so he was sending me up to fetch the briefcase for him. All the other wrestlers were down on the outside as I took off my hat and coat and pulled up my sleeves. The huge audience was just a blur in the background to me as I climbed, thinking, "This ladder's a lot taller than I remember . . ." with each step. The audience was going crazy, but I didn't hear anything. I just kept climbing.

Before I got all the way up, Ken rushed back into the ring, kicked Fit to keep him down (which, in reality, was so Fit could steady the ladder Ken was going to jump from) and climbed the other ladder to come face to face with me. As he stared a hole through me, I followed the advice Fit and Vince had given me right after I started with WWE — I counted to three in my head. That gave the crowd a chance to take in the moment, and then I punched Ken right in the face. On the video, you can hear the crowd let out a huge gasp, but at the time I didn't hear anything because I was so focused on what I had to do. I climbed up to the sixth rung of eight (which is high up for anyone but even more so when you're only 4'4"!), then lashed out at Ken again, connecting hard.

He hauled me up onto his shoulders and the audience gasped once more, louder this time. I was legitimately scared to death. When we'd done it in rehearsal, the ladder seemed smaller, there was a crash pad underneath us, and there weren't 80,000 fans watching. Before I had a chance to overthink things, Ken squeezed my leg to let me know it was about to happen. I tensed up and held on tight as he leapt off the ladder into a flip and we crashed to the mat in the corner, the hardest part of the ring. It looked like he about killed me.

There was no way of being able to hide that enormous bump from my dad but, to his credit, when I called after the match to let him know I was fine, he was supportive, encouraging, and proud that I'd had such a big moment on such a big stage. He did express his concern for me, saying, "Dylan, I worry about you." It would be that way throughout my career whenever he saw me take a particularly unpleasant looking bump or fall. He was always worried but always proud.

The landing from Ken's Lambeau Leap knocked the wind out of me worse than at rehearsal, but the bump itself hadn't hurt one bit and I was over the moon because I knew I'd just had a *WrestleMania* moment that everyone would remember. I rolled toward the ring post and spent the rest of the match lying there, selling the move, and watching as Ken eventually climbed the ladder, unhooked the briefcase, and won the match.

When Fit and I got to the back, I found Ken to thank him for our spot. He was so excited about having gone over — given that the last two people to win Money in the Bank had gone on to become World Champion, all signs were pointing to the fact that this was going to lead somewhere huge for him. Being able to share that moment in the ring with a fellow Wisconsinite, and a guy who trained me, was so rewarding and a highlight of my career. It still gets brought up whenever I meet with fans.

Unfortunately for Ken, he had a terrible run of luck. Less than a month after that *WrestleMania*, the Undertaker tore his biceps tendon and was going to be out for a while. He was the World Champion at the time, so it made sense that Ken would use his Money in the Bank contract to force a title match and win the championship. Ken was even told this was exactly what was going to happen — and then, days later, Ken got injured at a random house show in New York. He was told it was a triceps tear that would keep him out for around six months, so WWE hot-shotted the Money in the Bank contract over to Edge in a short match on *Raw*, then had Edge cash in and win the World Title from Undertaker on that week's *SmackDown*.

It got worse — further medical investigation showed that Ken's injury wasn't as serious as he'd first been told, so he ended up being out of action less than two months and, about a week after Ken came back, Edge got injured and had to surrender the title, which ended up going to my old traveling partner, the Great Khali.

During that post-*WrestleMania* period, as well as doing things here and there with the Boogeyman, Fit and I spent time working with Kane and Chris Benoit. When the Kane character first appeared in 1997, I was deathly afraid of him. His debut was awesome, one of the most memorable moments I've ever seen in wrestling. For a while, I was convinced it was Sycho Sid under the Kane mask and, because I didn't have access to the internet, it was some time before I found out that the role was being played by Glenn Jacobs, the guy who had played Isaac Yankem and taken over from Kevin Nash as Diesel. I was happy when I found out about that because I'd loved Fake Diesel, mainly because I was a complete Diesel mark in the '90s. More Diesel, whether it was Kevin Nash or not, was fine by me.

By the time Fit and I worked with Glen, he'd been unmasked for several years and was one of the most versatile guys on the roster. He was so easy to work with because he would always get a great reaction and the audience would buy him whether he was doing comedy or a serious angle.

I had a spot with him we'd do in almost every match, a variation on the one I did with the Undertaker the time I fell asleep under the ring. Finlay would take Kane down and come out to get me. Once I'd been thrown into the ring, I'd approach Kane, who would sit up like a zombie and stare me down. I'd look like I'd seen a ghost, panic, and then take my green derby hat off and put it on Kane's head. That would get a laugh from the audience. Then he'd grab me by the throat, get up to his knees, give me a chokeslam, and throw the hat at my carcass. After we'd done that a few times, he thought he'd mix it up without telling us. We did the usual chokeslam spot but he didn't take the hat off — this seven-foot monster decided he'd wrestle the rest of the match wearing a leprechaun's hat. I've seen pictures of him chokeslamming Finlay where they're both laughing because of how ridiculous it looked.

A Short Story: Finlay's Sense of Humor

I've never liked big dogs. When I was young, they would always jump up at me. To a normal-sized kid, that might be fun but, to me, it was terrifying. I was always scared they were going to knock me over and injure me.

On a tour of South America, I was sightseeing at a flea market on a hilltop with Fit and his wife when I noticed a huge, wild-looking dog staring at me. Fit, who knew about my fear of dogs, noticed it, too. "Oh, no," he said. "That dog's gonna get you, Dylan."

As if it had heard, the dog began slowly advancing toward me. As I backed away, Finlay, like any good father figure, suddenly shouted, "Get him!" and the dog sprinted right at me. I ran as fast as I could and managed to clamber up onto a ledge at the edge of the hill, the dog directly below me, barking its head off.

Instead of helping, Fit and his wife just laughed hysterically, although they did recover long enough to take some photos of me sweating bullets up on that ledge. That was typical of the relationship I had with Fit. He looked out for me like I was his own kid, but that didn't stop him from putting me through hell for his own amusement.

CHAPTER 9

THE CASKET ON THE STAGE

When Fit and I were working with Chris Benoit, I quickly discovered they had a similar sense of humor when it came to having fun in the ring, although Chris's fun-loving side didn't come out as much. We planned a spot where Finlay would be on the floor and I'd get in the ring. Chris would catch me and give me a German suplex, lifting me belly to back so we both crashed to the mat. He'd hold on and roll through, then go to give me a second when Fit would get back in the ring to break it up. Chris would then start suplexing Fit as I made my escape. I liked the spot because the German suplexes were easy to take from Chris — he would go up and then back and land you safely rather then flinging you across the ring. On the first night, Chris had given me two suplexes and Fit hadn't made it back into the ring, so he fired off a third before Finlay interrupted. The next night, Fit still wasn't there on the third suplex, so Chris kept going. I took five Germans. The night after that, the same happened and, on the fifth suplex, I asked, "Is he coming?" Chris just said, "Don't know," and suplexed me a sixth time. As we were getting back to our feet, I saw Finlay standing off to the side, laughing his ass off. I could also feel Chris holding in laughter as he gave me another five Germans before Fit finally broke it up.

Those eleven suplexes were fine to take but we had a near miss with a spot we only tried once. We had the idea that Finlay would pick me up around my waist as if he were going to dump me on Benoit, but Chris would get up, go behind Finlay, and give him a German suplex while he was holding me. Fit would let go just before he'd hit the mat and it would be like he was suplexing me, too. What we hadn't considered was that my head is very heavy compared to the rest of my body. As I flew into the air that night, my legs went right up in the air — when my head and shoulders hit the mat, my legs kept going. I landed in a heap, folded in half, with my feet hitting the mat above my head. I was just lying there on the mat, thinking, "Well, that's it — I'm paralyzed." I couldn't feel anything. Fortunately, I started getting feeling back pretty quickly, but for a few moments I was terrified. That was the scariest bump I took in my career. I definitely didn't call my dad afterward to let him know about that one. I knew exactly what he would have said though — the same as he always did when it came to my wrestling: "Dylan, I just worry about you." I knew he did — I just didn't want to worry *him*.

Chris was sure to check on me whenever we did anything physical in a match. He was often quiet and removed but he'd allow himself a smirk now and then and was genuinely a nice guy. I always found it funny that whenever anyone would describe another wrestler as a "nice guy," Chris would reply, "My pool guy is a nice guy, too — but that doesn't mean he should be in the wrestling business."

I rode with Chris and Ken Kennedy a few times and their schedule was to go work out in the morning, leaving me at the hotel as I still wasn't a gym guy. On the Monday, our day off, Ken asked me if I wanted to go work out with them. I told him I was fine and thought that was that — until I got a text from him later, saying,

"You should come, Chris wants you here." Shortly afterward, I got a call from Chris, saying he'd really been looking forward to us all spending the day together, working out, getting lunch, and going to a movie. When I told him I didn't really do the gym, he sounded so disappointed and said, "Whatever, man," before hanging up. Ken texted me a few minutes later, telling me Chris was really pissed off. As a highly respected veteran on the roster, Chris was one person whose feelings you definitely didn't want to hurt, so I grabbed my bag, hopped in a cab, and joined them at the gym.

Benoit led the session and started us off with a set of 500 squats before running me through every single exercise he and Ken were doing, nearly killing me in the process. As I was trying to catch my breath in the locker room afterward, I noticed Chris and Ken sniggering.

"What?" I asked.

"You didn't even have to be here, I just wanted to mess with you," confessed Chris, laughing out loud. After that, Chris took us to Outback Steakhouse and then to see *Jackass 2*. I've been a huge fan of *Jackass* since I was a teenager, but I never pictured Chris Benoit as the sort of person who would laugh his ass off all the way through that type of movie. He did though — and he paid for everything. I thought he was so awesome.

I'd be forced to reconsider that soon enough.

The main storyline on WWE TV in June was that Mr. McMahon had died. Not Vince McMahon the person in real life, just the on-screen Mr. McMahon, the evil corporate owner. There haven't been many wrestling angles that went as far as trying to put over that someone was dead, but they went all the way with this, rigging up a stunt where Vince got into a limo that then exploded. After years of appearing on the show, Vince had simply wanted to get rid of his TV character, which led to "I can't be on TV if I'm dead, god-dammit . . ." The company began preparing for a special episode of *Raw* two weeks later that would feature the funeral.

The weekend before the scheduled McMahon funeral, Chris

Benoit missed a house show in Texas. No one gave it too much thought, but there was a feeling that something odd was going on. It's pretty rare for any of the boys to miss a show without the office knowing well in advance (whether it was an injury or personal issue, for example) and Chris definitely wasn't the sort of person to ever miss a booking.

But then Chris didn't show up for the *Night of Champions* pay-per-view. It was one thing to miss a house show, but to miss out on the big paycheck that comes along with working on a PPV, especially when you were lined up in a title match, was a different matter. Chris was meant to be working with CM Punk for the vacant ECW title, and Punk was really let down that Benoit wasn't there. Punk ended up having a good match with John Morrison but was still a little disappointed as he'd been looking forward to wrestling Benoit in a featured PPV match.

The next night in Corpus Christi, Mr. McMahon's funeral was set to take place. All the wrestlers from *SmackDown* had been brought in and several of the top names from the past had come back to be part of the show, including the biggest star of the modern era of wrestling, "Stone Cold" Steve Austin. We'd been told to bring funeral-wear, so we were all there in suits and ties, hanging around ringside and chatting, waiting to do a dress rehearsal of the segment. There was a wreath in the ring and a casket on the stage, adding to the gloomy atmosphere. John Laurinaitis shouted for us all to be quiet and sit down. With a look around at the somber surroundings, Austin joked back, "Goddammit John, you're making it seem like someone died!"

The general laughter at Austin's comment was broken by Vickie Guerrero. Dean Malenko had whispered something in her ear and she'd let out a piercing scream and fell to the ground crying. Dean helped her up and quickly took her backstage. No one knew what was going on until Vince McMahon climbed into the ring and spoke to us over the house microphone, telling us all that Chris, his wife, Nancy, and their seven-year-old son, Daniel, had been found in their house dead.

We were all in shock. As we tried to process this information, Vince proceeded to tell us that the live show that night was being canceled and a tribute show would be aired instead, mixing some of Chris's finest moments in the ring with comments from his colleagues and friends, which he invited us to film before we left the arena. He told us that we would have matches at the *SmackDown* and ECW taping the next night, but if any of us just wanted to go home, we were welcome to do so.

I chose to record some comments before leaving, which ended up not being used during the tribute show. I talked about how Chris and I had become friends and how getting to know him backstage showed me a completely different side to the super-intense, double tough character people were used to seeing on TV. Retrospectively, I'm glad they chose not to air it.

Punk also recorded a tribute that *was* used on the show — understandably as Punk had been in a program with him and was one of the top guys on WWE's ECW brand. When we were finished, we left with Curt Hawkins and Zack Ryder, went to dinner, and then back to the hotel. None of us saw Vickie at the arena after Dean had taken her off. Her reaction had made sense, given that her late husband, Eddie, and Chris had been best friends. I never talked to her about it afterward, and she seemed as fine as any of us were when I saw her at TV the next week, but it had to have been horrible for her.

Later that night, Punk, Hawkins, Ryder, and I sat there in the hotel with the TV on, watching as *Raw* started and the tributes began. As we listened to the words recorded earlier by Austin, Triple H, Edge, William Regal, Chavo Guerrero Jr., and a number of others, updates from news outlets started coming in, suggesting that Chris had murdered his wife and child, then died by suicide. We set there, watching, waiting for more information, thinking, "There *has* to be more to it than this . . ."

It just didn't make any sense to us. We'd all seen how amazing Chris was with his family. Whenever I'd seen him with Daniel, I said to myself, "He's such a great dad." Sure, Chris could be quiet and removed but that was just his way. He never showed any signs that he could be capable of doing something like this and anyone who says they saw it coming is lying, plain and simple.

My first impulse was to think, "There's no way Chris could have done this." That was a feeling I held onto for a long time. What I'd seen first-hand was that Chris was a great wrestler, an amazing dad, and an incredible guy. What I was now hearing and reading was that he had finished his life in the most awful, terrible way imaginable. It's difficult for someone who knew him to reconcile the two.

As for all the reports and commentary that followed, I didn't pay much attention to any of it. Even now, I don't want to give it much thought, but I really want to believe Chris didn't do it, that there was a missing piece of the puzzle.

A week after everything happened, Vince held another meeting at the next TV tapings and told us that the press would be "out for blood." He said that any one of us could be contacted by some reporter, trying to turn even the smallest story into a big deal. He told us anything we said would be twisted, so we needed to make sure we were all on the same page. People who WWE sent to do media around that time were given clear points that they were expected to reiterate. Some of the boys came across well and some didn't — unfortunately, during his interviews, Ken said a few things WWE didn't approve of and lost some ground with the office.

From a selfish perspective, the biggest professional impact the fallout had on me was that it cost me a chance to have a match at *SummerSlam* — and not just any match. It would have been in a main spot, against one of the celebrities I looked up to when I was a teenager — and one of the guys that I'd seen Chris laughing at when he took Ken and I to the cinema.

The guys from *Jackass* were lined up to be involved with WWE over that summer and we heard the rumor backstage that there were going to be some of their guys against some of ours at *SummerSlam*. Hearing that, I went and pitched the idea of a boxing match between me and Wee Man. I figured it would be very different and get us some good coverage on *Access Hollywood* and shows like that. The creative team loved the idea and penciled it in immediately. On the back page of every show script, there would always be the card they were looking to build for the next big show and, as we got closer to *SummerSlam*, there it was, every week — Hornswoggle versus Wee Man: Boxing Match. Me against one of my childhood idols in a high-profile match at a huge pay-per-view event.

It never happened.

There was so much negative coverage of WWE after the Benoit murders that most companies and celebrities distanced themselves from the promotion, *Jackass* included.

The one good thing that came out of the tragedy was the company-wide crackdown on drug use. The WWE's Wellness Policy had been brought in during the previous year and it had started to work but, even though you'd never see the guys taking anything, you would see some people walking around clearly impaired, in so-called soma comas or similar conditions. Once the drug testing became more frequent and more sophisticated, the locker room was a different place. There were still a few casualties but it was nothing close to the number of wrestlers who died leading up to the Benoit tragedy. One of the biggest issues with the business was that people would just say "he's got demons," instead of acknowledging and tackling the underlying problem. After Benoit, things got so much better and it's a much healthier and more positive locker room now. Of course, the critics will always find something to complain about, but when the guys are playing video games instead of drinking and taking pills, that's definitely a step in the right direction.

CHAPTER 10

THE SHORTEST CHAMPION

Although I'd held a title on the independent circuit, it's not something I ever thought about when I signed with WWE. They didn't have a juniors' title. They didn't even have the juniors division anymore; it had been discontinued a few months before I came in. The Hardcore Title, which I could have won as a joke because of the 24-7 rule (the title was always being defended so, in theory — and in practice at one point — you could pin the champion when he was sleeping), had been retired long before I joined the company. So, I never entertained thoughts of walking down that aisle with a WWE championship belt strapped around my waist.

To my complete surprise, the week before *The Great American Bash* pay-per-view, the creative team called me and said I was needed for the show because I might be winning the Cruiserweight Title. I hadn't even been booked for the event and now I was being told I might win a title? I was excited, but I didn't dare get my hopes up.

Even that early in my WWE career, I'd learned how regularly things changed, often right up to the last minute before a show began — and even, sometimes, after a show had started.

I showed up for the PPV on the Sunday and didn't let on that I knew anything about what might or might not happen — I'd been asked to keep it a secret. Eventually, Dean Malenko found me and confirmed that I was going to be winning the title. I tried my best to act shocked as he told me I was going to be a surprise in the match and we'd figure it all out at rehearsal. After finding out for sure that they were going ahead with title change, I called my dad and Anne and asked them to order the show. I didn't tell either of them what I'd be doing, just that I'd be on it.

Later, I found myself in the ring with Jamie Noble, Shannon Moore, Chavo Guerrero Jr., Funaki, and Jimmy Wang Yang, putting the match together with Dean, who was producing. The match had been promoted (although I'll use that word loosely) as a Cruiserweight Open, so anyone under 215 pounds could enter. I needed to be in the ring when the opening bell rang but Vince didn't want me working the whole match, so the plan was that I'd be under the ring as usual and just before the ref went to start the match, I'd crawl out, get in the ring, and run across it as the bell rang — which would make me a legal competitor in the match — then roll out the other side and go back underneath until the finish. We wanted it to look like it was the leprechaun goofing around rather than tipping off the result of the match, so all of the other wrestlers were told to act confused, then go to work on each other and forget about me, hoping the audience would, too.

When it came to figuring out the finish, Dean asked me what I could do. I told him I had a decent frog splash off the top rope (which is part of what I'll always say about my in-ring talents — "Great ass bite, decent splash"). The frog splash had been my finisher on the indies, and I'd used it before on WWE TV against the Little Boogeyman, where I thought it had looked great. Dean wasn't convinced, pointing out that both Chavo and Rey Mysterio already used the frog splash, as well as Rob Van Dam, who'd only just left the company. Instead, Dean suggested I do a bulldog off the second rope. I tried it with Jamie Noble a couple of times, but it just didn't feel right. Still, I knew it wasn't worth complaining. This was a colossal opportunity for me and I would have been stupid to ruin it by whining about not getting to do the finish I wanted.

We were the second match on the main show that night. As the other five wrestlers made their entrances, Dean's voice came through on my headset. "Dylan, we're changing the finish." Immediately, I prepared the bad news — I wasn't going to get the belt and I probably wasn't even going to be in the match. Immediately, I felt so stupid for believing something like this could ever happen to me and, worst of all, I'd asked my friends and my dad to pay money for a show I now wasn't even going to appear on.

Dean spoke again. "Can you do the frog splash for the finish?" Hell yes, I could!

After Chavo's music had stopped, I scooted through the ring, the bell rang, and I scooted back under — it all went fine. The audience reacted when I appeared, but quickly got caught up in the action of the match and forgot I'd showed up at all. At the end of the match, Funaki, Shannon, and Jimmy were down on the floor, and Jamie and Chavo were both down inside the ring. As planned, I came out and started climbing the ropes as I felt the place start to buzz again. The crowd cheered when I hit the splash on Jamie. The crowd cheered even louder moments later when the referee counted three.

As Tony Chimel announced me as the new WWE Cruiserweight Champion, I stared at the title belt in my hands thinking, "This is insane — this never should have happened." Given my stature, the odds of me even having been hired by WWE in the first place had been so small, but for me to become a champion in WWE? It was an impossible dream come true.

When I got to the back, everyone in Gorilla gave me a standing ovation. All of the other wrestlers in the match came back and were happy for me to have had that moment in the ring. By the time I got to the locker room and checked my phone, there were about eighty text messages from various people wanting to congratulate me. Before I got back to any of them, I made the most important call first — to my dad. We talked about this incredible, unlikely achievement that just came my way. When he said he was proud of me, that was the pat on the back that meant the most to me of them all.

I didn't know where the company was going to go with me after this and, as it turns out, neither did they. Rather than playing me as an underdog champion who could actually wrestle, I ended up doing standard midget comedy segments with Jamie Noble.

As time went on, I started to sense that some of the other smaller wrestlers began to resent me for taking the title away from their division, not that doing so was ever my choice or intention. Jimmy Yang was particularly vocal about this. He'd do it in a humorous manner, but so regularly that I knew there must have been genuine annoyance beneath the jokes. A lot of internet wrestling fans also made their opinions clear from their keyboards — "Hornswoggle singlehandedly destroyed the cruiserweight division and cost a bunch of guys their spots on the card." I thought that sort of comment was unfair as I was just doing the job I'd been told to do but, at the same time, I did understand some of the feelings because the other guys had been going out there, working hard and having spectacular matches, then I came along for one match, won the title, and it became a prop in the comedy segment on the show.

I understood the anger, but I didn't feel bad at all. I never chose to be an inactive champion. Quite the opposite, actually — I was hoping that being the champion would give me the opportunity to start wrestling more. I kept pitching ideas to the writers and agents to put me in matches against the established cruiserweights but all they'd ever say was "maybe," and then I'd hear nothing else. The belt not being defended wasn't for a lack of trying on my part and I never understood why they would give me the Cruiserweight Title if I wouldn't be wrestling. I was capable of working and bumping, and I felt confident I could have done some fun stuff with people like Funaki or Shannon Moore, even if they weren't five-star mat classics. Still, the end result was that I was the champion and, keeping that in mind, whatever they wanted to do was fine by me.

I didn't get to do regular matches but I enjoyed the hell out of the comedy matches and segments I did with Jamie Noble. Some people wouldn't believe it because of his country bumpkin character and accent, but Jamie is one of the smartest guys in wrestling. If you want proof, go and watch the incredible Shawn Michaels versus the Undertaker match from *WrestleMania 25* — Jamie was heavily involved in putting that together as a producer. He's been an agent for a long time now and has been worked on countless big matches.

There was never any reluctance from Jamie when it came to working with or selling for the midget. He was always willing to do whatever was needed, no matter how incompetent it made him look. At times, he set traps for me, like he was Wile E. Coyote and I was the Road Runner. Jamie would set out Lucky Charms to catch the leprechaun but, in the end, I would end up trapping him. Either that, or I'd hit him with a pie, do something that would get him chokeslammed by Kane, or something between the two. At one point, Jamie and I were lined up to wrestle in a Hornswoggle's House Match at *SummerSlam*. Just like the boxing match with Wee Man, it was put on the next PPV lineup on the back of the scripts and, just like the boxing match, it didn't happen.

The idea was that we'd pre-tape a match which had taken place in my "house" under the ring. It was going to be shot movie-style to make it seem like I lived in a cave. It would have been very different, visually striking, and definitely enjoyable for the viewers at home, but the live audience would have been sitting watching a screen above an empty ring for ten minutes or more. That sort of thing doesn't ever work out too well with live crowds (plus Vince hates doing it), so the idea was dropped.

Despite the disappointment of not being allowed to work proper matches with the other wrestlers, being Cruiserweight Champion was still an awesome experience. I was also able to use the belt as a prop in one of my favorite photos of all time. Just a month before I became the champion, Binder became a dad and asked me to be his son's godfather. A while later, we took photo of my godson, Ayden, with the Cruiserweight Championship belt draped over him — a picture of two of the things that made my life so special at that time.

Another photo I got that was special at the time was taken just after CM Punk won the ECW Championship in September 2007. Right after he'd got backstage, I passed him as he was heading over to the area where they take the still photos for publicity. I asked him to not leave before I got back, ran to the locker room, and grabbed the cruiserweight belt from my bag, then ran back. When the photographer was finished with Punk, I asked if we could get a picture together with our respective belts. Punk loved the idea — two friends who no one thought could be champions in WWE with title belts in our hands.

CHAPTER 11

THE OTHER MCMAHON

In the fallout of the Benoit murder-suicide, the angle involving Mr. McMahon's death was dropped, and Vince evidently changed his mind about staying off TV. A new storyline was introduced where Mr. McMahon had an illegitimate son he didn't know about, and a big reveal of the "new McMahon" was set for a *Raw* in Green Bay. Given that was Ken Kennedy's hometown, a lot of people assumed Ken was lined up for the role. It made sense: despite his post-*WrestleMania* run of bad luck, Ken continued to be booked as a rising star after returning from his injury, he was still well liked by the office, his character had a lot of the McMahon attitude, and, on top of all that, Kennedy is Vince's middle name . . . a lot of the pieces fit together. If the rumors were true, it was going to be a huge break for Ken.

Just after *SummerSlam*, an investigation into online pharmacies prescribing steroids led to ten WWE wrestlers being suspended for violation of the company Wellness Policy. Among them, as I'm sure you could have guessed given his run of luck, was Ken. He was written off TV that week and suspended for thirty days — just a week before they were scheduled to reveal who McMahon's bastard son was. Years later, I asked Ken point-blank if he was supposed to have been Vince's son. He gave me a sly grin and just said, "I don't think so." We both knew it was meant to be him. Ken's luck didn't change over the next couple of years and, after a couple more injuries, and a match where Randy Orton complained about him being unsafe in the ring, WWE let him go. It was a real shame — Ken could have been a huge star.

The entire roster was brought in to *Raw* in Green Bay for the big reveal; no one had any idea who it was going to be. I figured it would be just another day at work but mid-afternoon, as rehearsal was about to start, Vince's right-hand man Bruce Prichard told me to meet him backstage. When I got there, the first thing he did was demand my phone. I could tell from his expression he was dead serious, so I handed it over. Then he said the words that changed my life: "You're Vince's son."

The big reveal was going to be me. All I could do was stare at him blankly and mumble, "Why?"

"What do you mean, *why?*" Bruce replied. "You're going to be in a storyline with the boss. Don't question it!"

I asked if I could have my phone back and was told I'd get it back after the show. The office was determined to keep the identity of Vince's son a secret and didn't want any risk of the news getting onto the internet. I told Bruce I understood but if I was going to be featured in the main event on *Raw* in my home state, I wanted to ask my dad, Anne, and her mom to be there. Bruce agreed to arrange complimentary tickets for them and watched me like a hawk as I texted, asking them to come to the show that evening. Then he took my phone away again.

Meanwhile, the rest of the roster was in the arena rehearsing the final segment of the night. Vince was explaining how a "private investigator" would appear on the screen and read out a series of clues about the identity of his son. He told everyone that when something came up that took them out of the running, they should go backstage. Then everyone was told it would come down to Vince and Hunter in the ring and that was the end of the rehearsal. They didn't even clue the roster into the payoff of the angle to avoid spoilers getting out.

As the rehearsal was ending, Bruce told me that he'd get me my bag later but that I needed to get under the ring immediately. I made my way to ringside and snuck underneath just as everyone else was making their way to the back. Once I was settled, I got on the headset. Kevin Dunn was waiting for me and instructed me to not speak on the headset unless I was directly spoken to.

Around 6 p.m., as the crowd was beginning to be let into the building, my bag was slid under the ring apron and Vince checked in to make sure I was all right. He repeated what Kevin had said, explaining that when they spoke to me, they could block other people from listening in and only he, Kevin, and I would be able to hear each other. They were taking every precaution to keep this secret under wraps.

That night was one of my longer stays under the ring — I'd already been under there for a couple of hours before the show started. The dark match and *Heat* tapings took another forty-five minutes and I only emerged in the final moments of the last segment of the two-hour episode of *Raw*. Every twenty to thirty minutes, Vince would check in and ask if I needed anything to eat or drink. I always appreciated his concern for my comfort under there. Later on, he went through my cue with me, then asked if I was changed yet. When I said I wasn't, he asked, "How are you going to change under there?" I simply said, "Vince, I'm a midget," which earned me a signature Vince laugh.

When I eventually decided to get changed, I opened my bag and saw the Cruiserweight Title belt sitting there. I started to panic, wondering whether I should bring it into the ring with me or not.

I didn't want to screw up in my first moments of this new, high-profile role, and I couldn't ask about it because I'd been forbidden from talking to anyone. I thought I'd mention it when Vince checked in next but when that didn't happen for a while, I grew increasingly worried. Finally, during a commercial break, I pressed the button to allow me to speak on the headset.

"Kevin?"

Nothing.

"Kevin?"

Still nothing.

"Kevin?"

"We told you not to talk."

"I'm sorry — I just wanted to know if I should bring the Cruiserweight Title out with me."

"It's about *that*?" he asked, sounding like he couldn't believe I'd ask something so stupid. "Wait a second."

After a while, I heard Kevin's voice again, saying, "Vince, the son's asking if he should bring the goddamn belt out with him."

I was relieved to hear Vince say, "That's a great question! Yes, Dylan — you should bring it out because one of the clues is to do with titles."

When the final segment of the night went ahead, the field was thinned out before one final clue was delivered — the new McMahon liked to "play the game." With Triple H's nickname being the Game, the other final contenders cleared out, and Vince and Hunter were left together in a moment made more awkward because Hunter is married to Vince's daughter — and the audience knew it. Vince screamed that something was wrong and demanded the name of his bastard son. The "investigator" then explained that the game the son liked to play could be hide and seek, horseshoes, or marbles, and that things were "looking up." Not for Vince, but for his son, Hornswoggle.

The crowd erupted as my music hit. I got in the ring and danced around like a kid at Christmas. Vince looked disgusted and Hunter looked like all his birthdays had come at once. The most-watched weekly show in the wrestling industry went off the air with Hunter pointing and laughing as I hugged Vince McMahon's left leg.

Appearing in the main event segment of *Raw* felt incredible and it was made even better by the fact that it was happening in Green Bay, with all the people closest to me at the time right there in the crowd. When I talked to my *real* dad afterward, I was relieved to hear that the angle didn't bother him at all. He understood that working with the most powerful man in the entire business was a huge opportunity for me. When he went to work the next day, people obviously knew what had happened because they joked with him, asking "Hey, is there something you need to tell us about Dylan?"

Immediately, I went from being involved in a segment on *SmackDown* most weeks to being a major part of several segments on *Raw* every week, usually interacting with Vince himself. Over the first couple of months in this run, a lot of the physical stuff I did was with announcer and interviewer Jonathan Coachman. It would invariably be cartoonish, the best example being an episode of *Raw* in England where I lured Coach under the apron, then jumped in the ring where there just happened to be a TNT detonator waiting, and I "blew up" the underneath of the ring. An explosion sound effect was played over the speakers and smoke came out from under the ring but, miraculously, Coach was fine again the next week.

I loved working with Coach because he had such a great character and personality, but he seemed to get a little frustrated with always being on the losing side. One night, he went to Vince and asked if he was ever going to win a match against me. Vince shot back, "Goddammit, Coach, why would *you* beat a midget?" Coach stammered that he felt he should beat me at least once, or everyone would assume that I'd always win. Vince just asked, "Who the hell wants to see *you* win anything?" Coach decided to leave it there.

After my shenanigans with Coach, Mr. McMahon started sending other wrestlers after me in an attempt at "tough love." This led to an infamous segment with Carlito where I spray-painted a hole in a wall and then ran through it to get away from him. Some people online have referred to this as a low point in wrestling history, when things lost all semblance of being presented as real. I'm sure there's been a lot worse than that and I didn't mind being presented as a Looney Tunes character if it meant I was featured on the show.

The only downside to becoming Hornswoggle McMahon was that I was told I wasn't going to be the Cruiserweight Champion anymore. The office didn't want there to be any focus on my character other than being Vince's son. They also didn't want me to be beaten for the belt, so instead they retired the title and disbanded the division.

The company clearly never placed much value in the cruiserweights, but the thought of giving up the title still upset me. I could already imagine the inevitable comments about how I killed the whole division and I knew that would make me feel terrible. What upset me the most though was that I never got to work a real match as a cruiserweight to show the fans and the boys what I could actually do. Something else that was phased out was my on-screen association with Finlay. However, despite being separated on screen, we still worked together on the house shows. This made for an interesting dynamic because Fit was still a heel but I'd become a babyface along the way, without ever really doing anything to turn.

As my on-screen relationship with Finlay was put on hold, my real-life relationship with Anne was coming to an end. At work, things were going great but, at home, they couldn't have been going worse. Sometimes, I was only doing the first show on a weekend and then saying I had to go home to sort things out with Anne. I was sure my behavior was getting me a lot of heat with the office, but I just wanted to deal with our problems.

I loved Anne. I thought she was the one. She'd talked about never wanting to get married again because of having gone through a bad divorce but a ring and a ceremony didn't matter to me. I just wanted to be with her.

Our relationship had never been smooth sailing. A few months after we'd started dating, I began to notice things about Anne that confused me. She'd get the shakes, her eyes would glaze over, and she'd just seem out of it. When I began to regularly find pill bottles in her purse, it all fell into place. Even though she was still in her mid-twenties, she had arthritis and used pain medication to cope. Unfortunately, this had led to her becoming addicted.

We kept going around in circles, with her swearing to me she wasn't abusing the pills, me telling her I couldn't deal with it and that she needed to get some help, her promising to stop — and then I'd find her zoned out a week later with more pill bottles rattling around in her bag.

Anne's mom was aware of all of this and, together, we tried to help her get clean but, whenever I was on the road with WWE, there was one less person to keep an eye on her. After Anne and I moved out of her mom's and into our own apartment, there was nothing or no one to stop her doing whatever she wanted whenever I wasn't there. Soon enough, her habit got out of control. We lived three miles from the airport in Green Bay, so she would always take me there and pick me up rather than have me pay for parking or cabs. One morning, she wasn't there to collect me. I called her repeatedly, but she didn't answer, so I took a cab home. When I got there, she was sprawled out on the bed with two empty bottles of pills beside her.

Terrified that she was dead, I shook her until she drowsily opened her eyes. My initial relief that she wasn't dead gave way to anger. "Why are you doing this?" I screamed. All she could mumble was "I'm so tired . . ." I yelled at her that she had a problem, she started crying, and the cycle continued.

As much as her behavior caused us problems, mine was just as bad. Somewhere along the way, I started being unfaithful. I'm not proud of it. I was a twenty-year-old who had never had much attention from women before. Now, I was on TV each week, traveling the country, and being noticed. If a woman showed interest, especially if I had a few cocktails in me, I would just go with it and see where it went. Sometimes it went nowhere. Sometimes it didn't. Worst of all, this wasn't just on the road. Sometimes it was in town and right under Anne's nose. I don't know how, but I convinced myself that my apologies would be enough, and we'd get through it. Looking back, between her addiction problems and my infidelity, it's amazing we lasted as long as we did.

When Anne was out one day, I was on her computer and she'd left her MySpace logged in. Maybe I shouldn't have looked but I did and, straight away, I found messages between her and a guy named Aaron who used to be an indie wrestler. They'd been to Milwaukee Brewers games together. They'd been away to the Wisconsin Dells for a weekend. She had told him, "You complete me," and "You make me happier than I've been in a long time." I was crushed. I'd helped her with a bunch of debt, I'd done my best to help with her drug addiction, and, above all else, I'd loved her. I'd *also* cheated on her several times but in that moment, I couldn't see past my own pain. When I confronted her about it, she told me that it had started with them being friends but turned into something more. She wanted to leave, but I couldn't let her go. I told her we could work it out and tried to convince her to stay, but when I got back from my next tour, it was to an empty apartment. Everything was gone, because everything was hers. All that she had left behind were the things I'd moved in with — a PlayStation and my wrestling figures.

I couldn't help but take my heartache with me to work. I was miserable but everyone in WWE was so supportive, even people I didn't expect it from. Soon after Anne and I split up, I was at *Raw* doing a segment where I chased Melina out of the shower and through the building. Vince's daughter and EVP of creative, Stephanie McMahon, was producing the spot and, between takes, she pulled me aside to say, "Hey, I heard what's going on at home and I'm sorry about what's happening. But let me tell you, in this new role, you're going to get a *lot* of attention. You're going to have a lot of fun with this." I thought that was thoughtful and supportive, especially since I hadn't been doing right by her family's company when I was missing so many shows to try to fix my broken relationship.

Something else that cheered me up was when Finlay and I were reunited on screen at the *Survivor Series* that year. Vince's ongoing attempts to make me "McMahon tough" had led to him arranging a match between me and Khali for the PPV show. The tale of the tape for this one was insane — he was almost double my height and more than triple my weight. We started out with some comedy spots, including my "Irish Mist," but then Khali got his hands on me. Just as it looked like the jokes were over and I was going to get ripped apart by the giant, Finlay ran out to save me, turning himself babyface in the process.

Another memorable segment I had with Khali was on the fifteenth anniversary edition of *Raw*. That whole night was incredible for me because I was in a number of segments, including both the opening and the closing ones — something not many people get to do on a regular *Raw*, let alone a huge milestone edition like the fifteenth anniversary. I couldn't believe my luck.

After the opening segment, an in-ring "family portrait" comedy spot with all of the McMahons (including me) and a host of other hilarious characters like Bastion Booger, "Big" Dick Johnson, and Gerald Brisco, my next part in the show built up to a rematch against Khali. I assumed it would be similar to our *Survivor Series* match and Fit would come out to save me, but when I got to the arena that night, one of the producers told me that it wasn't going to be Finlay coming to my rescue — it was going to be Hulk Hogan.

Even though I'd been more of a Warrior guy, this was Hulk Hogan, *the* face of wrestling of the '80s. I couldn't help myself and simply had to ask, "Can we do a pose down afterward and can I rip my shirt like he does?" The writer loved the idea and went off to check with Hulk. An hour later, he came back and said the pose down was on, but the shirt ripping was off. Hulk "wasn't feeling it." I wasn't going to let it go that easy, so I thought I'd try my luck later at rehearsal.

When the time came for everyone in the segment to talk it through, I noticed Hulk was wearing a tight, black Under Armor shirt rather than his usual Hulkamania T-shirt, and I took that as a sign that he didn't feel in good-enough shape to do his trademark shirt-tear. Still, I had to try. Vince, Hulk, Khali, and I went through everything we were going to do later on the show, and when we got to the pose down, I looked hopefully up at Vince and said, "Then we rip our shirts, right?" Vince glanced over at Hulk, who smiled and chimed in, "Not tonight, brother." Between that rehearsal and the live show, I considered going ahead and ripping my own shirt anyway in the hope that Hulk would join in, but when the moment came, I decided it was better to stick to the script.

Even without the shirt-tear, sharing the ring with Hulk was incredible. When I was standing with Khali and Hulk's music hit, every hair on my body stood straight up. I can't begin to describe the feeling. Being able to join Hogan in his trademark pose down was an incredible experience — and it wasn't the only trademark routine I was going to be involved in that night.

The closing part of the show saw Mr. McMahon and his biggest on-screen rival, Stone Cold, get into an altercation which, inevitably, Vince lost. Afterward, Austin called everyone down to the ring to join him in a beer bash. I couldn't believe my luck to be out there as Austin was tossing beers around the ring and smashing cans with everyone. Right as *Raw* was going off air, I saw Vince sitting on the floor outside the ring and thought it would be pretty funny if I poured beer on him, so I stood by the ropes and made it look like I was accidentally pouring beer on my "dad" over my shoulder as I talked to Triple H. It was a spur of the moment idea I had because I thought it would look good on TV. They got a great camera shot of it, too, and that was how the fifteenth anniversary of *Raw* finished.

It had been an amazing night — I'd been in the ring interacting with two of the biggest names in wrestling history and got to pour beer on the most powerful man in the entire industry. Once again, I wondered how and why it was all happening to me. Then as I walked backstage, I started to get a little nervous about what I'd done to Vince. Austin and Hunter had poured beer on him as well, but they were both in a very small group of people who can pretty much do whatever they want on the shows. I was definitely not in that group. As soon I got through the curtain, Vince found me and growled, "What the hell was *that*?" I immediately went into apology mode, but he cut me off with that trademark laugh of his and said, "I bet it made great TV." Vince is very much like that — he wants people to take chances.

Maybe I *should* have gone off script and ripped my shirt after all . . .

A Short Story: 3:16

When I was young, my dad let me order one WWE pay-per-view a year. In 1996, I went with *King of the Ring* because the Ultimate Warrior was fighting Jerry Lawler. That was the only match I cared about because I knew the Warrior was going to kick the King's ass. On that same show, "Stone Cold" Steve Austin won the King of the Ring tournament and cut the Austin 3:16 promo that pretty much launched him to the top. Here's the funny thing — at the time, that now-legendary promo didn't even register with me.

Warrior left WWE soon after that, but Austin was on the rise heading into a program with Bret Hart. That's when I really started to like Stone Cold, because anyone who beat the hell out of Bret Hart was someone I was going to cheer. Now that I know Bret, I think he's great, but I just wasn't a huge Hitman fan back in '96. When it came to Austin, I loved the glass smashing and I loved the storyline feud he had with Vince.

I got to meet Steve a few times when he came in to do something for WWE while I was there and we got along well. After he'd just got his podcast going, I told him that I'd love to do his show if possible and gave him my number. A while later, I got a couple of calls from an L.A. number and didn't pick up because I didn't know who it was. The one time I did pick up, a voice said, "Hey, is Hornswoggle there?" I asked, "Who is this?" "It's Steve," said the caller. Because he'd asked for Hornswoggle and not Dylan, I thought it was a fan, so I said, "Wrong number, sir," and hung up.

The next time I was at a show with Austin, he walked over and said, "Hey you — you kayfabed me!" I was confused. "When I called you, you kayfabed me and you hung up on me." As I explained that I didn't realize it was him and I'd thought it was a mark calling, John Cena walked past. Steve stopped him, pointed at me, and said, "He thinks I'm a mark." I got the hell out of there as quickly as I could. Fortunately, Steve actually thought it was funny and I ended up doing the podcast with him. Believe me, hearing your phone ring and seeing the name "Steve Austin" come up on the screen is about as awesome as it gets.

Even though so many great things had happened for me in 2007, there was one more surprise to come. I still picked up *Pro Wrestling Illustrated* magazine now and then, especially their year-end awards and top 500 issues, which I've loved since I was a kid. As I was flicking through the 2007 PWI Awards issue, I found myself staring at a full-page picture of *myself*. I'd been named Rookie of the Year, an honor I now shared with Ric Flair, Steve Austin, Goldberg, Randy Orton, Owen Hart, Kurt Angle . . . and Prince Iaukea. I couldn't believe what I was seeing. PWI is a staple in the industry, and I can't describe how great it was to be included in the awards issue I'd read religiously each year. (Although, despite apparently being the top rookie, I didn't make it into the PWI 500 that or any other year. Getting on that list is still an ambition of mine.)

I can see how some people thought it was bullshit that I beat out Ted DiBiase Jr. (the guy in second), given I wasn't a regular in-ring worker, but what I *do* know is that I probably wouldn't have been in a position to win that award if I'd been six feet tall. Honestly, if I had been normal-sized, I don't think I would have had the same sort of drive to prove I could do this. For all the downsides that come with being small, it's made me what I am and got me what I have. If I'd been 6'2", I wouldn't have been as motivated to prove myself. I still would have loved wrestling and wanted to go as far with it as I could have, but if I didn't stand out physically the way I do, I'm not sure I would have made it to WWE.

CHAPTER 12

THE BATTLE FOR THE BASTARD

As 2008 started, Fit and I were both babyfaces, so I got to be more involved on house shows, either in Fit's corner or as his tag team partner. Fit hated being a babyface. He'd been a heel for most of his career and he was great at it. When we turned, he was taken out of his comfort zone. He'd walk to the ring, waving to the crowd and high-fiving the fans, the whole time muttering, "This isn't me" through gritted teeth. He still found a way to have fun with it though — we started doing a pose in the corner of the ring every night where I'd climb on the ropes and he'd climb up behind me and we'd do the "I'm the king of the world" from *Titanic*. Because I was sandwiched between Fit and the turnbuckles, he had to get back down first, and when he did, he'd "accidentally" bonk me in the head with the shillelagh, followed by his signature chuckle. After a few occurrences, I realized it wasn't an accident. That shillelagh was even harder than it looked and hurt like hell. I started putting one arm above my head to protect myself but Fit would grab my hand and spread my arms out, so he had a clear shot at my skull.

On TV, Vince's behavior toward me was growing more sinister. He started trying to turn me against Finlay and, when that didn't work, put me in situations where he'd make it look like they were in my interest but were designed to put me in danger. Just like in a cartoon though, something would usually happen to derail his evil plan.

Mr. McMahon sent me to the ring to face two big, bearded Scotsmen, the Highlanders, in order to qualify for entry in the 2008 *Royal Rumble*. My partner was an unknown local talent named B.K. Jordan, so it was clear we were both about to get our asses kicked. I'm sure everyone was expecting Finlay to save me as usual, but this time, it was Mick Foley who stepped in and helped me overcome the odds to win the match and a spot in the rumble. It's always incredible when you're working with a legend like Mick because he gets a great reaction from the crowd no matter what the storyline is. He's also one of the nicest guys you'll ever meet.

With my place in the big match secured, Mr. McMahon decided I needed to get some rumble experience. This led to a Mini-Royal Rumble on *Raw*, where I was the first entrant. They brought out a series of midget wrestlers, all dressed up to look like other WWE superstars — there was Mini-Kennedy, Mini-Mankind, Mini-Kane, and Mini-Batista (who later got thrown out of the building for sneaking pictures of the female wrestlers backstage).

The little person playing Mini-Kennedy had the same condition as me, but his legs were a lot thinner and it made him look awkward, especially in trunks. Despite that, he was easy to work with and didn't complain when I almost took his head off with a clothesline. I even managed to gorilla press him up above my head and throw him clear over the top rope in a homage to my hero, the Ultimate Warrior. I also got to hit Finlay's finisher, the Celtic Cross, on Mini-Kane. That was easy because he was really small. The segment ended when they had the full-size Great Khali come out as the last entrant and, once again, Finlay came to my rescue. I loved the entire thing

— getting to show some of what I could do as a wrestler and having that whole segment based around me was flattering and showed me the company believed I could deliver.

After all of the buildup, my appearance in the *Royal Rumble* that year didn't amount to much. I came out at number nine, walked down the short aisle at Madison Square Garden all fired up, took one look at the Undertaker staring down at me, then crawled under the ring as the Garden crowd booed. I sneaked out a couple of times during the match, once to pull the Miz over the top rope and eliminate him, then later to attempt the same thing with Mark Henry. I had less success with Mark, who hauled me up and into the ring, where I ended up caught between him and the even bigger Viscera, who was now shirtless and horrifying as Big Daddy V. Before the two behemoths could squash me like a bug, Finlay rushed out and attacked everyone with his shillelagh, saving me but earning us the dubious distinction of being the only people in history to be disqualified from a *Royal Rumble*.

A Short Story: Keeping a Secret Secret

A few minutes after Finlay and I got to the back that night, John Cena came out at number thirty. To say everyone backstage was surprised would be an understatement — no one knew John was going to be in the rumble. He'd been injured in a match late the previous year and because he was expected to be out of action for the majority of a year, he had to vacate the WWE Championship. Three months later, he was back in the ring and winning the *Royal Rumble*. It was incredible. Whenever anyone would ask how he'd managed to recover so far ahead of schedule, he'd just say, "I worked my ass off." Whenever he's had to rehab an injury, he always blows the recovery date away.

We knew there was something that we weren't being told that night, because the lineup for the rumble match backstage only had twenty-nine guys on it. At the pre-show meeting each year, they'd get all the people in the rumble together, go through the key spots and eliminations until they brought it down to the final few, then they'd ask everyone else to leave. I'd assume, that year, they then told Batista, Hunter, and Kane what was going on, as well as maybe mentioning it to Mark Henry, Chavo Guerrero Jr., and Carlito, all of whom John eliminated as soon as he got to the ring. But for all I know, they might have taken those three guys aside and only said, "Hey, there's a surprise guy coming out at number thirty, he'll eliminate you as soon as he comes out." From what I know, John got there after the show started and hung out in a bus until just before he came out.

It's been tough to keep things surprising in wrestling in the age of social media, but it's great when it happens. And on that night, it made for one of those moments no one will ever forget.

After the *Rumble*, Mr. McMahon was not pleased that his son had let him down. As punishment, he demanded I become the newest member of the "Kiss My Ass Club," which was exactly what it sounded like — the person he was attempting to humiliate would have to kiss his bare ass on national TV. This idea was presented to me with absolutely no tact — before the show that night, Vince simply told me, "You're going to join tonight," and that was that. No discussion, no argument. The payoff to the segment was going to be that instead of kissing his ass, I was going to bite it. (Once again — great ass bite, decent splash.) Biting an ass is a standard part of a midget's wrestling repertoire but usually the recipient was one of the women and it was through some clothes. I didn't mind doing it because it got me in a main segment on *Raw*, but putting my mouth on a sixty-year-old man's bare ass wasn't on my bucket list. Still, the crowd seemed to enjoy the segment, and I liked it because it was another chance to have the spotlight on me.

That bite led to Vince ordering me to face him on *Raw* the next week in a rare singles match for us both. The "match" was pretty much just Vince daring me to slap him, and when I finally did, he took off his belt and prepared to deliver some more "tough love." Finlay got to the ring before the whipping started and stopped Vince getting to me. Vince then got on the microphone, told Finlay he was interfering with "family business," and threatened to fire him. When Fit backed down, Vince pointed out to me that he and Finlay weren't the same sort of Irish because Finlay was a coward. Vince then threw me down and turned around to find Fit grinning his gap-toothed smile at him. Fit cracked Vince in the head with his shillelagh, immediately raising a goose egg, then sent me up to the top rope. I hit my tadpole splash on Vince and the ref counted three. With that, I became one of very few people to pin Vince McMahon. I know it's not *real*, but it's still a cool piece of trivia! "Stone Cold" Steve Austin has never pinned Vince McMahon but Hornswoggle has.

Finlay was involved in one of the Elimination Chamber matches at the next PPV, *No Way Out*, along with Undertaker, Khali, Batista, MVP, and Big Daddy V. I'm sure the gigantic cage surrounding the ring can be intimidating for the regular-sized wrestlers, but to me, it was overwhelming. The metal grating between the ring and the chamber wall had zero give to it. As I was walking around in the cage during rehearsal and looking doubtfully at the grating, Fit came over and casually commented, "I'll take a chokeslam on that. That'll look good." I suggested he should rethink that but he simply chuckled to himself and walked off. Sure enough, the Undertaker chokeslammed

Finlay on the grating later that night and it looked great — but it had to have destroyed his back.

During the match, my part was to appear between one of chamber's four corner pods and the edge of the ring, then throw Finlay his shillelagh. There was very little room between the cage structure and the ring and as the chamber was being lowered around the ring before the match, it looked like it was going to be too tight for me to squeeze my head through. From underneath the ring, I started trying to push this massive structure. It must have been comical to anyone who noticed the midget heaving against a multi-tonne mass of metal but I was determined to push it even a single inch because I knew production wanted a shot of my face poking up in the corner rather than just an arm holding a shillelagh. When it was time to do my spot, I was *just* able to squeeze my skull through the gap.

Mr. McMahon wasn't happy with me for interfering in that cage match so, later in the show, he told Finlay that if I wanted to be involved in cage matches so much, I could have a cage match on *Raw* the next night . . . against Vince himself. This was when John Bradshaw Layfield was brought into the fray.

A Short Story: Overserved

There's been a lot said about how JBL was one of the biggest bullies in the WWE locker room. He didn't hold back in the ring, that's for sure, and he'd take verbal shots at almost anyone on the roster if he felt like it, especially if there was an audience there to listen. John's not the only person who did it though. To me, that was just boys being boys on the road.

During the weekend of my first *WrestleMania*, we'd all been at the TGI Fridays near the hotel. I'd enjoyed a few too many drinks, got into the Hurricane's rental car, and proceeded to throw up everywhere. Bob Holly, another guy who got an unfair reputation, hauled me out of the car by the back of my pants and carried me across the parking lot — under one arm — toward the hotel lobby. As he was doing that, JBL and Bruce Prichard drove up and told us that Vince's limo was just around the corner. John and Bob got me into the hotel, onto a luggage rack, and pushed me into the elevator and up to my room.

Even though I was still the new guy, John and Bob took care of me when they easily could have messed with me or left me to get fired when Vince showed up. That doesn't strike me as something a "bully" would do.

Over the previous few weeks, there had been several backstage segments where Finlay had been yelling at Vince about a secret that I needed to be told, a secret he didn't want to hide anymore. The big reveal we'd been building up to was that Vince *wasn't* actually my dad — Finlay was. I found out years later that this angle was supposed to lead to a match at *WrestleMania 24*, which would have been the Battle of the Irish between Finlay and Vince himself. I can't imagine how much promotion that would have got but, unfortunately, it didn't happen. Somewhere along the way during the backstage segments, Vince apparently changed his mind and kyboshed his own physical involvement.

At the time, I had no idea that Fit's match with the boss had been canceled, so I couldn't feel disappointed. In fact, it was completely the opposite. I couldn't believe my luck. When I started wrestling, I never thought I'd be on *Raw*. I never thought I'd be in a cage match. And I definitely never thought I'd be in a one-on-one match with the most powerful man in the entire industry. And yet there I was, about to have a cage match on *Raw* against Vince McMahon.

Before rehearsal started that night, Fit took me aside and prepared me for the fact that I was going to get roughed up, but that Vince would take care of me financially for my involvement. Later, Vince reiterated that it was going to be a tough night. "It's going to be snug tonight, Dylan," he warned me. He wasn't kidding.

Finlay accompanied me to the ring for the match and was just leaving the cage when JBL, unannounced, slammed the cage door on him, causing him to drop the shillelagh. John then handcuffed Fit to the ropes so he would be forced to watch what was about to happen. With no one to protect me this time, Vince removed his belt and whipped me — to say it stung would be an understatement. Instinctively, I put one of my hands over my ass to cover up, at which point Vince went to town with a series of lashes which hurt my hand even more than my ass. He didn't hold back at all and, as much as it hurt, I'm glad. If anything physical had looked less than brutal here, the whole segment would have fallen flat. After he'd finished whipping me, Vince left me in the ring with JBL. John grabbed me and flung me hard into the cage wall, face first. I intentionally didn't put my hands up to cushion the impact because I was hoping that if I hit the cage hard enough, I might get busted open and that would just add to the drama. I didn't draw blood, but I got a perfect bounce off the wire fence and it looked vicious. John then kicked me very hard, right in the face. Again, I'm glad he didn't hold back. The crowd were booing the hell out of him at this point, which was exactly what we wanted. Fit was playing his part perfectly, too, half-threatening John and half-begging him to stop.

JBL then picked me up and got ready to deliver his signature fallaway slam but instead of throwing me overhead and to the mat, he was going to fling me over the ropes and into the cage wall. This was the bump I was most nervous about. I knew that once I hit the fence, it would be hard for me to control my fall. Earlier in the day, I'd asked Fit how I could take the move safely and he told me to grab the top rope and cling onto it — that way I could make sure I didn't fall on my head.

As John held me up, taunting Finlay with what was about to happen, I noticed something that scared the hell out of me. The way John had me lined up, I wasn't going to collide with the fence — I was going to fly directly into one of the thick metal poles that held the cage sections together. Fortunately, the camera wasn't on me as I told him, "Pole! There's a pole behind you . . ."

Fortunately, John heard and adjusted his position before he threw me. It felt like I was in the air for minutes instead of seconds. I collided with the cage, failed to grab the rope on the way down, and landed kidney-first on the club end of the discarded shillelagh. The jolt of pain that shot through me was insane. I may have looked unconscious on the outside, but my body was screaming on the inside.

After JBL and Mr. McMahon had left, Finlay finally escaped his handcuffs, then scooped me up and carried me to the back. He was convincingly distraught; since the viewers had never once seen him show *any* form of emotion before, it was a truly powerful moment. A couple of weeks later, it would be revealed that it was Finlay who was my storyline father, not Vince.

After the cage match, everyone was happy backstage, especially Vince, who made sure to check that I was okay physically. This was the end of my regular on-screen interaction with Vince, which was a great shame as through all the stories and segments we did together, he was amazing to work with. He's an absolute perfectionist. When he thinks something should be done a specific way, he'll have it done over and over again until it's exactly how he wants. Working with the most powerful man in the entire industry each week over several months taught me so much about the wrestling business.

The company got me a red-eye flight back home that night and told me I wouldn't be at the *SmackDown* tapings the following day as I'd be off selling the injuries from the cage match. On the Wednesday, I got another call from the office telling me I wouldn't be needed for the following week's tapings either. They brought me in the week after that to film one short scene in a hospital bed where JBL attacked me. That was played live on *Raw* just after Finlay had finally admitted that he was my father. After that, my diary was empty. When WWE didn't bring me in for a show in my hometown of Oshkosh later that week — a show where all the local advertising had heavily featured me — I started getting concerned. I wondered if, rather than being off the shows to sell my injuries, I'd been written out of the storylines and the company altogether. Maybe they were going in a different direction now and would carry on without me. The sudden realization that it was a possibility was more terrifying than being thrown into any cage. The program continued to move forward toward the big blow-off, a "Belfast Brawl" no-disqualification match between JBL and Finlay at *WrestleMania 24* in Orlando, Florida. As they built toward this on TV, I still had no idea if I would be involved in any way. No one was telling me *anything*.

Even so, I was still under contract so I assumed I'd be brought along to 'Mania if only to appear at the fan festivals, and the event being in Orlando gave me a perfect excuse to plan a vacation with all my friends. I figured that even if I wasn't used on the *WrestleMania* show, I'd come in early, do some appearances, and then spend as much time as I could at the Disney parks. I booked everything in and a group of us were set to arrive in Orlando four days before 'Mania.

That plan went out the window with one call from Michael Hayes, who was now the head writer on *SmackDown*. "Hey kid, we're not bringing you in until really late on the night before *WrestleMania*." I told him that I'd planned a big vacation with my friends and everything was already booked. Hayes paused a moment before replying, "Do you realize what you're saying to me right now? We're giving you a big comeback on the biggest show of the year and you're telling me you can't do what we're asking?" Like an idiot, I began to argue but Michael cut me off and told me, "Just listen to us." I knew not to push my point, but I was so angry. Like an idiot, all I could think about was how I was going to miss out on everything I had planned at Disney when I should have been thinking about my job, my career, and the company giving me such a huge opportunity. It was so selfish and stupid of me.

WWE likes to surprise its audience whenever it can, but that can be hard to do given how quickly information leaks out on the internet. Even though my return wasn't a big deal in the grand scheme of things, they thought bringing me back after I'd been off TV for a month would a nice extra for the show. They were going to fly me in at 11 p.m. the night before the show so as few people as possible knew I was even there. When I thought about it, I realized that I couldn't be walking around at Disney World in the few days leading up to 'Mania. I'm not saying I was so famous at this point that people would have instantly noticed me as the WWE's leprechaun, but with my stature, I don't really blend into a crowd. Before long, someone would have recognized me, word would have got out, the surprise would have been ruined, and the office would have been pissed at me — and maybe even changed plans because of it, something that isn't unheard of when word of a surprise leaks too soon.

On the morning of the show, John Bradshaw Layfield, Fit, and I stood in the middle of the Citrus Bowl, this huge, empty stadium, and talked through what we were going to do. There was a spot planned where JBL would be about to hit Finlay with the shillelagh, but I was going to run in and hit him from behind with a kendo stick — and not the homemade type that I used in my backyard wrestling days. John instructed me to hit him as hard as I could. I wasn't convinced but he explained, "If you don't hit me hard, it won't make a sound, but it'll still hurt. If it's going to hurt anyway, I'd rather it sounds painful, too." I couldn't argue with that logic and that's John — he didn't hold back when he gave me my beating on *Raw* a month earlier, and he didn't expect me to give him any less in return.

I don't generally go back and watch events I appeared in — I find I get critical of everything I did or how I looked — but *WrestleMania 24* is one of the exceptions because I remember how excited I was all through that day. We were scheduled to be the first match on the main card and that's a big deal — because it sets the tone for the night, opening *WrestleMania* is a huge responsibility.

JBL came out first, followed by Finlay who stopped at the top of the ramp and waved backstage. That was my cue — I ran out from the back as my music hit and the crowd popped. It was a relief to hear the fans were excited I was back. I couldn't believe that I was on '*Mania* again and this time, I wasn't just sneaking out from under the ring, I was getting to make an entrance down the ramp next to Finlay and they were playing *my* music. I never expected to hear my music at a *WrestleMania*. The two main recollections I have of walking to the ring that afternoon were that I could feel the Florida breeze on my face, and that I couldn't hear much. Open air stadiums can be difficult to judge because the sound goes up and out. Just like the year before, being in front of a crowd of that size was overwhelming. I looked around to see if I could figure out where my friends were sitting but quickly realized I had absolutely no chance.

The bout got off to a quick start when Finlay rushed the ring, leading to a hard-hitting match where two of the toughest guys in wrestling beat the hell out of each other as you'd expect — after all, the story was about a father looking to get revenge on the bully who'd put his disadvantaged child in the hospital. The crowd was with them the whole way. As they were wailing on each other, I kept saying to myself, "You've gotta hit him, you gotta hit him," psyching myself up for my spot. When the time came, I swung the stick as hard as I could at John, then got the hell out of the ring.

Later in the match, something happened that wasn't planned and it ended up being pretty memorable. Finlay was down, I was standing on the floor, and JBL was walking over to pick up one of the trash cans that was in the ring. Seeing me standing there at ringside, he grabbed a dented can and, without any warning, hurled it at me. Everything happened so quickly that I only just managed to turn a little and throw my hands up in time to protect myself. If I hadn't done that, the can would have knocked me out for sure. As it was, the can hit me mostly in the hip. It hurt like hell, but it looked absolutely awesome on the replays.

I could never understand why Finlay lost the match. It didn't make any sense. At *WrestleMania*, the babyfaces usually win, and given the storyline behind this match and the fact it was the opener, there was even more reason for the good guy to come out on top. But since JBL went on to work with John Cena, I guess they figured he needed a big win to make him look like he was a threat to the top guy in the company.

The whole *WrestleMania* experience that year was incredible. I particularly loved watching Ric Flair's retirement match against Shawn Michaels live with Binder, because Flair is his favorite wrestler of all time. Even though it was Ric's final match in WWE and he was almost sixty years old, I think it was one of his best matches and, for my money, the most emotional match in wrestling history. And because my friends had been able to change their

plans, we stayed on in Florida for a few days and I got to go to Disney World after all.

Not all of my off-screen activities at this point were as wholesome as going to Disney World. I was a young, single guy, on TV every week, making more money than I'd ever thought I'd make. It was a blessing and a curse. After I broke up with Anne, my behavior became even worse.

One of my regular tricks was to go to the local college bar in Oshkosh with a hundred singles in my pocket, climb on top of the speaker, and start throwing dollar bills on the dance floor. I was "that asshole" at the bar, shooting money around, hitting on all the women, and talking shit to all the guys. If anyone talked shit back, Binder would step in and beat the piss out of them.

Some nights, however, I was on my best behavior. And fortunately, on one of those nights, at a bar called the Rail in Oshkosh, I met Kim. She came over and opened with "Hey, are you that guy from *Raw*?" Within weeks, she'd moved in with me. We were crazy about each other. I just wanted to spend as much time as I could with her. When I was off the road, I didn't want to go out anymore — I just wanted to stay home and do nothing, because doing nothing with Kim by my side made me so happy.

CHAPTER 13

THE FRENCH OPEN TENNIS BALLS

From 2004 to 2011, WWE held a yearly draft where people would be moved between the *Raw*, *SmackDown*, and ECW rosters to keep the matchups fresh. Whenever these drafts happened, very few people knew whether they were going to be moved or where they'd end up. I don't know how, but Fit had found out what was happening in advance of the 2008 draft — he and I were going to be moving to ECW. We both had mixed feelings about it. I knew Fit would be one of the biggest stars on the brand, so we'd be in a lot of the main storylines. But then again, WWE's version of ECW wasn't watched by as many people as *Raw* or *SmackDown*, so we'd be the proverbial big fish in a much smaller pond.

Shortly after we got there, we found ourselves in a program with Mark Henry and Tony Atlas. Tony was a former wrestler and powerlifter who had been brought back to be Mark's manager.

My first big moment, scurrying out from under the ring for the very first time on WWE SmackDown! *I couldn't have imagined it would lead to me performing at several WrestleManias, including in front of 74,635 people in Orlando, Florida.*

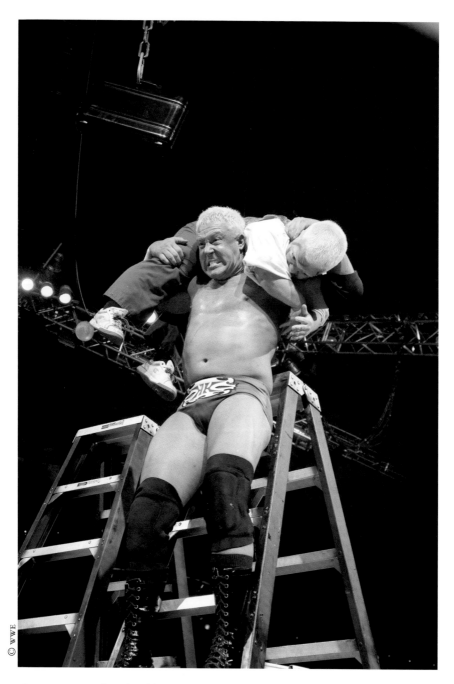

On Ken Kennedy's shoulders, about to take the biggest bump of my career at WrestleMania 23.

Hitting the tadpole splash on Jamie Noble moments before the biggest win of my career.

The new (and final, for a while) WWE Cruiserweight Champion.

It was a privilege to meet some of the guest hosts on Raw, *including Ozzy Osbourne, Verne Troyer, and future president Donald Trump.*

Two highlights of my career — being part of D-generation X and my WeeLC match with Torito.

Binder, Weimer, and yours truly — "The Suits" at Weimer's wedding.

With Dad at the Muppets Most Wanted *premiere, and rare proof that he does, once every few decades, wear a suit.*

Me and a bunch of Muppets. Also, me with Miss Piggy, Fozzy, Kermit, and Gonzo. (Sorry, Ricky, Ray, Danny, and Bill — couldn't resist it!)

Zack Lipovsky (bottom left) had big plans for my prosthetics in Leprechaun: Origins *(top row), which my dad and Dorothy got to see on their visit to set. The designers of* WWE SmackDown vs. Raw *saved a lot of time and went the motion capture route instead (bottom right).*

The best moment of my life, holding my son for the very first time.

Grandpa's Rock: Landon and me at the exact same age, on the same rock in Grandpa's — now our — backyard.

Disney trips have become a yearly tradition. By 2018's visit, Landon had outgrown me but neither of us has outgrown Disney.

A Warrior to the end — meeting my childhood hero was the ultimate experience.

Feeling the power of Hulkamania with Landon.

One of the great joys of working on the local indie circuit is Binder and I are able to bring our sons, Ayden and Landon, along with us.

How ACW has grown — from December 2013 in front of 125 people to April 2018 about to run an arena show in front of 2,500. I'm here with Binder, Weimer, our business colleague Nathan Gust, and arena manager Toni.

With some of my best friends in the business: Tyson Kidd (top right),
Kofi Kingston (top left), and Curt Hawkins (all three).

In the end, everything comes down to family. Four generations of Postl men and, below, the whole clan in 2019. From the left: me, Landon, Ben, Laura, Averie, Julia, Ezra, Tim, Dorothy, Elias, and Dad.

That was a role he didn't just play on the shows — he was legitimately managing him on the road as well, encouraging him to get to the gym and get back in shape, because Mark sometimes needed a little extra motivation. When he was interested in what he was doing, Mark could be a very good performer, but when he wasn't motivated, he was difficult to get to do anything. Tony annoyed Fit a great deal. His regular speaking voice was as loud as how most people yell, and if Tony wasn't talking, he was chuckling to himself, usually for no apparent reason. He was an odd character who could easily get on your nerves.

Tony was good at motivating Mark, but when it came to helping him in the ring, that was Fit's job. Mark had been with the company for more than a decade but still needed some guidance between the ropes. I don't think that was entirely his fault. He'd signed a big contract with WWE just as he was going to the Olympics as a weightlifter, and the spotlight was on him immediately. Mark never got the chance to properly hone his craft: he wasn't given the opportunity to work with many people who could help him along, plus he kept getting hurt, too. (He'd been injured at one point or another during seven of his first ten years with the company.) In Fit, Mark had a guy who could guide him through longer matches, show him how to play to his strengths and hide his weaknesses, and generally give him the polish he'd never had.

The key was to slow him down. Once Mark started taking his time, he was able to look much more aggressive. That's when it all started to come together, and Mark started wrestling like a big, mean, scary strongman. After Fit was finished with him, Mark went on to have some great runs with Randy Orton, John Cena, and a series with the Big Show that shocked a lot of people because it was so much better than anyone ever expected. Mark wound up a World Champion and Hall of Famer. Finlay would never claim any credit for that, but I'm sure Mark would be the first to tell you Fit had a lot to do with helping him along the way.

A Short Story: The Highest Heights

Touring with WWE meant I had the opportunity to see a lot of the world. When we were in Ecuador, a group of us wanted to check out a volcano so we rode to the top of one of the mountains in gondolas. I was with Fit and his wife, the Undertaker and Michelle McCool, Scott Armstrong, and Mark Henry. We couldn't all go in the same gondola, so Undertaker and Michelle rode together, Fit and his wife went with Mark, and I rode up with Scott.

When I got to the top, Mark was freaking out, spouting profanities. It turned out this big, mean wrestler was actually afraid of heights. He thought he could cope with the ride up, but what he didn't count on was that Finlay *knew* he was afraid of heights. All the way up, Fit was shaking the gondola, telling Mark it was moving on its own and that he could hear funny noises from the cable.

However, I didn't hear that story at the top of the volcano. I only heard it after I'd traveled back with Finlay and was given the exact same treatment. Fit spent the whole journey talking about how unstable the gondola was and how there was nothing but empty space beneath us. The whole time, I was scared out of my wits.

One of the guys who I'd heard a lot about from the boys but never met was Christian. He'd left the WWE to go to a smaller promotion, Total Non-Stop Action — or TNA — a little before I first came in. Now, we found out he was coming back to start with ECW. I was traveling with Edge and Tommy Dreamer at that time and Edge told me, very pointedly, "He's going to *love* you. You'll see." When we finally all met up, Christian first hugged his best friend Edge, then Tommy, then grabbed me, pulled me into a hug — and started dry humping me. Edge quickly joined in, yelling, "See? I told you he was gonna love you!"

Christian is one of the funniest guys I've met in wrestling, with a great, dry sense of humor. Edge refers to him as "The Dick" because that's what he is — he's a dick who messes with everyone. He made it a particular priority to annoy the hell out of Tommy. Not that Tommy ever minded because he's always up for anything that would get a reaction. Backstage, Tommy would put his face in a cake like Mrs. Doubtfire, hang things out of his mouth, or walk around with his ass hanging out to make the boys laugh. The positive vibe he brings to any locker room is one of the many reasons I respect him so much.

It was Dreamer who introduced the locker room practice of "Mr. Fuji-ing" when we were on an overseas tour, where a lot of the boys were happy for any distraction. Mr. Fuji was a wrestling manager in the '80s and '90s who would interfere in matches by throwing "ceremonial salt" into the eyes of his wrestlers' opponents. Tommy would casually stroll up to someone and ask questions like, "Who was Demolition's manager?" then when they answered "Mr. Fuji," he'd fling whatever he was holding — usually salt or talcum powder — in their face. He not only got me but also Edge, Matt Striker, and Kane with this gag. It quickly got out of control and people started getting "Mr. Fuji'd" any time and everywhere. Ring announcer Justin Roberts was "Mr. Fuji'd" three or four times by different people during one live event. Everything came to a head when Tommy managed to get Big Show to say "Mr. Fuji" in catering one night — then threw a handful of rice at the seven-foot goliath. With rice stuck to

Tommy Dreamer, living up to his name and making an excellent pillow.

his head and face, Show calmly stood up and left the room. Everyone at the table thought, "This could be bad." Moments later, Show came rushing back in and let a fire extinguisher off directly in Tommy's face. It was hilarious, but that was when we all knew "Mr. Fuji-ing" had to stop.

Tommy was also the creator of the infamous game "Tommy Ball." He'd sit against a wall with his testicles hanging out, and players would each get to throw a tennis ball at his groin. The first one to hit a nut was declared the winner. The original players were me, Edge, Kane, and Justin Roberts, but in time the roster grew to more than twenty — the line would often stretch out of the locker room and down the hall. The main rule of Tommy Ball was no rocketing the ball at Tommy's testes. Doing that could get you a lifetime ban from the sport. Edge and Kane always went last, because they were the best at the game by a considerable margin. If no one else had won by the time it got to them, you could guarantee one of them was going to connect a ball to a ball. I have no idea how Tommy didn't get seriously injured doing this. If he did, he kept it to himself and, honestly, I don't think he would have cared. Sacrificing his testicles to entertain the boys is the sort of thing he'd do without thinking twice.

A Short Story: A Short Date

Since Tommy Dreamer worked in the office, he'd get to stay at the "TV hotels" — great places that the company covered. Sometimes Tommy would let me room with him and I'd always leap at the chance because it meant I'd save some cash and get a major upgrade from my usual standard of accommodation on the road. We were in Seattle one time and headed to the hotel bar to grab a drink and, in Tommy's words, "meet some of the guys." The guys he was referring to turned out to be Vince McMahon and his son Shane. Soon enough, I found myself sitting at the bar next to Vince, drinking a rum and coke while the boss had a Dewars. While I was there, I was texting a little person friend of mine who lives in Seattle, arranging to meet up for dinner.

Tommy knew what my plans were and mentioned them in front of Vince, who was immediately interested. "Going to meet this little friend of yours?" He reached into his pocket, pulled out $300 in cash, and handed it to me, saying, "Here, you treat her nice." I thanked him but said no, I wasn't going to take the money. We kept drinking and Vince kept insisting, each time more forcefully until he went into his Mr. McMahon voice, saying, "You need to take it, goddammit. You take it!" I took it.

After we'd left the bar, I gave the money to Dreamer and told him to make sure it got back to Vince. I met the woman, took her to dinner, we had a nice evening, she went home, and I went back to Tommy's hotel room.

The next day, I saw Vince in the hallway at TV and he didn't say anything about it. I checked in with Dreamer later and asked if he gave Vince his money back. Tommy smiled and said, "No, he won't remember." I assume that money ended up in the *House of Hardcore* creation fund . . .

Tennis balls (not Tommy's balls) found their way onto WWE shows when Finlay and I worked with Hawkins and Ryder. One of our regular spots involved me putting my impressive juggling skills to use. (That's a little known fact about me — I can juggle really well because I used to go to juggling club with my dad every Monday. I was taught by a guy named Mike Price, who ended up appearing on *America's Got Talent* and now performs in Vegas and on cruise ships.) After I'd juggled the balls, I threw them at our opponents. I'd always be sure to start with Ryder because that meant I'd get to throw the third ball at him after I'd flung the second at Hawkins. I'd also be sure to always aim right at Ryder's groin, and my aim was good enough to score a hit at least once a night. I only ever aimed at Hawkins's leg or chest. Once the match was over, we'd either kick the balls out of the ring or, usually, toss them into the crowd.

On a French stop of our European tour, the guys backstage decided they wanted to play some Tommy Ball but we didn't have any tennis balls. I said I'd take care of it. I found Fit and suggested that we should send a runner out for tennis balls so we could get the juggling spot in our match. Fit was immediately suspicious and asked if they were for the show or if they were for Tommy Ball. I lied through my teeth and thought I was pretty unconvincing, but Fit send a runner out to get them anyway.

When the runner got back, she handed me a pack of three tennis balls, telling me, "We can take these back if you don't want them." When I asked why I wouldn't want them, she told me they cost $400. My head almost exploded. I was expecting to pay a little more than usual since we were dealing with international currency but *four hundred dollars* for three tennis balls? I asked why they cost so much and she told me that because we were in France and the French Open was underway, all of the regular tennis balls were sold out and the only ones left were these professional-grade tennis balls.

I couldn't let the boys down and I couldn't let them know I'd spent that much money on balls either. I'd sold Finlay on the idea that we needed them for the show and I couldn't go back on that or let him know how much I'd paid or he'd think I was an idiot — and *then* tell the locker room, too. It was a no-win situation, so I handed over the money and took the balls.

We did our match, I juggled, I threw the balls — and as they rolled out of the ring, I sprinted after them to stop them going too far. If I was going to pay $400 for tennis balls, I wasn't going to let them get away! Fit had other ideas though. He slapped them out of my hand one by one and threw them into the audience as I stood there, working out how much money I was losing as each one went flying into the crowd.

Backstage, Finlay noticed me sulking like a sad puppy and asked what was wrong. Eventually, I came clean and told him how much the balls had cost. When he asked why the hell I'd paid that much for them, I told him we needed them for the show. "And for Tommy Ball . . ." he continued. Then I finally confessed what he'd suspected all along.

Later that night, in the locker room, he came over to me with a huge grin on his face and something in his hand. "Don't ever pay that much for tennis balls again," he said, handing me back my money. "Even if they are 'French Open' tennis balls." That was when I realized he'd set the whole thing up as a rib on me. He couldn't stop laughing as he told me, "You should have seen your face when I was throwing the balls into the crowd." For the rest of that tour, people backstage kept coming up to me and asking what I'd be willing to pay for all sorts of random stuff.

By the way, I learned later that French Open tennis balls actually *do* exist — and they cost about four bucks for a can of three.

Hawkins and Ryder were still fairly new to WWE at that point. They'd come in the previous year as the Major Brothers, then undergone a gimmick change to become a couple of Edge's followers. Doing that was their own idea, but when they approached Edge with it, he loved it so much he went to bat for them with management. Without Edge's support, it probably wouldn't have happened. Edge was getting a huge push as one of the top guys in the company and the fact that he was willing to share that spotlight with a couple of new kids tells you a lot about how much he cares about helping to elevate talent. Brett and Brian Major became Curt Hawkins and Zack Ryder, the "Edgeheads," and to this day, they both still call Edge "Uncle Adam" out of respect for what he did for them.

A Short Story: Rough Ryder

Zack Ryder and I have always had the kind of love-hate relationship where we go out of our way to mess with each other. A couple of times, when we've been on the road for a while and are both very tired, it's got a little out of hand . . .

When Hawkins, Zack, and I would share a hotel room, I usually slept on the floor on a couple of comforters. One particular night, and I have no idea how it escalated to this, Zack messed with me so much that I decided to jump bare-assed onto his pillow. Zack, a germaphobe, freaked out and responded by grabbing *my* pillow and farting into it. I then went to the bathroom, took a dump, wiped my ass, and chased Zack around the room with the toilet paper. He was screaming while Hawkins was calmly sitting on his bed, texting everyone else in our group to say, "You guys are missing the weirdest thing ever." He wasn't wrong.

Zack's had such a strange run with WWE. Everything with him has been so stop-start. He's gone from winning singles titles to doing absolutely nothing for weeks. I truly believe he's the reason WWE started using YouTube. They were doing nothing with the channel (or with Zack) and then Zack came up with his *Z! True Long Island Story* show. WWE didn't understand what he was doing at first with the whole Internet Championship thing — in fact, when someone asked him to bring the belt in to a show, Hunter saw it and said, "Look at this mark — he made his own title," absolutely crushing Zack. After a while though, when WWE finally realized how well he was doing, they started getting on board with YouTube. Unfortunately, none of it came back to benefit Zack, which is a real shame.

He's a great guy and he's got so much drive. He's a childhood cancer survivor, too, something I don't think WWE ever really mentioned. I'm not saying he should be pushed just because of that, but I think it makes a hell of a story that could inspire a lot of kids going through some rough times. He deserves so much more than the stop-start treatment.

Just don't tell him I said that.

Hawkins and Ryder were great traveling partners but they weren't the only people I rode with at that time. Over the years, I traveled with Deuce and Domino, Matt Striker, Dreamer, Daniel Bryan, Ted DiBiase Jr., Tyson Kidd, and CM Punk, and we had some great times, as well as some weird encounters. The strangest random celebrity meeting happened at a sports bar in Alabama. Punk, Hawkins, Ryder, and Domino, Jesse (Ray Gordy), Festus (Luke Gallows), and I were having a few cocktails and some food when a waitress tapped Punk on the shoulder and said, "Sir, Charles Barkley would like to meet you." Punk laughed and blew her off, asking why the hell the famous basketball player would be in some bar in Alabama, but she came back a few minutes later and repeated herself. Punk rolled his eyes, but he leaned back and looked around the wall behind him into what was the VIP section. He then looked back at us all and said, "Holy shit, it's Charles Barkley!"

Gallows got up straight away and went over to introduce himself, so we all followed and soon enough, the Patrón shots were coming by the trayful. I didn't speak to him much, just enough to say hello, thank him for the tequila, and get a picture with him; from what I saw, he was a nice guy. It just seemed so random that we'd run into a legendary player from the Phoenix Suns and Philadelphia 76ers in Alabama, of all places. (Only later did I learn that Barkley was born and raised in Alabama and moved back there when he retired — so it wasn't that random after all.)

Someone who missed out on meeting Barkley that day was Kofi Kingston, the guy I probably traveled with the most. He'd just started out on ECW TV at the beginning of the year as the "Jamaican Sensation" with the worst fake Jamaican accent I've ever heard. There are two things about me (that I know of) that Kofi can't stand. One, he won't get in a car if I'm driving. He absolutely refuses. Two, he's not a fan of my hotel choices. When we traveled together, our deal was that he'd get the rental car and I'd arrange the hotels, but he'd tell me "three stars and above." I didn't get it. We'd be getting in at 2 a.m. a lot of the time, then waking up early to go to the gym, eat, and get back on the road, so I thought it was pointless spending $100 or more on a room we'd be using for no more than four to six hours. I'd regularly book a two-and-a-half-star hotel and when Kofi asked to see the itinerary and questioned it, I'd say, "It must have got a bad review since I booked and lost half a star." Enough of the guys experienced my questionable hotel choices for me to end up being known backstage as "ol' two-and-a-half star." I even got two and a half stars tattooed on my leg. It's not as meaningful as the cross I've got on my back with "Clint" written on it, but after that first tattoo, sentiment went out the window. Since then, I've added many more tattoos, including the Warrior's face paint, the kanji symbol for wrestler, lyrics from a New Found Glory song, and a bunch of Muppets.

As *WrestleMania 25* approached, we found out Finlay was once again going to be in the Money in the Bank ladder match. Before we even began discussing what we'd do in the match, I started thinking about our entrance gear. I remembered that Fit had worn a black leather jacket when he'd wrestled for wcw — it had one sleeve missing, a metal football pad over the shoulder, and a bunch of metal studs on the lapel. I found out that he still had it and asked if he'd wear it for 'Mania. He gave me his gap-toothed grin, immediately figuring out what I was up to. "Are you getting one?" I told him I was going to get one in green — and he loved the idea.

It turned out to be easier said than done. First, I had to get a green leather jacket that would fit me. That ended up being impossible, so I found a small black jacket that would work, sent it out west to a guy who'd been recommended for airbrushing, and had him paint the jacket bright green. After that, I sent it on to Robert Adams from Main Event Gear, who removed one arm and added the metalwork — Robert worked his ass off to make sure I had it in time and got it to me the night before *WrestleMania*.

I wasn't the only guy with new gear specially made for that 'Mania. On the day of the show, as everyone involved in Money in the Bank was going through the match, a very excited Rey Mysterio approached and asked me to come with him. I told him I had to go through the match, but he insisted and I soon found myself running up the long entrance ramp to get behind the curtain. Once we were there, Rey said, "Look at this!" and showed me the gear he was going to wear that night. Rey had a tradition of dressing like superheroes during his *WrestleMania* matches and, because *The Dark Knight* had come out the previous year, I'd suggested that he should get Joker gear made for 'Mania. He told me that he wanted me to see it first because I was the one who'd given him the idea. His match that night didn't last long but that gear was *sweet*.

I didn't miss too much in that meeting because we'd already gone through the key spots in the secret ring at the hotel. Just like the ladder match two years before, my first impulse had been to ask to take everyone's finisher, especially Kofi's since it was his first *WrestleMania* appearance. Then, just like the time before, I realized a midget taking everyone's finisher probably wasn't going to work, so I looked for something else to do. When I heard they were putting a bunch of dives into the match, I thought I could get involved in that. My dive would have to be through the first and second ropes but I thought it would still be memorable. Finlay didn't agree. "This is *'Mania*," he said. "We've got to make it big." As usual, he was right. Shelton Benjamin was going to do a flip dive from the top of a ridiculously tall ladder, so me pretty much falling out of the ring under the middle rope wasn't going to impress anyone.

Finlay himself was going to do a dive out of the ring and onto Kane to start the sequence — Fit doing a dive was impressive by itself because he wasn't known for that sort of thing. After that, almost everyone in the match was going to get in on the action. MVP, Christian, CM Punk, Kofi, Shelton — all of them were going to do a dive. Someone suggested Mark Henry join in, but fortunately that conversation didn't go too far. Mark leaping and hoping someone would be able to catch his 400-pound frame would have been a disaster that could have potentially killed someone. Finlay saw potential though. "Why don't we take it away from him? He could climb the ropes like he's going to jump, then I'll hit him with the shillelagh. Dylan can crawl up on top of him and jump off onto everyone on the floor." It wasn't going to be a 400-pound-man-crushing-another-guy-to-death sort of disaster, but I still thought it could go wrong. Mark always got heavily watered down before he went out for matches, and then he'd sweat buckets, so I was worried I'd slip and fall. That's a long way down — especially when you're my size.

We decided to see if I could even get balanced up there. Mark lay facedown across the turnbuckles and I used a stepladder to climb on top of him. He was so big that he covered the whole corner of the ring, so I couldn't get to the ropes, and it was tough for me to get up on his back. Without thinking, Fit reached out his hand to help me up — it worked perfectly, given our on-screen father-son relationship.

Even though I'd managed to climb Mount Henry, I still had my concerns. Up there, it looked even farther down than I'd imagined, and it scared the hell out of me. It would be even trickier when Mark was watered down and sweating. Plus, the spot called for me, a 140-pound midget, to jump onto a group of six grown (and, in the case of Kane, overgrown!) men and knock them down like bowling pins. I told Fit no one would buy it. He just smiled and said, "It's *WrestleMania*, Dylan."

Once again, he was right. We did the spot the next night and it looked fantastic. Fit even gave me a boost by shoving me in the ass as I jumped, shooting me onto the guys with far more momentum than I could have ever managed by myself. On the video, you can see me blatantly thanking CM Punk for catching me.

Something that I loved that year was that I got to be part of WrestleMania Axxess, a huge fan fest where people could come in, meet the wrestlers, take photos, and get autographs. When this was being planned, someone from the organization team came to me and said that part of the display that year was going to be "Hornswoggle's House." I had no idea what that meant and being told, "We're spending a lot of money on this" didn't clear anything up. It turned out that they were planning to set up a ring with the apron removed so everyone could see underneath — and rather than the "cave dwelling" that had been suggested for the Hornswoggle's House match at *SummerSlam* against Jamie Noble, there was going to be a bedroom, a kitchen, and a living room, all designed in miniature and lit up so it looked like a livable space. I felt so special that year at Axxess because they set me up my own booth right outside of my "house," surrounded the ring with a white picket fence, and did everything they could to make it look different to everything else. Most of the other guys do their signings at a generic booth, so I was honored that the company chose to invest such a lot of time and money in me.

It's also an incredible privilege to meet so many fans. I didn't know how to approach autograph signings at first and had to ask Fit for advice. My first signing was at a Best Buy and I asked him if I should talk with the fans — not because I didn't want to but because my character on TV *couldn't* talk. Fit told me I couldn't just mumble and grumble my way through the signings, so I'd have to speak properly. I always found it funny when people would be surprised when I'd start talking to them and say, "Oh wow, you actually *can* talk!" — as if they genuinely thought the midget could only grunt and growl like he did on TV.

It was during those autograph sessions that I began to truly understand my connection with kids — they would visibly light up when they met me. For most of them, it was clearly the first time they had met an adult of my stature, so they'd be standoffish at first but warm to me soon enough. I'd like to think that meeting me prepares some of these kids for what to expect when they meet another little person later in their lives. Hopefully, it won't be an "oh my gosh look at him" moment, because they've already met someone like me.

Something that WWE has in common with Disney is fans of all ages, and you'd see that at places like Axxess. The year we had Hornswoggle's House, I had a sixty-eight-year-old couple waiting in line to meet with me. When they got to the front, I got to talking with them and the woman told me I was her husband's favorite character on the wrestling shows because I made him laugh more than anything else in his life. I just couldn't believe that. I thanked them profusely, then asked which wrestlers they were going to see next. They told me they were going home now because they'd only come to see me. That was so deeply humbling.

When you're on TV regularly, you get to reach so many people — and to hear their stories, in turn, is so humbling. My dad called me one day to tell me he'd been contacted by a lady from Fond du Lac, Wisconsin. This woman's son is a little person who'd been through so many problems because of his condition, and he was a huge wrestling fan. Dad asked me if I'd go to meet Keegan. I was hesitant at first, simply because I still couldn't grasp the idea that anyone would want to meet *me* in the way that I had wanted to meet the Ultimate Warrior when I was a kid. In the end, I agreed to it and I'm so glad I did.

Keegan is the strongest little guy in the world. When I met him, he'd already been through more than fifteen surgeries, including operations where the surgeons had to literally break his legs in order to repair them. Despite this, he still wants to play soccer, basketball, and baseball when he gets older. The doctors all tell him he can't, but he's got that never-say-never attitude. For his most recent birthday, he went paintballing with a bunch of normal-sized kids. I've spoken to him regularly for years now, got him tickets to come see *Raw* and *SmackDown*, and I love that he's just as fearless as I tried to be when I was growing up. If what I've done has had even the slightest bit of influence on him, it's one of those situations that makes everything worth it.

CHAPTER 14

THE COLLECTOR

Shortly after *WrestleMania*, wwe once again had their yearly draft and I was moved to *Raw* — alone. For the first time in three years, I was going to be without Finlay. It was terrifying; it felt like I'd had my security blanket taken away. I'd always felt that as long as I was with Fit, I'd have something to do and someone to go to bat for me. There were no such guarantees for a midget alone on *Raw*. On the final episode of wwe *Superstars* before we were separated, Fit and I had a mixed-tag match against Tyson Kidd and Natalya. After we'd won the match, Fit led the crowd in singing "When Irish Eyes Are Smiling" to send me on my way. (I only found out he was going to do that in Gorilla just before we went out, when Fit leaned in to me and said, "Well, I guess I'm singing to you after.") It ended up being really emotional, even if Finlay didn't know any of the words apart from the chorus. When I hugged him, I told him I was going to miss everything about working with him. He just replied, "You're going to be okay."

I was told the reason I was being moved away from Fit was because I was going to be paired up with a new Irishman who was coming in. Sheamus was a tall, muscular guy with a pale-skinned, red-haired look that stood out from the rest of the roster.

He got a big push as soon as he first came in and it took a lot of people by surprise. I know he's the stereotype of the sort of wrestler Vince has always tried to promote, but there were a lot of talented people in WWE at that time who had more experience. Despite that, they put the WWE title on him before he'd been with the company a full year.

It was good that I wasn't paired with him because he wouldn't have worked as an Irish-jigging babyface and I think it would have been tough to turn me heel again at that point.

Without anything for me to do on *Raw*, I mostly ended up doing backstage comedy segments with Goldust. I worked with him on live events as his manager-slash-sidekick and, even though they were just ways to get me on the shows, working with him was a great experience, especially since he'd been one of my favorites when he first came to WWE in the mid-'90s.

Although I was on the company's flagship brand, the move started to feel like a step backwards, as I'd gone from appearing on TV every week with Finlay in ECW to being on *Raw* only once in a while and on the secondary show WWE *Superstars* the rest of the time. Also, Finlay was higher up in ECW than Goldust was on *Raw*, so that limited my opportunities, not that I ever expected to be paired up with a World Champion.

To keep me busy, they had me go out and shoot T-shirts into the crowd using a pneumatic cannon. You were meant to charge it for a couple of seconds and then shoot the T-shirt out into the sea of hands for someone in the crowd to catch. On a couple of shows, they had a heel wrestler come out, grab the cannon, and shoot a shirt, point-blank, at *me*. When the Miz did it, it hurt but no more than I expected or could cope with, but the time R-Truth did it, he charged the cannon for about eight seconds and fired it right into my mid-section. After that, I had a bruise that went from my stomach to my groin and hurt to touch. That was one of the first times I remember feeling like the people in the back were screwing with me.

WWE found more of a use for me later in the year when *Raw* began to have a guest host each week. A star from the entertainment world would be brought in and there would always be plenty of backstage segments involving them. As the WWE's resident little guy, I was almost always used in at least one of the segments. I loved getting to meet so many celebrities. The best of the best, as far as I'm concerned, were Mike Tyson, who is a genuine wrestling fan and was so enthusiastic about everything he did with us; Bob Barker, who was easily the best guest to interact with on screen and absolutely stole the show that night; and Ozzy Osbourne, one of my dad's favorite rockers.

Working with all these celebrities also gave me the chance to get a bunch of memorabilia signed, all of which I now display at home in my basement bar. Among my prized collection: a signed Ozzy Osbourne CD, signed boxing gloves from both Floyd Mayweather and Mike Tyson, as well as a DVD of *The Hangover* signed by Mike (which he was super excited about, saying he'd never been asked to sign a movie before), a Pete Rose signed baseball, Shaq signed basketball, and a Bob Barker signed DVD of *Happy Gilmore* (again, apparently the first time he'd been asked to sign a movie).

Some of the fans didn't care for the guest host gimmick but I understood what they were meant to achieve. A throwaway match between a couple of undercard wrestlers wasn't going to get us on an entertainment news segment but, for the same investment of time, someone like Jeremy Piven could get us some mainstream coverage, even if he did refer to our big midyear pay-per-view as *SummerFest*. I couldn't believe he flubbed that line, because Jeremy is right up there with Mike Tyson in terms of being a legitimate wrestling fan.

Of all the guest stars we had on *Raw*, Donald Trump is

unquestionably the most famous. At the time, I couldn't have known I was having my picture taken with the future President of the United States but there it is, a photo of me with the Commander in Chief. When Trump was on *Raw,* they ran a storyline that he had bought *Raw* from Vince McMahon and, to say thank you to the fans (and, of course, get a lot of publicity for the company), he was going to refund everyone's ticket. They legitimately did that, right there in Green Bay. Also, when they did the angle where Trump dropped money on the crowd, it was *real* money. Not all of the notes were hundred-dollar bills though, they had the cameramen find the people in the audience who'd picked up a Ben Franklin and focused on them to make it look like everyone was getting a C-note. The rest of the money was smaller bills, but WWE still must have given away a huge amount of cash that night.

Although the majority of the guest stars were great, there were a couple who were disappointing. Reverend Al Sharpton complained every time we had to do more than one take of anything and refused direction. It was his way or no way. But the guy who really surprised me most was Jonah Hill. It was so obvious that a WWE show was the last place he wanted to be. He blamed his behavior on being sick, and maybe he was, but that didn't change the fact that he was difficult with all the writers and producers. I had been a huge fan of his, and to see him acting up so much upset me. I was involved in three segments with him and although he was nice enough to me, he kept moaning to anyone in earshot that everything was taking too long. He couldn't wait to finish and get out of there. After all of that, WWE ended up not airing any of the footage he shot with us anyway, which I don't think was a bad thing.

During the guest host run in 2009, I spent a lot of time working with Chavo Guerrero Jr., both on TV and on house shows. Chavo was tremendous — he could do anything you asked him to do, and he was always professional when faced with the idea of regularly losing to a little guy. He probably could have played the "I'm a Guerrero" card to get out of it, but he was smart enough to realize that working with me meant a spot on *Raw* each week and that *any* screentime on a major cable network, even if being beaten or outsmarted by a midget, was more valuable than winning an eight-minute match on an online show like *Superstars*. Sometimes, I'm sure that he must have felt like Coachman and wondered if he was ever going to get one up on me, but he never came across as bitter or resentful about what we were doing. Plus, because I was almost always doing something with the guest stars each week, that usually meant Chavo would get to be involved, too.

Most of the time, the guest host would put us in some sort of gimmick match. We had a boxing match, a bull rope match, a one-arm-behind-his-back match, a Chavo-wrestles-on-his-knees match, and even a Sharp Dressed Man match when ZZ Top was hosting. WWE had a tuxedo specially made for me for that one, and I got to take it home with me afterward. I always got to keep the gear that was made for me, so my garage is now full of costumes. I don't have to worry about Halloween for at least the next twenty years.

The planned payoff of my run with Chavo was to see us mend fences and form a tag team. One week after we'd run an angle where he saved me from an attack by Chris Masters, I came to *Raw* and met him in the ring for rehearsal, Shawn Michaels and Triple H, who were back together teaming as D-Generation X, were sitting by the commentary table. While Chavo and I threw ideas around, Hunter turned to Shawn and said, "You know, kids *really* love him." Shawn, confused, said, "Really? Chavo?" Hunter corrected him, "No, *Hornswoggle*." That made more sense to Shawn. "You're right. My kids talk about him all the time." Both guys told me that story later, almost word for word, independently of each other. As Chavo and I talked about our tag team, I had no idea that in the stands, the groundwork had just been laid for the biggest money run of my career.

CHAPTER 15

═══════════════

THE "WORLD'S LITTLEST MEMBER"

Not long after my rehearsal with Chavo finished, we were taken aside and told our segment was going to be canceled. Hunter had enough pull to get his idea authorized immediately, and a producer told me I was going to be working with D-Generation X. I thought it was a joke, and that this was just his way of telling me I wasn't booked that night. When the producer assured me he was serious, I couldn't believe it. I felt terrible for Chavo because it left him with nothing to do, but how could I say no to working with D-X? I was a huge D-Generation X fan when I was younger, especially when the 1-2-3 Kid came on board as X-Pac. The D-X I'd grown up watching was aimed at the teenage male to mid-twenties demographic and their antics could be a little adult-themed. At the time, I didn't get a lot of what they were doing because I wasn't even a teenager. For example, when they did a spot with a super soaker that was imply-ing they were jerking off, I just thought it was fun that they were shooting a water gun into the crowd. This version of D-X still had a lot of humor involved, but it couldn't push boundaries like before because WWE had gone PG. Using me for a while gave the presentation a lighter tone. Hunter and Shawn themselves were both married with kids by then, which changed D-X, too.

The angle started with me dressing like Shawn in a backstage segment. They had to make a custom-fitted costume for me, right down to a set of Shawn's trademark chaps. Each week, I'd do something to try to impress them so that they'd let me join D-X, and each week, I'd get under their skin a little more. All this built up to an episode of *Raw* that was going to take place at Madison Square Garden.

A Short Story: MSG Sucks

I might be one of the only wrestlers to say this, but I hate Madison Square Garden. I know it's a special place for a lot of wrestlers but, in many cases, that's because they grew up watching their idols work there when it was the center of the northeast wrestling world. Bruno Sammartino, Pedro Morales, and Bob Backlund built their legacies in MSG but, without wanting to be disrespectful, that doesn't mean much to me. I wasn't even alive when they were selling out the Garden. I wasn't even alive when the first *WrestleMania* happened there. I understand that the history of the business is important; I just don't hold the Garden as holy ground like a lot of the older guys do.

Because of that, performing there didn't mean as much to me. First off, I hate New York City for the traffic alone. It's the worst city in the world to drive in. There's also nowhere at the arena for the talent to leave their cars. You have to pay for parking across the street in a garage, then walk across the road and through the fans to get to the backstage entrance. If you get there early enough, it's fine, but getting out of the building and back to your car after a show is a different story. On top of that, the changing rooms in the building are tiny — and if *I* feel that way, think of what it must be like for Big Show.

After I'd checked "working the Garden" off my bucket list (and it *was* there), it wasn't special anymore. I much prefer working at the Resch Center in Green Bay in front of my family and friends. The Resch is my MSG.

When we were finally at the Garden for *Raw,* Triple H called me out from under the ring and invited me to join him and Shawn with their typical D-X catchphrases. In the middle of it all, he kicked me in the stomach, hooked me for his Pedigree finisher, and, after working the crowd for what seemed like forever, planted me face-first in the center of the ring. The crowd reaction was huge and some of them even booed him for that, which I thought was amazing, given that Garden crowds have a tendency to support heelish tactics. Being part of that moment with a couple of guys I'd grown up emulating was crazy. I had to play dead for the rest of the segment, but the twelve-year-old fan in me couldn't stop smiling on the inside.

The funniest part of that whole day came earlier at rehearsal. We had a crash pad in the ring, so we could try the move and make sure it looked good. Hunter doubled me over and grabbed my arms. As I was staring down at the pad, waiting for him to give me the cue to jump with him, he started laughing. Then I heard Vince laughing at ringside. I asked what was happening and Hunter replied, "There's not much for me to grab onto here. You don't really have arms." I started laughing, too, then we did the move and it felt fine. It was easy to take. Hunter was happy when he watched the recording of the rehearsal back. "It looks like I'm killing you," he grinned.

That segment at MSG led to me serving D-X with papers to appear in *Little People's Court*, where any little person can go to get justice when wronged by a normal-sized person. What made this idea even better was that the writers were planning to do this the week that Verne Troyer was scheduled as the guest host of *Raw*, so he could play the court judge. Verne was iconic as Mini-Me in the Austin Powers films and I knew having him in the segment would get a *lot* of people watching. Beyond that, Verne was a genuine hero of mine as someone who had made a name for himself as a little person. I couldn't wait to meet him and shoot the segment.

When the day came to shoot the *Little People's Court* footage, I was given the bad news as soon as I walked into the arena. Not only had Verne refused to be the judge but the whole segment was going to be moved to another week. Whenever that happens, you start worrying it'll never go ahead.

It turned out that Verne wasn't keen on working with other little people, and while he agreed to appear briefly in a segment with me, he didn't want to be one of a number of little people on the show. I got the feeling he thought that would have taken away from him as the guest star that week. He was nice enough when we met, but I sensed he was going through the motions with everything he did. I also didn't understand his reluctance to do more with me. Part of me understood him not wanting to be surrounded by other little people, but if you're a little person coming into a place where there is already an *established* little person on the show, that meeting is the main thing people are going to want to see from you. After all, if I'd somehow been cast in the third Austin Powers movie as Mini-Austin (or, more likely, as Mini–Fat Bastard), they wouldn't have kept Verne and I apart from each other for the entire film, they would have built us up as opposites and had us end up in a big (or little) showdown.

Incidentally, I couldn't believe how *tiny* he was, even compared to me. Meeting him was one of the few times in my life I've felt tall.

I was relieved when the *Little People's Court* segment finally went ahead three weeks later for the Christmas episode of *Raw*. It was a show-long angle where they filmed Shawn and Hunter going under the ring and entering "our world," which looked suspiciously like the backstage corridors of an arena. Shawn and Hunter wandered into the trial room, which had a midget judge, midget bailiff, and midget jury. The "trial" ended with Shawn declaring that if I wanted to be in D-X, I'd need to "do something big" to impress them, I'd have to "climb mountains" or "pull on Superman's cape." I couldn't pull on Superman's cape, but I could tug on Santa's beard. Later that night, the Big Show was doing an interview in the ring with Santa where he was asking for his friend and tag-team partner Chris Jericho to be allowed back on *Raw*. After Santa told him his wish would be granted, I came out from under the ring, climbed through the ropes, and yanked off Santa's beard, revealing Jericho himself. The grown man and the giant chased me away, but I came back out surrounded by a midget army (well, six other midgets), all dressed in D-X gear. After we swarmed Jericho, Big Show got involved and that ended badly for us. The smallest guy got absolutely crushed by Show with a sidewalk slam. The size difference between them was so huge that it looked like Show killed the guy, especially when he picked him up by his leg with one hand and dropped his limp body over the top rope. (For the record, the little guy was absolutely fine, he just sold the bump *really* well!)

Show got his hands on me next, lifting me way up high for a chokeslam, but Shawn and Hunter intervened before he could bring me crashing down to the mat. After Hunter told Shawn he still wanted to "squash" me, Shawn said I was growing on him, prompting Hunter to confess he didn't hate me as much as he used to. They decided I'd proved myself by going after Show and Jericho and agreed that if I dropped my little lawsuit against them, I could be the official D-X mascot. When I was first told I was going to be a "mascot" and not a "member" of D-X, I took that as a slight, but I quickly realized it really didn't make any difference, so I let it go.

As the D-X mascot, not only did I get to add two more words to my on-screen vocabulary ("suck" and "it"), but I was involved in a lot of their matches on TV and at live events, when I'd get to whip glow sticks out into the crowd. Whenever I'd do their signature crotch-chop with the pyro going off behind me, twelve-year-old Dylan would be going crazy. Hell, I was twenty-three then and I was *still* going crazy on the inside. It was a dream come true.

I got to do a number of backstage segments with D-X. One of the more memorable spots had us playing midget bowling, where Shawn and Hunter were firing me down a corridor on a skateboard so that I'd collide with an unsuspecting Jillian Hall. Doing something with a skateboard reminded me of when I was a kid trying to skateboard with my stepbrother Ben. Even though he was a year younger, he was so much better because the size difference meant I had to take five or six times pushes for every one of his. I also thought back to the skateboard shoes I'd got covered with blood during one of my early hardcore matches and couldn't believe how much had changed for me in just four years. As we were rehearsing the midget bowling sketch, the writer wasn't happy with the bump Jillian was taking and told her to stop trying so hard to protect herself. That was when Shawn absolutely lost it. "Are you kidding me?" he yelled. "She's falling on concrete and all you can say is 'do it better'?! You do it — jump in the air right now and take a bump." After that, the writer made sure that Jillian had a crash pad to land on.

Another memorable segment was when Hunter was trying to use the new range of WWE action figures to motivate me to follow his commands, and each time he'd mention the name of one of the superstars, I would do their trademark pose. Moments later, Shawn turned up and brought in Santino Marella to do the world's worst impression of Chris Jericho. The sketch ended with Hunter commanding me to "get him," at which point I jumped on Santino and attacked him like a tiny, angry dog. After Hunter called me off, a beaten Santino staggered to his feet to deliver the immortal line, "Good luck with the sucking it."

Santino was so great, especially in those sort of segments. I called him the man of 1,000 stories because you could throw any word at him and he'd have a story involving it. I have no idea if the stories were real or not, but he told them so well and in such detail that you'd always believe him. It was impressive seeing him switch his accent and personality so quickly backstage whenever he needed to — one moment, he'd be talking to you in his usual Canadian accent but the moment a fan or a kid was nearby, he'd switch right into his on-screen Santino character.

During my run with D-X, the guest host I was most physically involved with was Jon Heder, who played Napoleon Dynamite. He teamed up with Miz and Big Show for a match against me, Hunter, and Shawn. Heder was great, one of the best guests we had on *Raw* since he was up for anything. He got in the ring later, wearing a fancy Ric Flair–style robe, which he removed to reveal a less than Herculean physique. Instead of wearing track pants and a T-shirt like most of the guest stars did when they stepped into the ring, Heder went all the way with proper wrestling trunks and boots. I don't know if he was a legitimate wrestling fan but he really *got it*.

His big spot in our match was to nail me with a kick. When we discussed it in rehearsal, he was concerned about his lack of training and asked how hard he should kick me. I told him to not worry about me: "Just make it look good." I'd regret saying that later when, live on TV, he kicked me square in the throat. I hit the mat, gasping for air, but I couldn't be mad at him because I'd told him to just go for it. I managed to recover enough for the finish — when Big Show accidentally fell on top of Jon, I did my tadpole splash onto them both, and won the match by pinning Heder. Everyone says I've always been pretty stiff with my splash but I think it hurt me just as much as it hurt the other two that night because landing on Show meant I couldn't plant my feet or hands on the mat to absorb the impact like I usually did. I just had to leap directly down onto his back. When I hit, all the air went out of me and I heard this huge, deep grunt come out of Show. I didn't hear anything from Heder, so Show must have done a great job protecting him.

Being part of D-X was the most fun I'd had in my career at that point and it wasn't just the on-screen involvement that was rewarding. The money I made from merchandising during that period was unreal. I'd been featured on merchandise before and I'd get more merchandise later in my career, but nothing ever came close to the royalty checks I got from the "World's Littlest Member" D-X T-shirt. There were a bunch of other D-X shirts, too, plus individual shirts for Hunter and Shawn so I can't imagine how much they must have made from merchandise.

Being a lifelong WWE merchandise collector, I made sure to get my hands on everything that came out featuring me. My grandpa would as well. It meant so much to hear he had started collecting my merchandise. In time, he had so many items that he couldn't fit it all on the table he'd put aside specifically for all my stuff, so Dad built him a shelf unit where he could display all my figures, shirts, bobbleheads, photos, hats, and anything else WWE brought out.

Grandpa was always so interested to hear about my travels. He had a world map on the wall in his house, and every month, he'd ask me where I was going and add push pins to keep track of every place I'd visited. He even came to a few of the WWE shows when we were in the area. It was so great to have him see me doing what I loved. Sometimes, around town, people would tell me that every time they saw my grandpa, he would produce a wallet full of photos of me and regale them with stories about my travels and my wrestling career. It felt great to know just how proud he was of me.

A Short Story: Gold Heat

Even though it wasn't a fraction of what I made from the D-X run, I made decent money from royalties on merchandise when I was with Finlay. There were T-shirts, green derby hats, and inflatable shillelaghs (which I loved).

However, I got nothing at all from the first T-shirt I appeared on since the office considered it a Finlay shirt. It looked like the Notre Dame Fighting Irish logo and said "I come ta fight." I loved it, but after Fit pointed out that his catchphrase was "I *love* to fight," they halted production after one week and changed the slogan. I've still got a ton of the originals in my garage.

As a lifelong action figure collector, it was a big deal for me when my first figure came out. It was an Unmatched Fury model, which didn't have moveable limbs, but there were two of me in each pack (I guess because I was a smaller than the others, so they felt they would be short-changing the collectors with just one small figure) and one in every 500 contained a gold special-edition figure. After they'd been released, Fit brought one of the gold figures to TV and showed it to Arn Anderson. "I didn't get a gold figure," Fit told him. Arn gave me the signature Anderson look while scratching his beard and said, "You've got heat there, kid. He brings you on the road, he makes your career, and *you* get the goddamned gold figure?" Whenever Arn would see Fit and me together after that, he'd walk over and ask Fit, "Did you get a gold figure yet?" Fit would always say no and Arn would shake his head and mutter, "Little son-of-a-bitch," as he walked off.

It was an amazing feeling when the first moveable figure of me came out. I took the figure to the checkout in Walmart, where a fifty-year-old woman scanned it then paused. She looked at me, looked at the figure, looked back at me, and back at the figure. This went on a while. Eventually, I just said, "Yep," and she said, "Okay." That was cool, if odd.

John Cena taught me the trick of throwing a piece of my merchandise (which ended up being a hat) into the crowd at shows so a kid could catch it. Other kids would wish they had caught it, so at the interval, when they saw the hat at the merchandise stands, they'd be pulling on their parents' sleeves.

Over the years, I was lucky enough to be on a number of T-shirts. Some I loved, but one in particular didn't work for me. The design concept was that I was holding a shillelagh but, and there's no other way of putting this, the cartoon drawing looked like I was clutching a huge penis.

Royalties from the WWE video games were also excellent for each of the two games I was in, even though I wasn't a playable character. The developers told me it would be too hard for them to do the motion capture for my moves, which didn't make sense to me as I was already doing mo-cap for my character's entrance. There were also a lot of other games with playable smaller characters, like Yoda in Star Wars, but developers just didn't want to do it. I was disappointed, but I can't complain too much since the checks were still pretty sweet.

Looking back, that period toward the end of 2009 was the best run of my career. Plus, it contained the greatest moment in my life. However, the two weren't connected in any way.

Back in April of 2009, during the European tour after *WrestleMania 25*, I was in the production office when I got a Facebook message from Kim asking me to call. I knew it had to be something important because I was overseas. I immediately started worrying that someone had died, so I called right away. No one had died — in fact, it was completely the opposite.

"Dylan," she said, "you're going to be a dad."

CHAPTER 16

THE CHANGED MAN

I was going to be a dad.

The first thing I did was hang up on my pregnant girlfriend, earning myself an instant nomination for the Asshole of the Year award. That was how we *both* were with each other though — when things got too emotional, one of us would hang up. Finding out she was pregnant sent me straight into panic mode. It had never occurred to me that I might get someone pregnant when I was so young, if ever. I couldn't even form words. I wasn't ready to be a dad. I was barely even a grown-up; how could I be a dad? I didn't know anything about kids. I'd spent some time with my godson, Ayden, since he'd come along, but being a dad was an entirely different world.

I ran — literally — out of the production office to find Fit. When I tracked him down, I grabbed him and said, "I've got to talk to you right now." We went off to the side and I told him I was going to be a dad. He dropped to one knee with a huge smile on his face and gave me the biggest hug. If there's one thing Finlay cares about more than wrestling, it's his family and his kids especially. He told me he was so happy for me, but all I could say was "No." Over and over, that one word. He asked what was wrong and I told him I didn't know if I could do it. I was only twenty-two, I wasn't ready to be a father. Still grinning, he just told me, "Stop it. This is going to be the best thing to ever happen to you, Dylan."

Larry Heck, WWE's trainer, was walking by and saw me with Fit, still freaking out. I told him what was going on and he gave me a huge hug, too. Then I told them both that I'd hung up on Kim as soon as she gave me the news.

"What?" said Fit, suddenly frowning.

"Why would you do that?" Larry said. "You need to call her back right now."

I knew he was right, so I got myself together and went back to make the call. Kim was crying when she picked up. I apologized, and we talked. Fortunately, my friend Josh Weimer was living with us at that point, so he had been around to offer her some extra support. He had actually found out about the baby before I had; Kim was scared about how I would react so she told him first and asked how to break the news to me. Weimer was the voice of reason and pointed out she'd have to tell me at some point, and it wouldn't be good for her to know for a long time and say nothing.

Since I was away so much with WWE, Weimer often found himself the focus of Kim's pregnancy temper. The tiniest thing would set her off and he eventually had to move out because of it. He called me when I was on the road, letting me know that she'd just flipped out for no reason and started throwing DVDs at him. Trying to be supportive, I took my pregnant girlfriend's side and that led to Weimer and I not speaking for a couple of months. That ended up putting even more strain on my relationship with Kim because I missed my best friend.

I didn't help things with my behavior either. After the first six months or so of our relationship, things had begun to sour between us. I'm ashamed to say it but, being young, selfish and stupid, I'd started being unfaithful to her long before I found out we were going to have a kid together. I wish I could say that I stopped that behavior the moment she said "you're going to be a dad" but I can't. I still just didn't "get it."

When I was in Chicago at CM Punk's birthday party, I didn't know when to say enough was enough, and ended up in my car with one of Punk's sister's friends. Neither of us realized it but her driver's license fell out of her bag and onto the floor, where it was found several days later by Kim. At the time, WWE was in Green Bay, and Kofi and Punk were staying at my house. While I drove Kofi to the airport to catch an early flight, Kim went into my phone and found a couple of text messages between me and the woman whose license Kim now had.

When I got back, I walked through the living room past the still sleeping Punk and into my bedroom, where Kim was waiting, red-faced and furious, holding out my cell phone accusingly. "You want to tell me something?" she asked. As I was attempting to answer, she punched me square in the eye with a right hook, then shoved me onto the bed and began hammering me in the back of the head. I didn't defend myself at all, partially because I didn't want to risk any physicality with a pregnant woman, but mostly because I knew I deserved it.

When she stopped hitting me, I staggered out of the room to find Punk gone. I texted him and asked if he'd heard anything. He wrote back, saying, "No, what's up?" I told him in person the next time I saw him, and he couldn't believe it. He said that if he'd known something was going on, he would have tried to help. Given that he'd only been in the next room, it seemed a little weird that he hadn't heard anything, but I let it go. I had other things to be concerned about.

It wasn't until a month after I found out about the baby that I started worrying about my child being born with achondroplasia, too. That was one of my biggest fears — I wouldn't want to put anyone through all the surgeries and medical issues I'd had as a child. However, I decided that if we did find out the child would be born with dwarfism, we would do our best, rather than reconsider the whole thing. When we found out through an ultrasound that the baby was going to be normal-sized, I was beyond relieved.

We also found out the sex of the baby before the birth. Kim really wanted a girl and I really wanted a boy. Mentally, I could cope with the idea of a son, but I worried about what it'd be like to have a daughter because of all the unfamiliar things I would struggle to relate to as she grew up. When the nurse told us it was a boy, I stood up, pointed right in Kim's face, and said, "Ha! Told you!" She began to cry and I immediately went from nominee to outright winner of Asshole of the Year.

For all the negativity that came during the pregnancy, everything in my life changed right before the new year. I was flying back from a show in Hartford when Kim's aunt Lori called to tell me it was time and that she and her daughter, Kayla, were driving Kim to the hospital. As soon as I landed, I drove home, grabbed some clothes for us both, and headed out to see my son born.

A little more than twenty hours after Kim was induced, we were almost there. I was sitting by her head and there was a sheet up across her stomach so neither of us could see what was going on down below. When I was a kid, my mom had shown me videos of my back surgery and, ever since, I haven't been able to cope with anything involving the inner workings of the human body. Kim, on the other hand, wanted the birth filmed. There was no way *I* was doing that but, fortunately, we'd made up with Weimer by then and he was more than happy to play cameraman. Kim and I were both was fine with that. It says a lot about my friendship with Weimer that it didn't seem weird to me that he would be videotaping my girlfriend's parts, although I did question his decision to subject himself to looking at everything involved in childbirth.

It was a drug-free labor — Kim decided at the beginning that she didn't want anything. As the pain got more intense, she changed her mind but, by that point, it was too late. I felt so bad for her, especially when she looked up at Lori with a sad, defeated expression, and asked, "Why can't this just be over?" She was in so much pain that she even threw up. I was impressed she only did it once because *I* had to run to the bathroom to throw up three times. I've never been comfortable in hospitals because of all the bad memories I have of my constant visits there as a kid, and that combined with the smells and sights of labor made it all too much for me.

At 3:46 a.m. on December 30, 2009, time stopped as my son made his way into the world. That was the greatest moment in my life. I realized nothing else mattered except my son and his happiness. I was done with cheating. I was done with the childish bullshit. I knew it was time for me to grow up and be a man and a dad, to live up to the examples I'd been set by my own dad and grandpa. I promised Kim, then and there, I was going to do everything I could to make our family work.

The doctor asked me if I wanted to cut the cord, but that was still too much for me to handle, so Weimer stepped up again. My boy weighed in at eight pounds, three ounces and measured twenty-one and a half inches.

The nurse asked what we were going to call the baby and Kim just smiled at me, happy for me to make the call. It didn't even take a second for me to reply. "He's Landon," I told her.

We'd talked about names before the birth and our final three were Landon, Thor, and Xander. I wanted something different and we thought all three weren't names you often heard. We originally found Landon in a baby name book and thought it was perfect because no one else would choose it. That night, six babies were born in Mercy Medical Center and four of them were named Landon.

One of the other new dads came around with champagne for everyone in the maternity ward the next night and we saw in 2010 as a family of three.

It felt amazing to be able to introduce my dad to his grandson. The first time we went out to eat after Landon was born, we went to Red Robin. While we were there, I took a picture of them together and it's my favorite photo of all time, because Dad is looking at Landon with such love. That look is still there whenever they're in the same room. Introducing Landon to his great-grandpa was equally emotional. The first time he met Landon, Grandpa started grinning from ear to ear and couldn't stop.

CHAPTER 17

THE MOTHER'S RING

Two weeks after Landon was born, WWE was in Green Bay for an event, so I was able to bring my son with me and show him around. Everyone was asking me if I'd shown him to Vince yet, but I didn't want to seem like I was trying to score points with the boss. More and more people were telling me how important it was that I did it and, finally, Tony Chimel told me, "Vince absolutely loves children, Dylan. You *have* to do this."

Moments later, I knocked on Vince's door, went in, and held up my baby, saying, "This is my son, Landon." Vince grabbed him and held him, saying, "Oh, he's just beautiful, Dylan. Great job! You've got a really good little kid on your hands." Looking back now, I can't believe I nearly didn't do that because showing Landon to Vince was one of the most memorable moments I had at WWE.

A Short Story: Trolling Myself

When I started with WWE, the idea was for me to look as much like Finlay as possible, so I had to bleach my hair and stay clean shaven. I didn't enjoy shaving all the time, but it was part of the job. As I got more comfortable in my role, I started getting lazy and growing my beard out. No one said anything, so I grew it a little more. In the end, I found myself growing it just to see how far I could go before anyone told me to shave. That beard got out of control and, still, no one seemed to notice or care. By the time I looked like an angry troll, the beard had got to a point where even I couldn't deal with it, so I went to the office and asked if I could get rid of it.

"You can't cut your beard — that's your thing!"

We needed to get permission before changing our look because it could affect our marketing. It never looks good if a promotional poster, action figure, or a video game comes out and one of the featured wrestlers has since had an image overhaul. Of course, it depends on how drastic the change is and where you are on the totem pole — the higher up you are, the more flexibility there is.

My beard ended up growing to insane lengths, which caused some complications in childcare — whenever I would change Landon's diapers, he would latch on to my beard with his toes and start yanking on it.

At the beginning of 2010, TNA — the only other wrestling show in the U.S. at the time that had network programming, generally accepted as a distant number two promotion to WWE — attempted to start a new Monday Night War. The inter-promotional rivalry between WCW and WWE had led to a boom in the industry in the '90s, so the idea of having genuine competition was something that could have been great for business. TNA decided to run their flagship show, *Impact,* head-to-head with *Raw* on Monday, January 4, and did everything they could to generate interest, bringing in Hulk Hogan, Jeff Hardy, Rob Van Dam, and a host of other famous faces. WWE countered by announcing that Bret "Hitman" Hart would make his first appearance on *Raw* in thirteen years. He'd appeared elsewhere on WWE TV when he was inducted into the Hall of Fame in 2006, but this was the first time he would be on one of the weekly wrestling shows since the infamous Montreal Screwjob in 1997. There was a lot of buzz among the boys backstage — Bret was going out on live TV and being given a microphone, so everyone was excited to see what would happen next.

I was in Gorilla at *Raw* that night and I noticed there were more screens than usual. On some of them, the TNA show was playing. I asked Billy Kidman, who was running Gorilla, what was going on and he explained it was so everyone could see what was happening on the other channel. WWE monitored *Impact* again the next week but by the third week of the new "war," the extra screens had vanished, and WWE went back to ignoring the competition. Although *Impact* had done its best rating ever in the week Hulk debuted, it wasn't even close — the WWE audience was more than double TNA's. A couple of months later, *Impact* was quietly moved back to Thursdays. It was a shame, because TNA had the money to compete but they let the inmates run the asylum, which was one of the main things that had destroyed WCW. I thought one of the biggest errors they made was switching back to a four-sided ring when their previous six-sided ring was unique.

Being at *Raw* the night Bret came back was awesome. If I'm honest, I had never been a huge Hitman fan as a kid. I thought his matches were too repetitive, with the same moves in the same order. There were some of his matches I liked, especially *SummerSlam '93* against Doink, *King of the Ring '93* against Bam Bam Bigelow (who was a much better big man than Vader, in my opinion,) and, of course, the *'Mania 13* match against Steve Austin. Even if I never really got into him as a wrestler, as a human being, he's the best. When I met him, he gave me one of the greatest compliments I've ever received, telling me, "You're so damn entertaining — you're one of the only reasons I watch *Raw.*"

I was also able to do something nice for a friend of mine named Corey who had never asked me for any wrestling-related favors in all my time working for the WWE. He was a huge Bret Hart fan and, hearing that Bret was coming back and I would be there that night, Corey asked me if I could get Bret to autograph his *Hitman* DVD. When I met him at *Raw*, I handed the DVD over to Bret and asked him if he'd sign it. With a smile, Bret did and handed it back. I didn't look at the DVD again until I got home and gave it to Corey, not realizing that Bret had personalized his message. It wasn't signed it *To Corey*, it was signed to *To Dylan*. Even though he knows it was an honest mistake, Corey still gives me grief about that. It probably doesn't help that I kept that DVD and put it on display in my base-ment bar, right where he can see it every time he comes over . . .

As *WrestleMania* approached, I was hopeful I would be on the big show since I had been featured on TV a lot and was involved with one of the company's hottest acts. When I asked what I'd be doing, I was surprised to be told I wasn't going to be used. When I inquired why, I was informed it was because both Hunter and Shawn's pro-grams leading into *WrestleMania* were going to be "more serious," so there was no place for me in the buildup. Quietly and without explanation, I was separated from D-X and went back to either doing random backstage segments or, more often than not, abso-lutely nothing.

I was, however, asked to come to Axxess to do Hornswoggle's House again, and I was able to fly Kim, Landon, and my dad out to Arizona for the event. Landon didn't do so well on this trip — Dad told me he cried the whole time on both flights, and he clearly found everything overwhelming. I did, at least, get a picture of me and my son in front of Hornswoggle's House, even if he was bawling his eyes out.

In the end, Finlay made sure I had *something* to do on the show, even if it was just for a moment. He was in the pre-show battle royal, so he arranged for me to get involved. Near the end of the match, I came out, threw Fit his shillelagh, and distracted Mike Knox. Fit cracked Knox in the head, then I went up top and hit him with the frog splash. It was nice for us to have that little reunion at a *WrestleMania*. Moments later, Fit was eliminated from the match by Zack Ryder, who finished as runner-up to Yoshi Tatsu.

Later that night, Hunter beat Sheamus on the main card, and the show finished with Shawn putting his career on the line in an attempt to end the Undertaker's undefeated *WrestleMania* streak. After losing that match, Shawn went home to be with his family, but it was always nice to see him from time to time at shows when he'd come in to do a segment. Hunter began spending less time in front of the camera and more time working behind the scenes as an executive, but he still remained very polite to me backstage.

A Short Story: The Boss and the Best

Throughout the time I was with D-X, I was a little apprehensive around Hunter; the fact that he's a McMahon by marriage was always in the back of my mind. He can be curt when you're talking to him one-on-one, especially since he's become one of the most senior executives in the company. To his credit though, he always lets the boys be boys. Whenever he traveled with us on tour back then, he'd tell everyone to have fun and made sure we knew he wasn't going to go back and stooge anyone off to the office. He got treated more or less the same way as 'Taker did, in that he was still accepted as one of the boys. At the same time though, you didn't want to be a belligerent asshole in front of him.

He always keeps his finger on the pulse of the future of wrestling and he is genuinely a student of the game. He's watched Vince carefully and learned from him, but he's making big moves of his own now to expand the company. WWE never would have gone to places like Abu Dhabi or Saudi Arabia ten years ago. That's all Hunter.

Shawn was incredible to work with throughout the D-X run. I picked his brain a little about old-time stuff, but not as much as I should have. He owns up to everything in his past that was questionable. If you ask him if he was an asshole in the '90s, he'll laugh and admit that he wasn't in a good place back then. I know he legitimately regrets being involved with screwing Bret Hart over in Montreal because he feels it'll always be a black mark on his career. I don't think he needs to worry as a lot of people consider him the greatest of all time, myself included. All through my time with D-X, even though it was right at the end of his career, he was stealing the show every night whether it was a big pay-per-view match or the last day of a two-week European tour.

After *WrestleMania*, the draft had me move to *SmackDown* and I thought that might be a chance for a fresh start. It turned out to be a chance for a different bunch of writers to come up with the same excuses. For the rest of the year, I was in a few random segments on TV, but not in any program that would allow me to be seen regularly. Meanwhile, I was still on the road full time because, as Michael Hayes explained, I was a "special attraction." I didn't understand how someone could be good enough for house shows but not for TV. Being brought to TV and then not being used was depressing.

Every time I showed up for television, I'd sit in catering all day and eat. That's when the boredom and bitterness would set in. The only thing I was working out was my mouth, chewing my way through anything that got put in front of me. WWE was paying to fly me in, then paying for me to sit in the back and eat their food. Some people would say that's a pretty sweet deal, but when I was a kid, I'd wanted to be a pro-wrestler, not a pro–catering eater.

Life among the boys wasn't without its stresses either, thanks to one person in particular, that person being CM Punk. A few months earlier, CM Punk had brought a friend of his backstage — Chad Gilbert, who is the lead guitarist of my favorite band, New Found Glory. Punk knew I loved the band so he introduced me to Chad. When we finished talking, Chad gave me his number and said to let him know if I ever wanted to come to any of their shows.

When I upgraded to a new phone, the switchover didn't go as smoothly as I'd hoped and I lost all my stored numbers in the process. Going around all the boys to get their numbers again was a pain in the ass but I'd also lost Chad's number. When I found out New Found Glory were playing in Milwaukee during a time I'd be at home, I decided to take Chad up on his offer, so I texted Punk and asked if he could give me his number. I didn't hear back, so figured I'd just ask him at the next TV tapings. When I got there though, people were coming up to me all day and asking what I'd done to piss Punk off. I couldn't answer them because I had no idea. As soon as I found him, I went to talk to him but he ignored me completely. I left him awhile and then tried again, but he just gave me a pissed-off look and then turned away. I had no clue what was going on. Later on, someone mentioned my name to him when I was nearby and Punk spat out, "Oh, you mean that user? The guy who only texts me when he wants something?" I jumped in and asked him what he was talking about and he came back with "You know what you did." Realizing this was about Chad's number, I told him I'd only asked because I'd lost everything in my phone, something Punk knew since I'd had to ask *him* for his number, too! He just told me, "Whatever, you're a user," and wouldn't say anything else.

From that point on, our relationship was terrible. I wouldn't say anything to him, figuring if he wanted to be angry over something like that, I couldn't do anything about it, but he'd go out of his way to be a dick. Sometimes it was physical, where he'd walk over to me and kick me for no reason; other times it was verbal and he'd say things like, "I can't believe you're still here. You'll be gone soon, I'm sure — there's a cut list and you've got to be at the top of it." If I'd go to sit with any of our mutual friends in catering and he was at the table, he would just get up and leave. It was like being back in high school. I'd heard that Punk was one of the hardest men in wrestling to be friends with, but I'd never seen it before.

Although I couldn't do anything about his change in attitude toward me, I wasn't going to take "no" for an answer when it came to New Found Glory. I managed to get in touch with Chad and the others without Punk's help and I'm great friends with them to this day. I talk to them all regularly and always go to see them when they're in the Wisconsin area. I've even got some of their lyrics tattooed on my arm. On one of my later WWE action figures, you can see the tattoo I got of some of their lyrics, and they all thought that was pretty cool.

Despite Punk turning on me, he still came to tell me that he'd suggested to the writers that I should be put with his Straight Edge Society. His idea was they'd treat me like a dog. Punk would explain that the reason I'd not been able to talk was that I'd been "chemically dependent" before he and his cult had "saved me." Even though it sounds humiliating, it would have made a lot of sense for everyone's character and given me some TV exposure. I was all for it but, unfortunately, the writers didn't like it.

I wasn't just waiting around for other people to suggest ideas for me or bring me something to do — I was pitching new ideas all of the time. A lot of my pitches would result in my character finally being able to speak. That was something creative was interested in discussing, but they wanted to be able to explain how I went from muttering and growling to speaking properly. They finally agreed to run with some of my ideas and we ended up doing a series of segments with Teddy Long where he'd try to get me to talk. One week, he had a nun try to teach me. Another week, he had me undergo electroshock therapy. We had six weeks laid out that would result in me finally finding my voice, but then after only a couple weeks of these, the angle was just dropped. Teddy and I showed up and we were told our segments were finished.

"So, what are we doing now?" I asked.

"Nothing," the writers replied.

I was shocked. It wasn't the first time WWE just stopped things dead in the middle of an angle, but it was the first time it had happened to me. I was so disappointed. There was more to it than the idea that having a voice would mean I might get more TV time or better angles. Because my character didn't talk, it limited what I could do for the company outside of the ring. Even though I was at Axxess *every year*, talking to everyone I met, talent relations would tell me that any other public appearance I did needed to be short because I shouldn't be talking at meet-and-greets.

After the learning to speak angle was dropped, the only thing I did that year on TV that came close to a program was when I did a few segments with Jack Swagger and his Swagger Soaring Eagle mascot, which was Chavo Guerrero Jr. in a bird suit. We always joked that whatever Chavo did, he could never get away from me and he was never allowed to beat me. It was all goofy stuff, like me shooting the eagle with a bow and arrow, or salting his leg before trying to eat it. It was a definite comedown after having been involved with D-X just a year earlier. As much as I told myself, "At least I'm being used on TV," this is when I started to lose hope. I found myself wondering if I'd already hit the peak of my career at the age of twenty-three, questioning if there would ever be another upswing. It's the same in any form of entertainment though — you might have a hit early on, but there's no guarantee that you'll ever have a hit again. That thought began to depress me.

That depression wasn't helped by what was going on in my personal life. Kim, Landon, and I had moved out of our apartment and into a house — my grandpa's. He'd decided it was time to move to an apartment, but I wasn't ready to let his house go to another family, so I bought it. Kim would have preferred a bigger place out in the country, but I loved the small-town feel of Oshkosh and didn't want to live out in the sticks. When my dad told me that Grandpa was moving into an apartment and it was now or never in terms of buying his place, I had to do it. I had so many great memories there. I don't think Kim appreciated me going against her wishes, but I couldn't cope with the idea of driving past Grandpa's house and not just being able to stop and go inside.

Although I'd been true to my word and never even thought about cheating on Kim after Landon had been born, no matter how hard I tried, I couldn't keep our little family together. Kim had checked out emotionally and there wasn't a connection anymore. I couldn't see it at the time but, looking back, everything changed when she found that girl's driver's license in my car. All the other times I strayed, I think she could have forgiven if not forgotten, but once I cheated on her while she was pregnant with my child, there was no coming back.

I was planning to get her a mother's ring for Christmas in 2010, and that meant I had to get Lori and Kayla to find out her ring size without her figuring out why. She got wise to what they were trying to do, and soon after, I got an irate call where she told me that if I proposed to her at Christmas, she would leave me.

After Landon was born, she started talking to other guys and didn't really hide it from me. It felt like she was doing all she could to undermine our relationship. Meanwhile, I wanted us to be a family and raise Landon together. She'd tell me, "Just let me go." But I'd keep fighting, hoping I could somehow get us through. In the end, when Landon was about eighteen months old, she left while I was on the road. I got a text saying, "I'm leaving, you can't keep me here anymore," and when I got home, half of everything was gone. It was scary how similar it was to what had happened with Anne.

Even though, deep down, I knew it had been coming for a long time and I knew things would never have worked out for us, I was heartbroken. I just wanted things back to how they were, no matter how much all my friends kept pointing out how unhappy we'd both been. It took me a few months to start pulling myself together. This was probably the lowest point of my life. I was off TV, starting to get *really* overweight, and having to figure out how to be a single dad.

As painful as it all was at the time, I wouldn't change anything about what happened between Kim and me, other than the arguments we had in front of Landon. (Fortunately, he doesn't remember them.) We're better parents apart than we would have been together. It's taken time and we still have our disagreements when it comes to parenting like any broken-up couple does, but I'd say that we get along fine ninety percent of the time.

I also have a better relationship with Anne these days. Her mom and her husband, Aaron, finally managed to get her to go to rehab and she got past her demons. I'm so proud of her for taking control of her life. I was sad when her mom died a few years back. I went to the funeral — I don't think Anne was expecting me but she seemed pleasantly surprised. There was no question about it from my perspective — her mom had been there for me so many times that I had to go and pay my respects. Despite all of the bad times Anne and I went through, I'm happy we can still be friends because, no matter what happened, she was always supportive of me.

I feel like I've been on a lifelong rollercoaster when it comes to the opposite sex. When I was a kid, I thought no one would ever be into me. When I got famous in my twenties, I thought, "They'll all be into me." (They weren't.) Now I'm in my thirties, off TV and with a kid of my own, I think, "Well, this is going to be tough . . ." The good thing is that my stature isn't so much of an issue any more. When I was younger, it seemed like a bigger deal but whenever I start seeing someone now, I'll always ask if my stature worries them in any way and make sure they know I'm comfortable talking about it openly and honestly. One of the biggest changes in the last ten years has been that conversations used to start with women telling me, "I know you from WWE." Now, it's "My kid remembers you from WWE." That's always a nice reminder that I'm getting old!

CHAPTER 18

THE MAKE-A-WISH KID

Like most wrestling fans, I've always loved the *Royal Rumble*, but I wasn't sure what to think when I found out that the 2011 *Rumble* was going to have forty entrants rather than the usual thirty. I didn't like that they messed with tradition, but at least it meant more of the boys would get to experience being in a rumble match. I was shocked when I found out I was going to be one of them and that I was going to get a chance to do something in the ring instead of hiding away like I'd done in 2008. Michael Hayes and Dean Malenko were producing the rumble that year. They told me when I was going in and when I was going out but, between those points, they told me, "Do whatever you want and have some fun."

I was going to be number twenty-three, right after John Cena had got to the ring and taken out everyone except for Punk. After the planning meeting, John came up to me and said, "All right kid, I've got my own stuff to think about for the match, so plan out what you want us to do and we'll do it." I found out who was coming out after us, came up with a few ideas, and told John, who was happy to do everything I suggested. It was amazing that the top guy in the company was so open to doing whatever I wanted and letting me shine, but that's John. As long as he thinks something will entertain the audience, he'll get behind it.

Punk and Cena were down on the mat when the countdown began for the next entrant. The clock hit zero and my music started up. As I ran to the ring, the audience popped for me, which was more than I'd expected. I climbed through the ropes and faced off with Punk, mimicking the little hand dance thing he did before he spin-kicked me right in the chest. It was hard, but it was safe. Despite our problems, he was always professional in the ring.

Tyson Kidd was the next in. Cena bounced him around a bit and I did a spinning headscissors before John gave Tyson his Attitude Adjustment finisher. I motioned to John that I wanted to do the move, too. So, with the audience cheering, I got Tyson up on my shoulders and nailed him with my own take on Cena's move. Tyson had no problem at all selling for me because he knew he was being involved in something memorable. He just "gets it." I always thought Tyson deserved a much better run than he had, but he ended up in the "good hand" category like a lot of the guys who never get used at the top. It was tragic that his career ended just when he was starting to have a good run as a team with Cesaro. Due to an accident in a match with Samoa Joe in 2015, he suffered a spinal cord concussion and wasn't able to wrestle again.

Heath Slater, the next guy to hit the ring, didn't "get it" quite as much. A couple of years later, Tyson told me that just before they went out that night, Heath was whining backstage, saying, "Aww man, why's the midget doing shit to us?" Tyson tried to point out to Heath that it was actually a good thing, but Heath couldn't see it. When he got to the ring, I hit him with Steve Austin's Stone Cold Stunner, then Cena and I both gave him John's signature five-knuckle shuffle (they were dramatic fist drops — we just slammed our fists into his forehead). After John threw Heath out, Kofi joined us in the ring and I mostly faded into the background until Sheamus kicked me off the top to eliminate me. It was a great night, especially since I wasn't being used a lot at that point. In the end, I was in that *Rumble* for almost ten minutes, longer than the eventual winner, Alberto Del Rio. It made me feel that WWE still believed I could go out there, play a role, and be entertaining to the fans.

However, after the *Rumble* that year, it was back to not doing a whole lot. When I was done with whatever my part was on the show — which usually wasn't much — I'd get cleaned up and back into my smart clothes in line with the WWE dress code, grab my gear bag and backpack, and go sit in the production office. If I was in Heavy Hornswoggle mode, I'd stop by catering on the way and grab a corn dog.

A Short Story: Dressing for Dinner

Something that added to my frustration was that even when I wasn't working on the shows and just sitting in catering all evening, I'd still have to adhere to the company dress code. That dress code was something that annoyed a lot of people but, for me, it was even more of a pain in the ass because of my proportions. I had to pack extras of everything because if I spilled something on my pants, I couldn't just go to the nearest store and get another pair. The rules called for us to wear a polo or dress shirt with slacks as a minimum, and wrestlers could be fined anywhere from $500 to $1,000 for not complying. WWE has calmed down on this in recent years and now allows the talent to wear WWE-branded sweatsuits instead.

Catering for the company has changed over the years, too. When I got there, it used to be city by city with a local caterer coming in to do the show. Some places were better than others; for instance, Milwaukee was known for being one of the best in the country. Now (or, at least, the last time I was there), there is one company that does catering wherever the company goes in the U.S. which, I guess, cuts down on cost and means WWE knows what it's getting. But when I was with WWE, we'd always be given lunch when we arrived, dinner later, and then a lot of not-so-great foods were put out during the show, things like pizza slices and corn dogs — stuff I shouldn't have been eating but did. As for the other meals, there was always grilled chicken and a salad bar, but they'd change things up to keep it interesting, so you'd also get ribs and steak. After every pay-per-view, they'd always have breakfast for dinner. Most of the guys loved it, but I hate breakfast foods. That aside, the food was always very good quality and definitely one of the perks of the job — albeit one that didn't help my waistline.

There was a *Raw* in February 2011 where the guest host for *WrestleMania 27* was going to be announced. No one, including any of the boys, had any idea who it would be. When The Rock's music hit, everyone backstage was shocked. Rock hadn't been back in the whole time I'd been working for WWE. I wasn't going to miss this chance to meet him, so I grabbed my gear bag and backpack and ran to Gorilla.

When Rock got to the back after finishing his promo, he saw me and headed straight over. I put my hand out and said, "Hey Rock, my name's Dylan. I just wanted to say hello and introduce myself. It's a pleasure to meet you at last."

Rock shook my hand and replied, "Hey buddy! Did you have a good time tonight?" The question confused me slightly, but not as much as his tone, which sounded like he was talking to a young child. When I told him, yes, I'd had a good time, he patted me on the shoulder and walked off. I was puzzled for a while and then I figured it out — he had *no* idea who I was and, worse still, he'd thought I was a Make-A-Wish kid! When I realized that, I was so embarrassed. The first rule of being embarrassed in wrestling is you never tell *anyone*, even your best friends. I did not stick to this rule on that night and told Kofi who then, obviously, went right ahead and told the entire locker room what had happened. By 3 p.m. the next day, everyone at the *SmackDown* tapings, including the cameramen and production team, knew about me being Rock's "buddy."

While The Rock was hosting *WrestleMania* that year, I wasn't surprised to find out I wasn't in any of the plans. I didn't even have Finlay to go to bat for me because, just before *'Mania*, there'd been an issue at a house show where Miz had interrupted the national anthem to generate heat. Some of the sponsors took huge offense and WWE had to make someone the scapegoat. Fit was the agent in charge of that show, so they released him. When Fit was let go, I really started worrying about my future. As long as he was with the company, there was the chance for us to reunite, but without him, I was more on my own than ever.

Even though I didn't step foot in the ring for the first time in five *'Mania*s, I did at least get to appear in a backstage segment. It was a "Well, it's better than nothing" situation — but only just. The segment was stupid, and that's being generous. Teddy Long and Snoop Dogg were doing a talent show parody and the punchline was that I came up to rap but couldn't because I couldn't talk. After Teddy and Snoop left, music came on, the Bella Twins came in, and I did some rapping, full words and all. It was always nice to be used but I was so awful. Forget white men can't jump, this was white midgets can't rap. I wouldn't have minded so much if the segment had a purpose and meant I'd "found my voice" but the next week, I went right back to grunting and mumbling. At least they didn't go forward with a rapping gimmick — that would have been even worse than the silence.

The Rock came in for a few more dates that year and at one, when he and I were in the same room, Big Show called Rock out for thinking I was a Make-A-Wish kid. Rock denied everything, but Show kept pushing until eventually Rock admitted, "Okay, *maybe* I did. I didn't know, I'm out of the loop . . ." Show kept going and asked him if Rock thought every little person he met was a Make-A-Wish kid. I never thought I'd see The Rock embarrassed, but he definitely was that night.

The next year, Rock and Cena were building up to their match for *WrestleMania 28* with an interview on *Raw*. I wasn't being used that night and I hadn't even been brought in, so I was watching the show from my local bar, Slade's, where I may have been "overserved." While Rock was cutting his promo, I noticed he had writing on his wrist. I couldn't help myself — I got on Twitter and called him out on his makeshift cheat sheet. Cena called him out on it later that night in the ring. A couple of weeks later at *Raw*, Rock was walking backstage and saw me. "*Hey!*" he said, pointing at me. "Hornswoggle! What's up with that on Twitter?!" I asked him if I'd been wrong. He just grinned and said, "No, you got me."

At least he knows my name now . . .

CHAPTER 19

THE MUPPET TATTOOS

Before *WrestleMania 27*, I was told that I'd be appearing on the next season of *NXT*. This wasn't like how *NXT* is now, it was back when they had finite seasons, public voting, and each rookie had a pro to guide them. I loved the first season of *NXT* because it felt real and ended up with the Nexus angle on *Raw*. That was an awesome start for a new group of heels, but it didn't live up to its potential. All of the Nexus guys quickly ended up trading wins on the main shows with the rest of the roster, turning them from something different into more of the same.

I was on the "never-ending season" and it was the *worst*. Believe it or not, I was cast as a pro. Titus O'Neil was my rookie, just when he was fresh into the company. He was very strong and very green — not a good combination. As for the show itself, it wasn't clear what was going on most of the time. At least in the previous seasons, there were weekly challenges for the rookies, which I always found entertaining.

There was some fan voting early in my season but that got dropped and then it just ended up being a bunch of matches between a bunch of people with no purpose attached to anything — and then the season abruptly finished. I have no idea what anyone was thinking. It just ended up being a watered-down version of *WWE Superstars*, which was already a watered-down version of *Raw* and *SmackDown*.

While I was doing whatever nonsense they told me to do that week for *NXT*, I made a few pitches to the creative team for me to go back to *SmackDown*. Even when it seemed like the writers liked the ideas, it would end up with "but he can't go back to *SmackDown* because he's on *NXT*" — as if that would somehow ruin one, or both, of the shows. I didn't understand their logic because there were plenty of other guys who would appear on either *SmackDown* or *Raw* as well as *NXT*. After that season mercifully ended, *NXT* was reinvented into the WWE's development system and started becoming what it is today — another WWE brand and not really a developmental system.

A Short Story: The Summer of Punk

Over that summer, Punk became one of the top guys in WWE, and I wondered if one of the reasons he'd been on edge before was because he was stressed about his position in the company. I thought it was worth trying to mend fences, so I found him at a TV taping and said, "I want to apologize if I came off as an asshole." He snapped back at me, "Well, you did." I told him that I hadn't meant to and apologized for upsetting him. We shook hands and put it all behind us, or so I thought. For a while, everything was great again.

I loved Punk's long title reign. He was starting to become like Austin and the nWo in the '90s, where you'd see people out in public wearing his white "Best in the World" shirt. That whole run felt so real, from the infamous "pipebomb" interview, where he ran through a list of his complaints about the company live on air, all the way to when he lost the title to The Rock. I especially liked the program he had with Jericho. I think it'll be a long time before we get something that feels so real again. I found out later that about ninety percent of that pipebomb promo had been approved by the office, but it got everyone talking.

Even though he had that huge run with the belt, he still seemed as frustrated as ever. He was the main champion but not wrestling in the main event all the time. For a while, he was selling more shirts than anyone, even Cena, but being treated at best as a distant number two. To an extent, I understand why he must have been annoyed, but how much can you really complain when you've got *that* spot? I think that no matter what he got, it would never have been good enough. He could have been successfully defending the WWE title in the final match of *WrestleMania* where he would be the one to break the Undertaker's streak and he still would have found something to complain about.

Near the end of 2011, I heard that the Muppets were going to appear on *Raw*. It was like Christmas had come early for me. The moment I heard, I was determined to do everything I could to be involved as much as possible. I also immediately booked myself in for a visit to my tattoo artist. I already had four Muppets tattoos on my leg and this was a perfect excuse to get lots more. Over the next week, I added another ten to the piece and I didn't stop there. As of now, I've got tattoos of Kermit, Miss Piggy, Gonzo and Camilla the

Chicken, Scooter, Beaker, Bunsen, Statler and Waldorf, Animal and the rest of the Electric Mayhem band, Rowlf, Walter, Fozzie, Lew Zealand, Pepe the King Prawn, the Swedish Chef, Sam the Eagle, and Crazy Harry with the TNT box. Sweetums will probably be the last one I get done because he'll be difficult to do without making him look like a big blob of brown. This is, without a doubt, one of the biggest downsides of my achondroplasia — short legs mean less room for Muppet tattoos . . .

In the week leading up to the show, I spent a lot of time tweeting #HornswoggleWithTheMuppets and managed to get that trending on Twitter. The guests on *Raw* always got a special tour from someone on the WWE roster and because people backstage had found out how much of a Muppets fanatic I was, I was given that honor. I couldn't have been happier. I got to the arena early and went straight to the green room. All the Muppet performers were getting ready and the puppets were laid out on tables. Seeing them all there as if they were dead legitimately upset me.

When I went around to introduce myself, I was amazed to find out that the performers already knew who I was. "You're all over Twitter!" they told me. "You're the one with the tattoos!" They seemed as excited to meet me as I was to meet them. Having Dave Goelz, Eric Jacobson, Steve Whitmire, and Bill Barretta all asking to see my tattoos of their characters blew my mind.

After more than a year of me pitching various ways of finding my voice, I nearly got my wish courtesy of the Muppets. One of the planned segments called for Miss Piggy to whack me and *that* would have magically given me the ability to talk. I was so excited, not only that I was finally going to get my voice but that I was going to get it from one of the Muppets! Unfortunately, WWE being WWE, plans changed and the four segments I was set to be in were reduced to just one. I still did the whacking bit with Miss Piggy, but it didn't lead to me speaking.

The best part of that night was something that didn't happen on TV. Landon was home with an ear infection, so I asked Eric Jacobson if he would FaceTime my boy as Animal. Eric was more than happy to do it. I called home to check in with Landon and found out he was crying because he was struggling with the pain. When I'd tried my best to help comfort him, I got off the phone and texted Kim that there would be a very special FaceTime call coming through soon. I sat off to the side of the screen, so I could see Landon's reaction and when he picked up Animal's call, his face lit up with happiness. They talked for five minutes and, afterward, I called Landon back. "Dad, Animal called me!" he yelled. "He called me from *your* phone!" I played along and said, "Animal took my phone?!" Landon laughed and told me he felt a lot better.

That's the power of the Muppets.

Even though the power of Miss Piggy hadn't given me a voice, creative finally found their own way to give Hornswoggle the power of speech. During a holiday episode of *SmackDown*, they had me win a Holiday Wish Battle Royal where I eliminated Sheamus, and then Mick Foley (dressed as Santa) granted me my wish of being able to talk. Unfortunately, Mick didn't give the creative team the ability to come up with anything beyond that for me, so we were back to square one. The only difference was now they could reject pitches that involved me doing interviews, too.

Early in 2012, I did a segment with Heath Slater on TV where I won a battle royal. This was just to set up Heath cornering me afterward so that Justin Gabriel could come to my rescue. Justin was very talented in the ring but couldn't connect with the audience. He wanted to create a character that showed off his love for high-risk, adrenaline-junkie activities, but couldn't find the way to translate that inside the arena. He talked to me once about coming out on a dirt bike and jumping it into the ring. I pointed out a few problems and asked him even if he could jump the bike into the ring, how he was going to land it static, how he was going to do it without ruining the ring mat, and how he was then going to get the bike out of the ring. The idea never got off the page.

I did a couple of things where I was in Justin's corner, including the *Elimination Chamber* pay-per-view in Milwaukee. I guess I was there to even the odds because Swagger had Vickie Guerrero in his corner. It was something to get me on screen when we were in my "hometown" (when you're from Oshkosh, apparently you can claim either Milwaukee or Green Bay as your home town — or Applebee, if you ask my wrestling friends) and that was, at least, better than the alternative of spending yet another show in catering.

The best thing about that day was it was the first time I was able to bring Landon with me to a show. I got to take Landon inside the Elimination Chamber — that was cool for both of us and a hell of a visual: a little person and his two-year-old son in this huge metal chamber. Landon had the time of his life walking around and inter-acting with the people he'd seen on TV. It was amazing to see how comfortable he was with my co-workers. When we got to catering, he walked right up to John Cena and said, "Hi, John Cena. Can you get me a cookie, please?" John looked at him for a second, smiled, and went off to get him a cookie. John's such a great guy that he even asked Landon if he wanted some milk. "No, John Cena. I'm okay — thank you."

Landon walked off, I mouthed "I'm sorry!" to John, and he just shook his head and smiled.

A Short Story: The Top Man

A while after Cena became the biggest star in the business, he got his own tour bus so he could get around the coun-try more comfortably. I'd travel with him in it sometimes, now and then with Kofi or Chimel. There was a big table, a couch, three bunks, and a master bedroom in the back. We'd play some cards, drink some beer, and talk about wrestling. Even now, I don't think people realize just how much John cares about the business. He is, genuinely, a wrestling fan.

People base a lot of their ideas about wrestlers on the ten minutes they spend in the ring each day without considering what they're doing the other twenty-three hours and fifty minutes. John is always doing something to promote the company, whether it's interviews, public appearances, hosting shows and award ceremonies, or appearing in films. The only thing more important to him than helping grow WWE is his work with the Make-A-Wish foundation — John's the top wish granter in Make-A-Wish history and he puts his work with them before everything.

John's careful about what he eats and drinks, but he's not as strict as you might think to look at him. We stopped at Whataburger more than once, and whenever we were in Wisconsin for a loop, we'd buy cheap random beers that we thought looked fun. The best worst one we found was called Beer 30, which comes in a purple can with a clock on it. It was so awful that it was good. Other times, we'd drink Coors Banquet with Jack Daniel's as a nightcap.

No matter what John eats or drinks, he works everything off so quickly — he's the craziest man I've ever seen in the gym. When I was gaining weight, he put me in Midget Boot Camp and made me work out with him. He kept me off the machines, telling me that everything I needed to do, I could do with free weights and it would be better for me. He had me using free weights, as well as doing push-ups into stair jumps, burpees with medicine balls — so many different exercises. It was exhausting but it got results. When he was done with me, he had me get on the treadmill until he was finished with his own workout — so, as you'd imagine, I spent a lot of time on the treadmill.

Even though my character being able to talk hadn't changed anything for me on screen, it was still a positive because it give me a chance to do something off screen that I'd wanted to do for a long time. That was being involved with the Be a STAR anti-bullying events that were held at schools and community centers around the country. After seeing my first presentation, Stephanie McMahon (who ran the events) put me on all of them for quite a while. Since children were my main fanbase and given my size, Stephanie knew that the anti-bullying message would mean a lot more coming from me than from anyone else in the company. Everyone else had bullet points to hit and eight minutes or so to do it. Steph just wanted my story in my words and told me that if it went long, it went long. She explained that the kids would listen to the other wrestlers but they would relate to me. And, honestly, if you're a kid and a guy the size of Mark Henry talks to you about how he was bullied when he was young, it's pretty hard to believe. It's a lot easier to accept the message from the midget. I loved doing those events and getting to help kids see that little people are normal people, too.

CHAPTER 20

THE TUB OF RANCH DRESSING

As *WrestleMania 28* approached, once again, there was nothing planned for me. I wasn't connected to anyone on the roster who would end up in a featured match, so I knew that if I wanted to get on the card, I was going to have to find my own spot. When a *SmackDown* versus *Raw* twelve-man tag match was announced, I saw my opportunity — not to be in the match, because they'd already announced the wrestlers, but to be on the outside. John Laurinaitis made Vickie Guerrero the "flag bearer" for *Raw*, so I marched right up to Vince and told him I should be *SmackDown*'s flag bearer. "Goddammit, that's a great idea," said Vince.

I was hoping I'd get to do something physical in the match, so I was relieved when John Laurinaitis spoke up in the planning meeting and said, "'Swoggle needs to do something, too." Several of the other guys were doing dives so I suggested I join in. I suggested a flip off the top onto the guys below, but it took too long for me to climb the ropes in rehearsal. Instead, we came up with a plan where Kofi and R-Truth would help me up to the middle of the top rope and, from there, I would leap out to the floor, where Mark Henry would catch me and fling me to one side. The problem with this was that it's fine to balance on the top in the corner because there are angles and the ropes are tighter, but it's much more difficult to get your balance in the middle of the rope, where it's the loosest. I told Kofi and Truth I'd need them to brace me once I was up there, and Kofi assured me he'd be there. I was also worried about Mark catching me. It was a long way down from the top rope into his arms, and he'd be watered down and sweaty. I was trying to take every precaution I could, asking him repeatedly how he wanted my arms so he could catch me better. After the third time I asked, Mark turned to Johnny Laurinaitis and barked, "Can you tell this guy he needs to stop worrying?" (He may have used a stronger word than "guy.") I kept my mouth shut after that.

On the night, Kofi and Truth hauled me up and Kofi forgot to brace me. I was yelling, "Hand! Hand!" and still nothing, so I thought, "Screw it" and just jumped anyway. Mark caught me with ease and threw me aside like a sack of potatoes. Backstage, I went up to Kofi and shouted, "You're my best friend and you didn't even hold my hand!" Kofi grinned back at me. "Do you realize how that just sounded?" I still sometimes go up to him and say, "Hand! Hand!" when I see him.

Someone else I saw backstage that night was Finlay. He wasn't working with the company at that point, but they had still invited him to 'Mania. He told me I'd done my spot well, but that it didn't make any sense. It was a huge dive for a guy like me but there was no payoff because Mark just threw me aside like nothing had happened. It was a dive for the sake of doing a dive, and he thought it should have done something to move the match forward and tell the story. Right there, I could see how much he missed being with the company — he would have been able to put that match together more logically. I texted him later to thank him again and he wrote back to say, "I want to make sure the stuff they do with you makes sense because you should have a huge role in the company."

By that point, I hadn't had a huge — or even a decent-sized — role in the company for two years, but that hadn't stopped me pitching ideas. I'd go to the writers or, sometimes, straight to Michael Hayes who was in charge of *SmackDown*'s creative. I got along with Michael, but I think he got sick of hearing my ideas. When I realized that, I got sick of pitching them. There's only so many times you can hear "we'll get back to you" without losing heart.

After *'Mania 28*, the writers' big idea was putting me with Brodus Clay. Earlier that year, Brodus had finally made his *Raw* debut after months of buildup. Everyone was expecting him to come out as a big, heavy destroyer and, instead, he came out as a fun-loving guy who couldn't stop dancing. That's when you make people fans again — when you manage to surprise them. Whether it be something like Cena's return at the *Rumble 2008*, my coming out unannounced at *WrestleMania 24*, or Brodus turning up in a totally unexpected gimmick, those are moments people remember and will go back and watch again.

Brodus's gimmick also had the added bonus of giving the boys something fun to watch during rehearsal. On any TV day, all of the producers and management had a production meeting that ends around 3 p.m. Meanwhile, the talent got to the building around 2 p.m., sometimes earlier, dropped their bags and changed into their sweats, went to catering to eat and then grabbed some coffee and sat in the stands to have what we call "cupversations" — talking about what's happening in the ring at rehearsal, using the coffee cup to cover your mouth.

Something that gets rehearsed over and over are the in-ring segments — like contract signings — and promos. Sometimes an in-ring promo was run through, word for word, in front of the writer, a producer, Hunter, or Vince. They might have to keep stopping the guy, saying, "Try it *this* way" or "I wasn't feeling *that*." And they keep going until they're happy. I've seen them spend thirty minutes making sure they get a short promo absolutely right. A lot of the time, rehearsal ends up overrunning and they have to hold the doors for an extra ten minutes before fans are let in.

They also rehearse any new or complicated ring entrances. Because Brodus had a couple of women dancing with him as he approached the ring, they needed to check the choreography, so they would run through his entrance every week. It was hilarious because he always looked so miserable. (I'm sure that's one of the main reasons they kept him doing it at rehearsal for three months.)

The women who were brought in for Brodus were named Cameron and Naomi and they couldn't have been more different. Everyone in the back figured them out pretty quickly and it became apparent that Cameron genuinely thought she was the star of the act. She rubbed a lot of people the wrong way, me included.

On one international tour, I was uncharacteristically the second person to get on the babyface bus after a 5 a.m. wakeup call and I still had a few drinks working their way through my system. I sat down at the back; put on my sunglasses, hat, and headphones; leaned against the window; and tried to get some more sleep. Cameron sat down right in front of me and, in the most annoying voice imaginable, said, "Hey Horny . . . are you okaaaaay? Are you druuuunk? You can't show up druuuunk! You should know better than that." I then, extremely impolitely, told her to leave me alone. She took offense and, given what I said, she probably should have . . . but I really didn't care. She shouldn't have been so obnoxious to start with, especially when she was only just starting out with the company.

That sort of behavior annoyed the boys, but what really turned everyone against her was that it was clear she knew nothing about wrestling and didn't even care to learn. She was only there because she wanted to be on TV. I can't remember anyone making less of an effort to improve than Cameron. Even Kelly Kelly, who gets a lot of negative comments about her time in wrestling, tried her best to get better and, when she was on the road, genuinely loved being in the ring. You never would have caught *her* trying to pin someone the wrong way up. Cameron was definitely in the wrong business.

Naomi was the complete opposite. Everyone loved her from the word go. She always understood her role, worked hard, and made an effort to improve. Even on the long European tours, you'd never see her in a bad mood — ever. She's one of the nicest people imaginable and she's turned into one of the best women wrestlers in the company. She deserves every bit of the success she's had.

Because I'd spent so little time in the ring or in the gym but plenty of time in catering, I was the heaviest I'd ever been — and this wasn't lost on the people in creative. Soon enough, I found myself on TV as Brodus's "little brother," stuffed into a tight singlet, shaking my ass around. Creative evidently thought that if two girls dancing with a fat guy is good entertainment, a fat, dancing midget would be the icing on the cake. I really didn't care if they were trying to rib me about my weight — I got some extra TV exposure and that was fine by me. I was only with the group for a couple of months, but it was fun even if it did mean having to deal with Cameron.

There were times when things didn't go exactly to plan. During one of our tours to England, we were getting ready to go to the ring and, just before we went out, Brodus turned to me and asked, "Hey, where are we?" I told him we were in Manchester. The music hit, Brodus ran out in front of the crowd, grabbed a microphone, and shouted, "How we doin', Manchester?!" — and was booed out of the building.

It was *then* I remembered we were actually in Newcastle. Oh well — as Brodus would say, "My bad." As I danced my way to the ring in front of him, he was ranting the entire time, yelling, "You're so fired! You're done! You screwed me!" He was laughing about it but he genuinely thought I'd given him the wrong city name on purpose so he'd get booed. It was the best rib I ever pulled off and I didn't even mean to do it. I couldn't stop laughing even when the match got started. As he was making his comeback and I was cheering him on, he stopped and yelled at me, "No! Don't you cheer, you don't care about me!" Even now, he'll bring that up to anyone who'll listen whenever I'm around.

I really liked working with Brodus and he was great to be around most of the time but he could be difficult to deal with when he was tired. He'd stomp around like he was pissed off at the world, wearing his Beats headphones and hauling a roller bag in each hand. Jimmy Uso did an absolutely dead-on impression of "Big Boo-Boo Face Brodus," as I called him when he was in a mood. Brodus had a decent run with WWE but I think he could have been a lot more. I know he thought they were making a mockery of him with the dancing character and I kind of understand because, seriously, how far can a character like that go? But, at the same time, it was memorable, and he got plenty of TV time. If he'd embraced it, who knows what might have happened further down the line. I don't think he appreciated the opportunity he was given until it was too late.

To be honest, my attitude was no better. On TV days, when it became clear there were no plans to use me on the show, I'd start checking online for early flights home. If I found one, even if it cost me several hundred bucks to switch my flight, I'd slip away and head to the airport. I wasn't the only person who did that; other guys who weren't going to be on the show did the same. I only got caught out once, where there was a last-minute change to the show and I was needed for something with Brodus. I was checking into my flight when I got a text from Mark Carrano, a friend of mine who worked in talent relations, asking, "Where are you?" In the end, they figured out a solution without me.

When we went to Mexico that year, my career hit a new low. Someone came up to me backstage to say I wouldn't want to go out front because they were giving one of the Mexican minis a tryout. I heard later that the midget wrestler absolutely nailed it. He'd worked in Mexico for years as the second version of Mascarita Sagrada before changing his name to Mascarita Dorada and, after WWE signed him, went on to become El Torito. Sitting there in catering, I was so depressed. I'd been dragged all the way down to Mexico, I wasn't being used on the show, and now they'd got a newer, faster, slimmer midget. That night, even the food was terrible. I grabbed three bread rolls and a tub of ranch dressing and sat there stuffing my face. Tyson walked by and said, "Do you realize how fat you're being right now?" but I didn't care. I just wanted to drown my sorrows in dip.

Before I'd given up on making suggestions, one of the ideas I'd unsuccessfully pitched a few times was me being a heel manager for a wrestler or a team, where I'd talk big and then hide behind someone else who would do the midget's dirty work. I also pitched the idea of being a heel general manager on *SmackDown*. Over on *Raw*, they had been running an "anonymous GM" angle for months, where someone would send orders by email to Michael Cole, who would deliver them over the house microphone to a chorus of boos. On *SmackDown*, the GM Teddy Long was well liked so I figured having a heel co-GM to get in his way at every turn could make for some good TV. I even managed to pitch that idea directly to Vince himself. He put me on the spot and said, "Let's hear it then." I tried, but let's just say I've done better promos in my time. Vince was polite about it, telling me, "It was all right, but it needs to be better."

Months later, I was at my dad's house on a Friday when one of the WWE writers called. He asked if I could do a Jersey accent. As proved by my attempt to sound Irish at my first tryout, I'm terrible at accents so I said I didn't think so. Undeterred, the writer explained what creative had in mind.

"They're going to reveal the anonymous *Raw* GM this Monday and it's going to be you. You're going to change characters and you'll be 'Big Nick' from Jersey, this guy with a Napoleon complex. You'll tell everyone you've been playing along with the Hornswoggle thing the whole time so that you could take money from all the stupid parents and their stupid kids — you're going to be a huge heel. So, get working on your Jersey accent!"

Three days. I had three days to learn how to deliver a convincing Jersey accent, so I didn't even have time to work with a dialect coach. I just watched *Goodfellas* and *Who Framed Roger Rabbit?* over and over and hoped the accent would take. I figured the character would be just like the talking baby with the cigar in *Roger Rabbit*, so that's who I focused on the most. I did my best, but it just didn't sound right.

At rehearsal on Monday, Hunter was in the ring with me and the writer, with Vince watching backstage from his office. When I told Hunter that I didn't have the accent down, he suggested we just try it, so we ran through the segment. Santino Marella and Jerry Lawler found me under the ring and pulled me out, then I launched into what was going to be my first *real* promo after six years in the company. The script had me talking about how I'd been playing the fans as pawns, getting the kids in the stands to beg for my "moichandise" and that their stupid parents had bought it all. It was building up to the big line, which was "this whole time, I've been swimming in the dough!"

The first run-through didn't go well at all. The second one was even worse. I looked up into the stands and saw Hawkins and Kofi having a "cupversation," wearing ear-to-ear grins and enjoying my agony. For the third run-through, they cut the house mics so only the people in the ring could hear what was going on. Kofi's voice echoed across the arena, "Awww, come on!" I turned and mouthed, "I hate you" right back at him.

Hunter was very supportive, making suggestions to try to make it easier for me, but I could see he was getting frustrated. Every time it went wrong, I was getting more and more upset and couldn't regain my composure. Here was my big break and I was screwing it all up. When it became clear I was never going to be able to pull off a convincing Joisey accent, Hunter told me to try it in my regular voice but like I had a hangover. That didn't work either. Then we tried me being a surly, disgruntled guy who was pissed off at the world. I was so flustered that I just couldn't get anything right. We'd been in the ring for a full hour at this point and needed to move on, so we took the rehearsal backstage and tried it again in Gorilla. Vince still wasn't feeling it.

I went off and kept working on it by myself. About an hour before the show started, I went to the writer to tell him I had it now. He told me it was too late, and they'd rewritten the segment. "We're not going to do any of the promo," he told me. "We're just going to reveal you, and you're going to bite Santino in the ass, kick Michael Cole, then get out of there." When I asked him to let me show Vince I *could* do the promo, he told me they were talking about other stuff now. I wouldn't stop. I told him I would go and interrupt the meeting if I had to. He just looked sadly at me and said, "Dylan, forget it. It's not going to happen. It's over."

This was probably the biggest opportunity I'd had in my career and I dropped the ball. The McMahon son and the D-X mascot angles were both huge, but I wasn't talking during either of those and I was the supporting character in the storyline. If I'd become "Big Nick," I would have had a ton of TV time and been talking every week. I was so upset but I knew it was my fault because I just couldn't pull it off the way they wanted.

We did the reveal later and it went all right. The crowd didn't love it, but they didn't reject it either. I heard that Vince spoke to Lawler later to apologize for having him appear in such a bad segment. I don't know if that story's true, but it was clear (and understandable) that the office was disappointed in me. They'd run the anonymous GM angle *forever*, and after they revealed it was me, it was quickly dropped and they moved on to something else. All of that time building it up — with no real payoff. I couldn't blame them for having nothing else for me moving forward. On the other hand, I do feel that if creative had had a long-term plan in place for how the angle was going to play out, they could have told me what was coming and given me some time to work on the new gimmick, even if it was just a couple more weeks. Also, if they'd given me bullet points for the promo instead of a inflexible script, I could have found a way to deliver it that worked for me. That said, given this was the very first promo of a character they had big plans for, I can understand why they felt they needed to micromanage. It has to go exactly how Vince envisions it, at least the first time out.

Even now, I can't go a week without hearing the words "swimming in the dough" from one of Kofi, Hawkins, Zack, Tyson, or Dolph Ziggler. I laugh it off, but it reminds me how I blew such a big opportunity. It still really frustrates me.

A Short Story: "Stupid . . . Stupid . . . Stupid"

A lot of wrestlers go through similar situations, where a great opportunity just doesn't happen because something doesn't quite click. Back when things were looking up for me in late 2009, they looked even better for Kofi. I remember him coming up to me one night and saying, "I've just seen what I'm doing at the Garden . . ."

The same night that Hunter was going to nail me with the Pedigree, Kofi was going to be involved in a brawl around the whole ringside area with main eventer Randy Orton, finishing up by leaping off a railing to put Randy through a table below. I was with him when they were walking through it at rehearsal and I told him, "You're gonna fall." Later that night, they did the segment and it went perfectly. Backstage, Kofi told me, "The whole time I was standing on that railing, I was thinking, 'If I fall, he'll never let me forget it.'" He was right — I wouldn't have. There was another near slip situation when Kofi dumped paint all over a race car that had pictures of Randy on it. I told him he was going to fall on his ass and, this time, I was nearly right. He started to slip on the hood of the car but caught himself just in time.

For a few weeks, it looked like they were going to push Kofi up to the very top of the card but then everything came to a halt. In a match on *Raw*, Randy thought Kofi was out of place for the finish and overreacted. We all have our triggers, I guess. That was "old Randy" behavior, back when he had one hell of a temper. After having kids, he became a completely different person and a much nicer guy. I never really spoke with Randy much until he'd become a father and then one day, out of nowhere, he came up to me to talk about being a dad. We talked for about ninety minutes. I couldn't have done that with "old Randy." Since then, we've spent a lot of time together, mainly playing *Call of Duty*.

I don't think Kofi ever resented Randy for their program not going through and, after a few years, Kofi got together with Big E and Xavier Woods as the New Day. I was traveling with them right at the start, when they were trying to figure out how to make their team work and they were so frustrated. They kept pitching ideas that would get shot down because Vince really wanted them to be a group of smiling, Gospel-church-going guys and genuinely thought it would catch on as a babyface act. Woods, E, and Kofi knew it wasn't going to work, but they ran with it because Vince believed in it. When the crowd turned on them, they went with it and, to his credit, Vince did, too. The act got over so much that they had to turn face and went on to have the biggest run of all their careers. I'm happy for Woods and E, who are both great guys, but I'm beyond happy for my buddy Kofi, who is probably the nicest guy in all of wrestling. There's not a single bad bone in his body. I'm so happy for him that, in 2019, he finally reached the top and became the WWE Champion.

CHAPTER 21

THE CLEAN MEALS

After I'd blown the chance to be "Big Nick," I went back to doing a whole lot of nothing. With no plans for me, I was put together with Khali and Natalya Neidhart in a group that had no explanation and no direction. It was just a giant, a woman, and a dwarf who didn't have anything else to do. Almost an entire year went by where we filled time on house shows and were used now and again on TV, never for anything of importance.

The experiences I'd had working with Khali before had been when I was in Finlay's corner, and while I'd seen Khali act like a diva on the road, I'd never seen him dare try that when he was in the ring with Fit. Whenever they were working together, Khali would do everything Fit told him to do, including taking bumps whenever he was asked, probably because he knew that if he refused, Finlay would make him bump anyway. Now that Fit wasn't involved, I saw a different side of him. Khali wanted to do as little as possible and the other boys would get frustrated when trying to organize anything with him. He refused to do anything he wasn't completely comfortable with and didn't care about how good his matches were. He didn't even care about being on TV. All he cared about was getting paid, preferably for doing as little as possible.

He wasn't the only person with that attitude, unfortunately. There were a few guys backstage who were content to stay under the radar and simply collect on their contract guarantee. In their eyes, the less they were in the ring, the less potential there was for them to make a mistake and get fired. I never understood that way of thinking. If I was going to be on the road as part of the team, I wanted to work in the ring and do whatever I could on the shows. If I was going to just sit in catering and eat, I would have rather been home with my son.

It wasn't just the lack of effort that put people off working with Khali. He could be incredibly stiff because he didn't know his own strength and didn't have the best level of control over his body. Everyone absolutely hated taking his overhead chop. He'd swing his massive hand down and connect so hard that some of the guys would say they felt the impact all the way down to their tailbone. Fortunately, I never experienced that move because I was too small for him to be able to catch me properly. Being small has its own benefits in the ring — working with big guys is a walk in the park because they're able to control my body easily and protect me more, even Khali. Mark Henry gave me his World's Strongest Slam at one point and it didn't hurt at all. It did, however, write me off TV for a while, and then later that year, I was off TV again — but this time, for the most awesome reason ever.

Around the time that the Muppets were involved with Tribute to the Troops, the WWE's yearly holiday season show for the U.S. Armed Forces, I heard a new Muppets movie was going to be made, *Muppets Most Wanted*. Naturally, I asked the WWE public relations team to get in touch and see if I could be involved in any way. I couldn't believe it when just two days later, WWE PR came back to me to say the Muppets producers wanted me to be a part of the movie. I thought it had to be too good to be true and something would get in the way, but I wasn't being used on TV or in a major role in WWE at the time, so getting time off wasn't an issue. Soon enough, everything was confirmed: I was flying to London for filming.

The flight from Detroit to London was the first and only time I've ever flown in first class. I'd been looking forward to enjoying the whole experience, having a nice meal and a few drinks, and seeing how different it was from being flown everywhere in coach by WWE. When I got on board, I found out that my seat was one of the pods that reclines all the way back. For most people, that means they can put their feet up comfortably. For me, it was legitimately a bed! In first, you can ask for your food to be brought whenever you want, so I thought I'd get some sleep first and eat later. I shut my eyes, drifted off — and woke up twenty minutes before landing. It was so comfortable that I'd slept the entire flight. I felt like an idiot for missing out on the meal, especially since this was during my big little guy phase.

I was not the sort of person to miss out on food and drink, as the movie producers must have found out when they got my room service bill. Every night, I'd order a burger or chicken sandwich with fries, and because I needed something to dip the fries in, I'd make my own special sauce using ketchup and mayo. It's no wonder I was putting on so much weight. That hotel was the best I've ever stayed in, definitely not one of my usual two-and-a-half-star specials. As an added bonus, I found out that Justin Bieber was doing a concert in London on the second day after I arrived, and I knew someone who was working in production for that show. I got in touch, said I was in London, and got invited to go along and watch from stageside. I don't care if it loses me cool points, I loved every minute.

After a couple of days settling in, everyone in the film was called in for several days of dance rehearsals. Because of the focus on footwork and body control you need for wrestling, I got to grips with most of the choreography quite quickly. Ray Liotta (*Goodfellas*) and Danny Trejo (*Con Air*) had no idea who I was but seemed impressed that the midget was picking everything up a lot faster than they were. When they came to ask me how I was doing it, I told them about what I did for a living. The next morning, Ray came over and said, "Hey, me and Danny watched your matches last night and we loved them!" The two of them spent the forty-five-minute trip to set that day bombarding me with countless questions about wrestling, asking how we knew what to do and when, how we avoided getting seriously hurt — they were genuinely interested in finding out how it all worked. I could relate because I was planning to find out everything I could about how the Muppets worked.

I was (and still am) a genuine Muppets fanatic to the point that I'd read so many books about them and was a regular visitor to Muppets news websites and message boards. Being on set offered me an incredible chance to see the ins and outs of how it all comes together.

All the sets were built on risers with trenches for the Muppet performers, so the humans would perform on sets several feet off the ground. All of the beneath-stage stuff would be hidden by props and set dressing. I found out that for ninety percent of the time when they are filming with the full-body Muppets, like Big Bird or Sweetums, one of the puppet's arms is pinned because the puppeteer needs one arm free to control the mouth and eyes. The other ten percent of the time, when control of both arms is needed, they'll use an animatronic head with someone off screen controlling it. And when anyone is taking photos of the Muppets, there will be someone behind the camera to direct the puppeteer so that everything is positioned correctly and the eyes are looking where they should be. Learning about little intricacies like that made the whole experience so much better.

I also appreciated being able to spend time with the performers. I'd met them previously at WWE shows but being on set with them gave me a chance to really get to know them. Early in the shoot, I approached Peter Linz, the performer behind Walter, told him I was a Muppets fanatic, and asked if he'd mind if I picked his brain. I ended up talking to him and Matt Vogel daily about anything and everything I could think of to do with the Muppets. They answered every question I asked — and I asked a lot. I also got a chance to hang out with Steve Whitmire, who took over from Jim Henson himself as Kermit, and Bill Barretta, who was Rowlf and a host of other characters, as well as being a co-producer and the puppet captain. They're such talented performers and I don't think they get the credit they deserve.

The whole Muppet experience was one of the best times of my life. A lot of the time on set, we would have trouble finding Danny because he'd go off wandering. It must have annoyed the producers, but we found it hilarious. Tina Fey, who was the lead non-Muppet in the movie, is one of the nicest people I've ever met, incredibly funny and

kind, and her kids — who were on set the whole time — were so well behaved. Having them around made me miss Landon even more. The month and a half I was in London was the longest I'd ever been away from my son and that was the only drawback about being in the movie. I made sure to send him videos every week to tell him I missed him, and I had some help in those from the Muppets themselves. Both Walter and Kermit did videos for me to send to Landon to tell him that all the Muppets were taking good care of his dad while we were making the movie.

With Tina Fey — wonderful actress, wonderful person.

I only had one talking scene in the movie and I got so nervous about remembering my lines. We filmed it at night and did it about twenty times from a bunch of different angles, so there really wasn't any reason for me to have been worried. I just wanted to do the best I could, not just because I wanted to come across well in the film, but because everyone had been so kind to me throughout the production. When we were nearing the end of the shoot, I wrote letters to everyone involved, from the crew to the makeup people to the drivers, to thank them for everything they'd done. I also had bottles of wine sent to each of them in their rooms. I was so grateful, and still am, to have been able to be part of the magic of the Muppets.

Shortly after I returned to the road with WWE, I got a message from Hawkins, telling me the midget wrestler who had tried out for the WWE in Mexico was now in Orlando at the Performance Center. Hawkins was trying to rile me up, saying, "You should see this guy — he can move and he's in great shape. You're nothing compared to him!" He followed up with a video of the guy flipping around in the ring. I knew Hawkins was just messing with me, but I realized I was going to get compared to this super athletic guy and that was frustrating, especially when I was just sitting around backstage most of the time.

I made a lot of excuses back then, telling people I couldn't reach the machines in the gym, or that exercising made my knees and back hurt, so I'd never worked out during my WWE run. Between that and the fact that I overindulged in catering, and ate and drank whatever I wanted when I was on the road, I had put on a ton of weight. Not a literal ton, of course, but when I started with WWE, I'd been 125 pounds and by 2013 I was up to 168 pounds. An extra forty-three pounds is a lot of weight for anyone to carry around but on *my* frame, it was ridiculous. People backstage poked fun of me because of my weight gain and it pissed me off, but not enough to actually do anything about it.

Eventually, it got so noticeable that Mark Carrano pulled me aside to tell me that people were worried about me. He told me that

Vince and Hunter specifically had mentioned my weight gain and were concerned about my health. I was informed that I was being put on a weight loss program, including meeting with the doctor and trainer at the WWE Performance Center so I could be given a workout and diet program. It hurt to hear that, but I only had myself to blame. WWE created a low-impact exercise program I could handle and provided me with clean meals that I'd take on the road, so I only needed to worry about cooking for myself when I was at home. They were pre-portioned meals for breakfast, lunch, and dinner. I was worried they'd taste terrible, but they were very good. The company covered the cost of these for me for three months.

Since the WWE was taking my health very seriously, I figured I needed to do the best I could in return and literally work my ass off. I also suspected that if I didn't lose my excess weight, they'd release me. I was asked to lose fifteen to twenty pounds but I ended up losing thirty-eight, getting back down to 130 pounds. The fact that I worked hard and exceeded their expectations won me a lot of support from management. At times, having to take my own personal containers of food on the road was embarrassing, especially when everyone else was in catering or at restaurants, but it was what I needed to do if I wanted to be taken seriously by the company.

Vince in particular was very complimentary about my weight loss, telling me I looked much healthier and saying he appreciated how much work I'd put in because it showed how much I cared about the company. I thanked him, then asked why I wasn't being used more regularly. He asked if I was pitching ideas to the writers and was surprised to hear I was doing it almost every week. "I haven't heard that," he replied. "Come to me from now on."

It didn't surprise me to hear Vince hadn't heard any of my ideas. The impression I got was that the last thing any of the writers wanted was to pitch something that Vince loved and then for him to find out it was someone else's idea. To avoid that, they only went with ideas they could alter enough that they could claim as their own, or things that were so old that they could pretend they'd never heard before. I also found out that you'd get heat with the creative team if they thought you were bypassing them. You couldn't win — if you pitched them something directly, they'd ignore you, and if you pitched to someone else, they'd get angry at you for going above their heads. It came down to this — if you were high on the company's roster, they'd listen. If they didn't have any real interest in using you, they didn't care about your ideas, no matter how good they might be. I'm confident a lot of the ideas I had *were* good because I'd always run them past John Cena, Kofi, or Fit to make sure they were worth pitching. Those guys always told me when I needed to hold back or rethink something. I'm certain I could have got some of my ideas green-lit if I'd asked John to push them, but I never wanted to use a friend's political pull to get my way.

Although it was great to have been given permission to pitch directly to Vince, getting to speak to him isn't easy. His schedule is always full and particularly crazy on TV days. Even if you do manage to get some of his time, you never know what kind of mood he'll be in. During one meeting with him, I got the impression he was getting annoyed and started fiddling with his phone. Moments later, someone ran in and said, "Vince, we've got something you need to take care of." The timing was far too coincidental for the two things to not be connected. Another time, we were in Washington, D.C. and I was waiting outside Vince's office to pitch him an idea. Hunter came out of the office and we exchanged small-talk as someone else went in to see Vince. A couple of minutes after Hunter left, one of the security guys, Scott Aycock, came over and said, "I'm supposed to tell you Vince isn't seeing anyone else today." I told Scott someone else had *just* gone in there, but Scott just said, "That's what I've been told to tell you." As far as I know, Vince didn't even know I was out there. I'm confident Hunter sent Scott to turn me away and I have no idea why.

A Short Story: Shirtless and Terrified

Scott Aycock was one of the guys I would rib on the road. He'd usually be in the group of people who would sneak me to the ring during a show, and one of my favorite tricks was to catch him in the groin just as I was disappearing under the apron. Predictably, he also had people (me included) teasing him for his name, pronouncing it "A Cock" as often as possible. He always kept a straight face and no-sold the name calling, and he always no-sold the ball-shots.

On a tour of Mexico in 2010, I'd been hidden under the ring as usual and was halfway through getting changed when I noticed the ring apron being raised. I still didn't have my shirt on when a camera was poked in under the apron. Then I saw it — there was a full-grown rooster under the ring with me.

I don't like big dogs, and I like big birds even less. They're unpredictable, uncontrollable, and they've got sharp talons and beaks.

The rooster tried to escape, but the photographer grabbed it and shoved it back under the ring. It was getting worked up, and all the bumps from the match above between Drew McIntyre and Chris Masters weren't helping. The bird noticed me and began approaching until it was only about ten feet away from me. I grabbed a kendo stick that was nearby and shouted, "If it comes near me, I'm going to kill it!" Then I thought if I *did* hit it, but didn't kill it, all I was going to do was piss it off even more.

After taking a few pictures of me, shirtless, terrified, and swinging a kendo stick, the photographer removed the rooster. When I got to the back that night, the boys were laughing their asses off. I told them not one single part of that had been funny. Scott just said, "I don't think you'll mess with me anymore."

Of course, I knew Finlay had to have had *something* to do with it. When I confronted him, he shook his head and said, "It wasn't my idea, Dylan. But if someone asks me for a chicken, I'll help them find a chicken."

CHAPTER 22

THE TWO-TIME MOVIE STAR

In the early 2000s, WWE had started up a film division, which led to the company's involvement in a number of movies of varying success. They were mostly action movies but one of the earlier films, *See No Evil*, was a horror film starring Kane that seemed to do well commercially if not critically. A few years after that, WWE Studios decided to go down the horror route again and reboot the Leprechaun film series. Looking at their roster, they evidently noticed someone who might be the right height to play the title character. There wasn't an audition — I was simply told I had the role. I wasn't given a script. I wasn't given a date when it would start filming. I'd just keep hearing, "We'll be starting in a couple of weeks." Then, nothing. I even asked Vince about it at one point. He told me it was definitely happening. If I pushed him for any more information, he'd just say, "We'll figure all that out." When I didn't hear anything more, I put it out of my mind until I got a call from Mark Carrano the next year, telling me I was needed in Vancouver in three weeks time to start shooting.

I flew out to L.A. before the shoot to meet with the director, Zach Lipovsky. Zach was clearly very passionate about the project and about movie-making in general, but he was a lot younger than I'd expected for a film director. During our meeting, he explained his vision for my character and it was almost the exact opposite of what I was expecting. His concept art looked a lot like Gollum from *Lord of the Rings* and required me to be in prosthetics and makeup from head to toe. I didn't understand that — if he was going to do that, he could have hired any little person to play the role. If they were going with me specifically because it would mean they could market the movie to people who knew who I was, those people would want to see that it *was* me in the film! Not only were people not going to be able to see it was me, they weren't going to be able to hear me either. When I mentioned that I still hadn't even seen a script, I was told that I didn't need one as I wouldn't have any lines. During the course of that one meeting, I went from being excited about having a starring role in a movie to being really upset.

A week later, having come to terms with how it was going to be, I flew back out to get fitted for my outfit and the prosthetics. Creating my mask was the scariest thing in the world. They wrapped my entire face in plaster and made me breathe through a straw. I never realized I was claustrophobic until that day. I was probably about thirty seconds from passing out before I told them to get it off me. The molding process wasn't even being done for the purpose of getting an imprint of my face; it was so they could fit their other prosthetics around the mold. When everything was put together, including freaky long arms that extended about a foot and a half, and an amazingly uncomfortable mask with a rigging system that dug into my head and neck, the whole outfit weighed about forty pounds. The fact that we were filming in the middle of summer made wearing all that gear almost unbearable. Despite the agony of being slowly cooked inside the leprechaun suit, I have to say that it looked awesome.

In total, the shoot took fifteen days. That's a lot less time than most people in the industry would say you need to shoot a quality film, but it's a fair indication of how much value WWE Films put in the project. At the least, they put me up in a nice apartment with a grocery store next door and a bar right across the road where I'd get dinner. I didn't know if I'd ever get the chance to be in a movie again, so I invited Dad and Dorothy out to visit. They came to set to see some of the filming and then because I had weekends off, we drove around the Vancouver area to see the waterfalls. It was a new experience because we had never been on a vacation where it was just the three of us. I was glad I could share that with my parents but found it hard to be away from Landon for so long.

Although the shoot was uncomfortable, there were some great moments. One came during a scene where a character is trying to kill the leprechaun with a shotgun. They were going to have an explosion off camera for the gun sound effect (although I didn't know why they didn't just put it in afterward in post-production) and Zach offered me some earplugs, telling me it was going to be really loud. When I turned them down, he insisted I wear them. I pointed out that I'd spent years at wrestling shows under a ring or a stage with some of the loudest pyro ever going off all around me. He still insisted, so I wore the earplugs, which didn't really work, and we shot the scene. The "blasts" sounded like high-grade party poppers to me. They weren't even close to the level of noise you get from Kane's ring-post pyro.

There was one scene in particular that stood out — the full-body reveal of the leprechaun. I was stalking one of the characters through a house and up to the attic. It was like the kitchen scene with the velociraptors in *Jurassic Park*, only the raptor was being played by a wrestling midget in a leprechaun suit. By the end of the shoot, despite my initial reservations, Zach and I thought we had something good on our hands, and I couldn't wait to see how it came out. I had to wait a long time.

Almost a year later, I was heading out to San Diego Comic Convention to do media for what was now called *Leprechaun: Origins* and even though I'd been asking to see an advance copy for months, I still hadn't seen the movie I was there to promote. Finally, someone brought a copy on a disk to my hotel room on the condition that I turn it back in first thing the next morning. I put it on my laptop and settled in.

Ninety minutes later, I texted Zach. The text simply read, "What did I just watch?"

There were so many things that we'd taken a huge amount of time to get exactly right that hadn't been used at all. Above all else, despite the fact that I'd been in the makeup chair for seven painstaking hours each day, there wasn't a single clear shot of the leprechaun. Instead, everything was dark and shadowy. There was a shot of my face here and a hand there, but I was on screen so little, and so little was shown of the creature, that my role genuinely could have been played by anyone. The part I thought would feel like that scene in *Jurassic Park* didn't even make the final cut. I was so disappointed.

Zach texted back: "I'm sorry. WWE Studios changed it around." He was just as disappointed and upset as I was. The producers had taken what we'd shot and edited it into something that neither of us was pleased with.

I was already angry after having seen the finished version of the film, but my evening got worse when I got a text from Summer Rae, one of the WWE's female wrestlers, saying, "See you tomorrow." I had no idea what she meant until she told me, "I'm hosting your Q&A panel tomorrow with the Miz. We're promoting the next *Marine* movie, too."

I was furious. I didn't go to their *Marine* promotional events. No matter how terrible the final film was, this event was to promote *my* film and now it felt like it was going to be all about Miz and Summer and *The Marine.* I went into the Q&A session the next day still in a bad mood. When Miz started fielding questions, I cut him off and told him I could do the job fine without him. Later on, taking my frustration out on him, I started jabbing at him about how I'd been in two movies and he'd only been in one. I knew Miz was only there because WWE Studios had told him to go, but I couldn't help myself from acting like a jerk. Later that day, I was lectured by Michael Luisi, the head of WWE Studios, about how I shouldn't have mentioned the Muppets movie because it wasn't a company production. I pointed out that I was part of the company, so they should have been promoting that I'd been in a massive Hollywood blockbuster but Luisi couldn't get past the fact that it wasn't a WWE Studios production and therefore shouldn't have been mentioned. I told him I was all for looking out for the company, but I had to look out for myself sometimes, too.

A Short Story: Miz-mode

From my behavior at that panel, it may sound like I don't like the Miz and that's not true at all. I traveled with him a number of times and we got along really well. He can just be a lot to take sometimes. It's very rare that you get "Mike" from the Miz, because he spends about ninety percent of his day in Miz-mode.

When he's in Miz-mode, he'll argue about *anything*. If you say the sky is blue, he'll tell you it's shades of green and purple. It's as if he hates silence and if arguing is a good way to break it, he's going to start an argument.

Whenever he'd do that, Kofi and I would tell him we wanted to talk to Michael, not the Miz. He'd insist "This *is* Michael!" but we knew better.

Some of the boys might have begrudged him his spot way back when he wasn't good in the ring, but everyone loves working with him now because he always knows what to do and when to do it to get the most out of an audience, especially on the microphone.

I might have been irritated that he was at my Q&A, but the truth is that he's probably the best PR person in the WWE because he can get his points across in a personable, charismatic way. He'll have a job with the company as long as he wants it for his PR work alone.

After a limited release in selected theaters, *Leprechaun: Origins* came out on DVD. On the night it was released, WWE ran the trailer on *Raw*. When I first saw it, it felt like something was missing but I couldn't put my finger on it. The next day, I watched it again and it hit me — my name wasn't anywhere to be seen! That didn't make any sense to me. I'm definitely not saying that I'm such a big star that my name should have been plastered everywhere but it was a WWE project being advertised on a WWE show and everyone watching that trailer would have known who I was. On top of that, I was the only person in the film who had anything approaching a "name."

I texted Carrano to ask why my name wasn't in there. He wrote back saying that it was just the first trailer and that they'd probably have another one next week. He was right — they did. They played it twice during *Raw* and my name *still* was nowhere to be found. The next night, I didn't even appear on *SmackDown* despite my film being promoted during it. I couldn't believe what was going on. I went to see Carrano in his office, and as we were talking, the trailer started playing on a monitor. When it was over, I asked him why I shouldn't just quit right then and there.

I unloaded on him, pointing out the company had kept me in the dark about dates for the shoot, not let me see the film until the last minute, screwed with the Q&A. I even pointed out that they'd asked me to lose a bunch of weight and that I'd done everything they'd asked of me. I said that if the company couldn't get behind me in their own movie, they might as well release me from my contract. Mark asked me to "be calm" and give it a week. He'd always ask me to "be calm." After a while, hearing those two words pissed me off more than anything else.

A week later, I was still angry. Soon enough, I found myself standing in front of Vince McMahon, asking why my name wasn't in the trailer. He thought about it for a moment and asked me a question in return.

"Were there any other names in the trailer?"

I told him there weren't.

"Well, that's why," he said. "They must not have wanted to put any names in there."

It made perfect sense. I walked out of his office, got to the end of the corridor, and then found myself thinking, "Hold on, that doesn't many *any* sense . . ." Vince had played one of his classic Jedi mind tricks and I'd fallen for it. Jericho talked about Vince's Jedi tricks a lot, but that was the first time I'd experienced one in person. From where I was standing, it was a WWE film and I was a WWE superstar so it didn't matter that no one else's name was mentioned, mine should have been. It benefited everyone. The problem was that I'd already accepted Vince's explanation, so I couldn't go back into his office and bring it up again.

I never found out how well the movie did, despite asking. All I heard was "we'll get back to you." The guys at Ringside Collectibles even pushed WWE for a *Leprechaun: Origins* figure of me to be made and said they'd market it. Nothing happened there. Despite all the money WWE must have put into the movie upfront, it didn't seem like they were willing to do anything that might help it succeed. I still don't understand why.

I also couldn't understand the WWE's behavior when it came to promoting my involvement in *Muppets Most Wanted*. After I got my invite, I went to Carrano and asked if they were going to send a camera crew with me to the premiere. I took his reply of "What premiere?" as a hard no. In the end, all WWE did was put a couple of pictures of me at the premiere and in the film up on their website.

That wasn't the first time they'd ignored an opportunity to capitalize on an association with a Disney project. I'd shot a lot of footage during filming, doing interviews with the Muppets and the stars in the movie. I even had interviews where both the director James Bobin and Tina Fey talked about working with me on the film. None of that stuff was used. There was Tina Fey, talking about how great it was to work with a WWE superstar, and WWE didn't use it on any of their shows. Not even on their website. Nowhere. The excuse I was given was that they'd just done the *Scooby-Doo! WrestleMania Mystery* film (which ended up being a straight-to-video special), so the Muppets was "competition." I couldn't believe that I'd just been in a huge Disney motion picture that made $100 million worldwide and WWE was ignoring the chance for some major publicity because of their Scooby-Doo deal. It seemed like such a wasted opportunity but, if nothing else, at least the Muppets premiere gave me a great excuse to take my dad out sightseeing around L.A. and get him to wear a suit for only the second time in his life (the other one being his first wedding — "and look how *that* turned out," he'd tell me).

I got to throw a premiere of sorts in my hometown, too — I rented a local movie theater for the day *Muppets Most Wanted* was released and invited all my family and friends to come see it with me. Landon was only four years old at that point, and while he knew that I'd been away the previous year to shoot a film with the Muppets, it just didn't click that *this* was the movie. When I popped up on screen for the first time, a wide-eyed Landon literally leapt out of his seat and shouted, "Dad, that's you!" I love that he got to see me doing something like that outside of WWE, and I was surprised and grateful that I was as visible as I was in the movie, since I thought I'd only ever be in the background. I definitely got more screentime in that film than I did in either *Leprechaun: Origins* or the next year at *WrestleMania 30*.

CHAPTER 23

THE WARRIOR PICTURE

Although I wasn't booked to do anything on the biggest show of the year, I was brought along to New Orleans for all the events that accompanied *WrestleMania 30*. I still loved going to Axxess, but it had definitely gone downhill because of cost-cutting. I didn't understand why Axxess was one of the main places they chose to cut corners because *'Mania* was making more money with each passing year. In the week leading up to *WrestleMania*, I always asked to do as many things as possible. First, because I didn't want to just sit around in a hotel room; second, because they were fun; and third, because we'd always walk away with plenty of complementary goods. Whenever I'd do the golf tournament, for example, I'd be given new golf shoes and gloves and, in 2013, as a result of winning the video game tournament, I'd come away with a new X-Box 360. I already had one, so I gave my prize to Tyson Kidd in an attempt to get him to realize the error of his Playstation ways. Tyson immediately sold the X-Box and told me, "I wasn't about to play *that*." Tyson's one of my best friends to this day but he'll let you know if he's not into something. One of my favorite memories of working with him was during a match which wasn't going to plan. I was on the other side of the ring, watching Tyson yell at my tag partner, kicking him between each word. "God [kick] damn [kick], tag [kick] the [kick] midget [kick], even [kick] he [kick] can [kick] work [kick] better [kick] than [kick] you [kick]!"

Even though I wasn't on the main show, I loved being able to bring my dad and Dorothy down for all the *WrestleMania* festivities that year. Whenever Dad came with me to 'Mania, he was happy to see me in my element among all of the other wrestlers, but he'd always make sure I kept my ego in check. One of the first times he came along with me, we walked past a mob of fans in the lobby and got into the elevator. On the way up to our room, he asked me if I was going to go back and sign autographs. I told him I wasn't because I thought it was dumb. He reminded me of when my mom had got me Dan Marino's autograph after I was recovering from one of my surgeries and how much that had meant to me, then asked me if *that* had been dumb. He told me, "You're going to put aside twenty minutes and you're going to go back down there and sign for those fans." Every year after that, I made sure to do that and if Dad was with me, he made double sure.

When the wrestlers' schedule came out for Axxess 2014, I found that I'd been booked for a signing while the Hall of Fame ceremony was going on. I wouldn't have been happy with that most years but this year in particular, there was no way I was going to accept that. My childhood hero, the Ultimate Warrior, was being inducted into the Hall of Fame and I wasn't going to miss his speech for anything in the world.

Once again, I went to see Carrano, this time to ask him to switch the schedule. When he said he couldn't, I pointed out that my name wasn't even listed on the schedule for the public, so no one would be coming to the signing expecting me. I'd just be another guy at another table so I said I wasn't doing it and suggested he find someone else who didn't care about the Hall of Fame to fill the spot. He said there was nothing he could do, and I left his office absolutely furious, an anger that only went away on the day before the Warrior's induction, when he called me up to let me know that I was off Axxess and, instead, would be in a segment at the Hall of Fame.

Usually, the Hall of Fame was kept to speeches only but that year, Vince wanted to do something slightly different, so they added a couple of entertainment segments between the inductions. Wade Barrett did an in-character speech that sort of worked but the segment that I was involved in was a disaster. This comedy interlude involved Torito, who had been brought on TV as the mini-mascot for Los Matadores, chasing me onto and around the stage until I ducked through host Jerry Lawler's legs and made my escape. Torito then charged Lawler and headbutted him in the balls. The crowd booed the segment and rightfully so. It might have been funny if the thing had started in the audience and we'd both been in tuxedos. A midget bull in a furry tux chasing a midget leprechaun in a green tux? That was so absurd that it might have worked. But, as it was, we were both apparently in our regular gear, hanging out backstage at the Hall of Fame for no reason and then Torito chased me on stage, also for no reason. It was terrible. At least I got to hear Warrior's speech. He made a brief appearance on the main *WrestleMania* show when they acknowledged the people who'd been inducted into that year's Hall of Fame class, but I didn't see him anywhere backstage. I promised myself that if he was on *Raw* the next night, I would do everything I could to meet him.

On the *Raw* after that *WrestleMania*, Warrior did another interview. Just like his Hall of Fame speech, it was great but I didn't like it when he put on the cardboard Warrior mask. I can't say why exactly, but it annoyed me. Still, I was determined to finally meet my hero. So, as he was doing his speech, I grabbed my bag and ran to Gorilla to wait for him. I'd heard he could get weird with people at times, but I felt like I needed to meet him and thank him for inspiring me as a kid.

When he got to the back, I waited for him to finish talking to other people and, as his wife Dana was with Stephanie McMahon, I saw my opportunity. I walked up to him and said, "Hello, sir, my name is Dylan and I work here." After the incident where The Rock thought I was a Make-A-Wish kid, I wasn't leaving anything to chance. I kept going, "I got into this business because of you. When I was growing up, you were the only wrestler I cared about. You're the reason I wanted to become a professional wrestler and you're the reason I'm here today."

Warrior shook my hand and said, "That means so much to me. That means more than anything anyone could say." He called his wife over, interrupting her conversation with Stephanie (which I thought I might get in trouble for later, but I didn't), and told her, "This is Dylan and he just told me I'm the reason he got into the business." I asked if I could take a picture with him and he said he would really like that. After I had taken my picture, he asked if *he* could take a picture with me. I was speechless. Dana took the picture and after Warrior went off to talk to someone else, she told me, "You have no idea how much what you said will have meant to him." After all the Ultimate Warrior got me through as a kid, I was glad I'd managed to give him something back, even if it was just a heartfelt thank you.

I couldn't believe I'd met Warrior, got to speak with him and take a picture. I couldn't believe he'd asked *me* to take a picture with *him*. I was on cloud nine.

The next morning, when I woke up, I noticed that there were a huge number of new messages in the group chat on my phone. Something big had clearly happened while I was asleep. When I saw that Warrior had died of a heart attack, I couldn't comprehend it. I'd been talking to him less than ten hours before and now he was dead? It felt unreal to me and all I kept coming back to was the thought that if I hadn't met him the night before, I wouldn't have ever met him.

One of the first people to text me was Rob Schamberger. He was the artist who designed the jacket Warrior wore on *Raw* the night before. He knew how much of a Warrior fanatic I was, and he wrote, "I know you must be hurting today and I want you to know I'm thinking of you." I couldn't believe how kind and thoughtful he was that day, in spite of how upset he must have been himself. He went one better several months later when I got a message from him telling me there'd be a package arriving that day at my house. When it came, I was blown away. Rob had painted the photo of Warrior and me. It was so thoughtful of him to take the time to do that and it means so much to me. It's the first picture you see when you walk into my living room.

CHAPTER 24

THE ROCK STAR

I was no longer the only little person on the WWE roster. When Eddie and Orlando Colón were repackaged as Los Matadores in late 2013, the former Mascarita Dorada became El Torito, a mini-wrestler in a bull outfit to act as the hook for their team. Torito being promoted to the main roster led to countless jabs at me from everyone in the locker room. Whenever we were in the same room, someone — usually Alberto Del Rio — would stir things up, saying, "Look at this! Something's about to go down . . ." in the same way some people would whenever Show and Khali were around each other. It was even worse whenever Torito was in the ring and we were watching on the monitor. The boys would comment openly on how impressive he was and even more jabs would come my way. "That's why he's on the show and you're not!" That sort of thing — just the usual case of bored wrestlers trying to get a reaction. It didn't cause any heat between Torito and me because we always got along well but, since he was getting used regularly on TV and I wasn't, the comments did get under my skin.

Having Torito around lit a fire under me. Since I was losing weight and getting in shape, I took the initiative and spent some time at a wrestling camp about ninety minutes away from home. I called on one of my original trainers, Shane Hills, and got in the ring with some of the local guys to bump around and sharpen my skills. When I was there, I got some video footage of me in action and gave it to Brian James, who wrestled in the Attitude Era as the Road Dogg and, by then, was one of the main producers on *SmackDown*. Brian told me he liked what he saw so, as soon as I'd got my weight down to where they wanted it to be, I started asking when Torito and I could start an in-ring program. The message that came back from the production meetings was "That's the easy thing to do." I told them that just because it was the easy thing, it didn't mean it wasn't the *right* thing. But they said that Vince didn't want to do it because putting the two midgets together was just too obvious.

I'd started to think I'd never cross paths with Torito on screen (at least not beyond our terrible Hall of Fame moment) when Brian came up to me before a *SmackDown* taping and said, "You got your wish — go get in your workout clothes and get in the ring." In the back, as I was changing, Del Rio tried to cause trouble again, telling me I couldn't hang with Torito and that I was going to be sucking wind out there. I just told him, "We'll see." Del Rio was a weird guy. If he was being pushed, he was great to be around. If he felt he wasn't being used properly, he'd be bitter and moody. You never knew which Alberto you'd be getting day to day.

When word got around that the two little guys were going to try something in the ring, the locker room emptied and, by the time we got out there, it was a ringside sellout. The boys were frothing at the mouth, like they were about to watch a gang fight. I could tell a lot of them shared Alberto's opinion that Torito was going to blow me up. I don't think they *wanted* to see me fail, but I'm sure they expected it. Del Rio joined me, Torito, and Brian James in the ring, translating for us. Brian asked us to bump around and work some spots, so we went through headlocks, headscissors, hurricanranas, and a host of holds we could use in a match. All I wanted to do was show everyone I could keep up with Torito and I think I managed that. It felt great to be working properly for once, even if it was only in rehearsal. I looked up and saw Kofi and Dolph grinning from ear-to-ear, knowing I'd stuck it to everyone who didn't believe in me. Now I just had to do it on the show later that night in front of a crowd of thousands, when I was going to be revealed as the newest member of the Three-Man Band, better known as 3MB.

A Short Story: Bottom of the Barrel

This new group, comprised of Drew McIntyre, Heath Slater, and Jinder Mahal, ended up being pretty low on the company roster but that wasn't how it was originally meant to be. WWE spent two full weekends shooting footage with 3MB for VH1 *Behind the Music*–like segments that were going to be played across our shows to introduce the group. It would have been different, and I think it would have got them over, at least as a solid mid-card act. Instead, maybe one clip was used and nothing was done with the rest. It was such a shame they got lost in the shuffle back then because Drew, Heath, and Jinder are all very talented guys.

The Matadores were another act that ended up at the bottom of the card after a decent start. Audiences loved the fun stuff with Torito, but when it was time for Eddie and Orlando to do the match, they weren't as interested. Eddie and Orlando got repackaged as evil travel agents (or at least that's what I *think* they were) after a while, and then once more as the Colóns, but they still didn't really catch on with the crowd, which is a shame since they can do anything you need in the ring.

―――――――――――――――――――――――――――――――――

Torito, Los Matadores, and 3MB had been working together for a few months; at one particular *SmackDown* and *Main Event* taping, I was called in as a late replacement for Heath Slater, who was on tour in Abu Dhabi. Rather than have Jinder and Drew with no one in their corner to counteract Torito during their *Main Event* tag match, I was going to be introduced as the newest member of the band, making it at least 2.5MB for that particular night. Later on, I was going to have a singles match against Torito on *SmackDown*. The problem was that I didn't have appropriate gear. I couldn't go out there and act like a rock star wearing my leprechaun outfit, so I went to see the seamstresses and was immediately told it wasn't possible to put something together for me in one night. When we found out that they were working on a pair of new pants for Heath, Jinder jumped in. "Cut 'em off. He can use those." The thought of cutting up something they'd been working on for a while clearly didn't appeal to the seamstresses but, fortunately, Road Dogg walked over and insisted that I needed new gear for that night's show. When he saw Heath's pants, Brian told them to go ahead and cut them down.

I asked Brian what he thought I should do for the rest of my costume. I had a pair of Chuck Taylors that I could wear and a vest I'd worn to the arena that night that I thought would work, but I had nothing to go underneath it. I hadn't wrestled shirtless since my indie days and I was still self-conscious about my body. Brian helped me with that, reminding me how much weight I'd lost and how I was in much better shape now. With his encouragement, I decided the vest would be enough and I wouldn't worry about finding a shirt. Once I was dressed, Jinder took a photo and sent it to Heath, who had no idea what was happening. Jinder told him, "We've got a new member and you lost your pants." Everything during the matches that night went smoothly and we even got a rare thumbs-up from Vince when we got backstage.

While everything went well during the first couple of times Torito and I worked together, we weren't so fortunate during later outings. At one taping, we had a bad night in the ring, blew a few spots, and ended up both getting lost. Everything was headed downhill quickly, so we finished the match before the audience turned on us. The moment we got to the back, Vince's headset came off. The headset coming off meant you were in *trouble*. He wasn't just annoyed about the blown spots, he was annoyed about the entire segment. "Goddammit, where was the ass-biting? These people don't want to see midgets beating the shit out of each other, they want to see the funny stuff."

A Short Story: A Not-So-Super Kick

Another time Vince took the headset off was after a tag match when Dolph Ziggler was across the ring from me. Early in the match, I ran at him, he went to kick me, and I bumped early. When we got to the back, the headset came off and Vince chewed us out. He made us watch the spot repeatedly on his monitor. Dolph took most of the heat, even though it wasn't his fault.

I never understood why Dolph wasn't one of the top guys in the company. The way I see it, a top wrestler needs to tick five main boxes: to be able to work both as a heel and a face, take good bumps, cut a good promo, make other people look good, and to be willing to work hard to promote the name of the company. Dolph does all of those things so well. Despite that, he's been put

Landon with Dolph backstage in Green Bay.

in the "good hand" category like Hawkins. Everyone backstage knows how special he is.

I think Dolph is so used to feeling overlooked that he brushes it off now. You learn to not get your hopes up because then you've got something to lose. It's just the way it works for most people — when you first go to WWE, you've got nothing but hope about what you could become. As time goes on and you realize what they want from you, the hope gradually vanishes and that's tough to come back from. That's not bitterness speaking, it's just reality and the way the business works.

Vince is a difficult man to please. Half of the time, he doesn't seem to know what he wants and he'll change his mind at the drop of a hat. One minute, he'll tell you he wants a match or a promo to go a certain way and then the moment you get back from delivering what he wanted, he'll ask, "What the hell was that?" When you tell him you just did what he said, he'll say, "Why would I ever say that?" It's frustrating, but understandable — with a massive company to run and so much on his plate, it's no wonder he sometimes forgets something he said just five minutes earlier. Since he's got to prioritize his time, he'll put more thought and effort into the main event programs and less into what he sees as minor parts of the show and that can lead to this lack of focus.

I was angry and disappointed with his reaction to my match with

Torito — I thought we'd got past the idea that "midgets are only for comedy." I figured our program would be immediately canceled and I'd go back to sitting in catering. I felt sorry for myself, but I also felt bad for Brian, who'd put a lot of effort into planning my segments and matches with Torito. He'd been so supportive of me and my determination to get back in the ring and I was worried I'd let him down. When I mentioned that to him, he told me, "It's just a speed bump — everything will be fine." Finlay, who had been brought back to the company as a producer, helped me see the bigger picture, too, explaining that as long as I gave Vince a little comedy, he'd be fine with me working the rest of the match properly. I was still a little resentful about being reduced to standard midget comedy spots but, eventually, I realized that Fit was right and giving a little meant I'd get a lot.

Despite Vince's anger that night, the good stuff we'd done had clearly made enough of an impression on enough of the right people because, soon afterward, Brian let me know that Torito and I were going to get a showcase match at the upcoming *Extreme Rules* pay-per-view. That was incredible news and more than I'd ever hoped for, but it meant we'd have to figure out a good gimmick for the match since most of the bouts at *Extreme Rules* had a stipulation, from falls-count-anywhere to last man standing. When we got together to go through our ideas, I suggested a mini-ladder match. Brian took it a step further and said we should do a mini-tables, mini-ladders, and mini-chairs match. Usually, such a match would be called a TLC (Tables, Ladders, and Chairs) match, but given it was going to be a mini-match, Brian said we should call it *WeeLC*. The creativity kept coming over the next few days. Before long, we'd also planned to have a mini-commentary table with mini-commentators and a mini-ring announcer. It was going to be the biggest little match in wrestling history.

About a week before *Extreme Rules*, I was disappointed to find out that our match was going to be on the pre-show rather than the main card. I didn't understand why something so unique would be on the pre-show, but that was their call to make. After months of being absent from TV, I was just happy to be in an advertised match at a big event, even if I wasn't on the PPV part of the event.

I was asked to get to rehearsal by 10 a.m. on the day of the show. When I got there and saw all of the small gimmicks they'd prepared for us, including a mini-replica of the main commentary desk, it started to sink in just how special this could be. There was so much going into this match, I knew Torito and I just had to deliver. He and I were joined at rehearsal by the Matadores and my 3MB teammates. I was relieved to find out that Finlay was going to help produce the match, along with Scott Armstrong. Fit hadn't been officially assigned to the match, but I'd asked if he could be involved because I knew everything would come together even better with his help. As the rehearsal got going, I immediately began pitching idea after idea until Fit calmed me down and reminded me that we needed to keep Vince happy with some comedy stuff. Of course, even *then* I wanted to have a great match without comedy, but I accepted we were going to have to give Vince what he wanted. We planned out a couple of comedy spots for early in the match and then worked on everything else we wanted to do.

There was one spot planned where I was going to climb to the top of a stepladder and act like I was scared of heights, even though it was only a couple of feet off the ground. When I pointed out to Fit that I'd climbed a ladder about six times that size at *WrestleMania 23*, he leaned in and whispered, "We'll just forget that." That was the one moment in the match he really wanted me to take my time with. He reminded me of the advice he'd given me at the beginning of my run with WWE — that if I thought I was taking too long, I should wait another three seconds. That's a piece of advice I pass on to my students now. When you're in the ring, time flies by and it gets easy to rush without realizing, so you need to slow down or nothing you do will have any impact on the audience.

The more we talked about the match, the more excited I got. Even though I'd been working with Torito for a few weeks and done fine, I thought this was the night where I was really going to get the chance to step up and show everyone what I could do. Even though I was excited, I was nervous, too, mainly because of where we were. The show was in East Rutherford, New Jersey, and Jersey's a wrestling town where they'll viciously boo anything they don't like. I told Brian I was worried the crowd might turn on us and he just said, "It's all up to you guys." (Which didn't help my nerves.)

Most of the little people they brought in added a lot to the presentation. Instead of Michael Cole, Jerry Lawler, and JBL calling our match, we had Micro Cole, Jerry Smaller, and JB-Elf. The guy playing Jerry Smaller was Short Sleeve Sampson, one of my opponents in the first midget match I was involved in, and Micro Cole and JB-Elf were played by Shovelhead Chuck and Robbie the Giant, respectively. They all did a great job. The same couldn't be said for the guy they brought in as the ring announcer. He had notes right there in his hand and he still somehow got my name wrong. It was the biggest match of my career and the ring announcer called me Horn Woggle. Fortunately, I didn't hear it on the night because I was so focused on the match.

Ours was the first match of the evening and when you open a show, the crowd is usually hot for you. The crowd in Jersey on that night was no exception and, to my relief, they were into the match from the moment we came out. I'd felt energy from crowds before on shows when I'd been in segments or with another wrestler, but never like this — it was a singles match on a major show and I felt that energy focus on me more than I ever had before. It was the first time in the WWE that I felt fully respected by the audience. I'm sure they expected the match to be nothing but comedy spots, but after I'd done the kick-to-my-own-head and the I'm-too-short-to-jump-over-the-ropes spots to keep Vince happy, we gave the crowd hard work and a legitimate wrestling match, and they were with us all the way.

During the match, we pulled off some spots that looked great and were fun to do. I definitely never thought I'd get to do an elbow drop through a commentary desk in WWE, that's for sure. There was also a spot where Torito was going to jump onto Jinder while he was being held up by the Matadores, then they'd all fall off the apron and break a bunch of tables and ladders set up on the floor. I was concerned that someone might end up getting injured doing that. When Torito leapt outside and looked like he'd landed badly, I started worrying he was seriously hurt. Seconds later, he popped right up and carried on, absolutely fine. Drew got his own crazy spot where he did a flip over the top and right through a table on the floor. The match definitely wasn't just me and Torito — all of the guys worked so hard and did such a great job to make the match work as well as it did.

For me, the highlight came when I climbed up a stepladder and got ready to leap off at Torito. Taking Finlay's advice to wait a few extra seconds to really make the moment matter, I made sure to look around at the audience and take in the atmosphere of 15,907 people watching *my* singles match. All I could think was "We got them." It was two midgets wrestling in New Jersey — they should have hated us, but the fans were on their feet and every face I saw was smiling.

When we got to the back, Torito and I were given a standing ovation by the producers and management in Gorilla. We got the thumbs-up, big smile, and "great job" that Vince only gives out when you've hit a home run. Michael Hayes, Fit, Scott, and Brian were all there, on their feet, all applauding — that was the only time I got that sort of reaction backstage at a WWE show and it felt great. Before going back to the locker room, I rushed over to the props department and made sure they saved me a piece of one of the tables we broke. I had everyone in the match sign it, got it framed, and hung it in my office at home. It's there among all the other memorabilia, but that piece of table is particularly meaningful to me because the match itself was so special.

We got a lot of praise from the boys in the locker room for our efforts. I'd felt respected before but never like this — I felt like I'd genuinely surprised many of the other wrestlers. I also got more text messages from friends after that match than any other match I'd ever been involved in. When everything had quieted down and the main show was underway, I called Landon to see what he thought.

"Dad, that was awesome! You did so good! I'm so proud of you! But I just want to make sure you're okay." I thought that was amazing. Even though he was obviously excited about what he'd just seen, he still wanted to check up on me and make sure I wasn't hurt. I always made sure to check in with him whenever I did anything physical, just to tell him, "Dad's okay." He was never too worried because he'd met all of the guys before and knew I was friends with them. I never had to "officially" smarten him up about wrestling being a work because he figured it out by himself.

As *Extreme Rules* went on, I sat there in the locker room with my gear on, taking everything in. All the other guys from the match got changed and were getting ready to leave and I was there, chilling in my gear, staring off into space, still enjoying the moment. I knew it would be the defining moment of my in-ring career and I just didn't want that night to end. Although I won't watch most matches I've been in, I'll watch that one back, over and over again. I'm still very proud of it today.

A Short Story: Drinking Shorts

As you may have gathered by now, I enjoy an adult beverage now and then. My friend Al Snow wrote in his book that alcohol and midgets sometimes don't mix well . . . and he's right, to an extent. I can become any one of the seven dwarfs after a few drinks — Happy, Grumpy, Dopey. (Probably not Doc, though. I'm not sure I'm ever that smart.)

Torito doesn't regularly drink but that didn't stop me from trying to persuade him. "No, Dee-Lan," he'd always say (that was how he pronounced my name), until

I insisted we drink on the bus when we were on tour overseas. We got a bottle of tequila for him and a bottle of vodka for me, sat at the back of the bus, drank, and talked for the three-hour ride. His English was broken but good enough for us to communicate and we had a great time. On the last night of that tour, after finding out Torito also liked Bailey's, I put a full bottle on the table right in front of him in catering and told him we were going to finish it on the bus later. "Oh no, Dee-Lan, oh no," he said — but we did. The next day, he walked up to me looking a little worse for wear and the first thing he said was "Too much Bailey's."

It was funny to see Landon's reaction the first time he met Torito backstage. Without the mask, Torito looks like a short, regular guy. When we saw him, Torito shook Landon's hand, and as he was introducing himself, Landon was looking at him, then me, then him, then me, and clearly trying to figure it out. Once Torito had gone, he turned to me and just said, "He's kind of like you, huh?" When I told him yes, Landon processed this for a moment, said, "Oh. Okay," and that was that. To this day, whenever we see another little person, he'll say, "Look, he's like you, Dad," and that's it.

Traditionally in wrestling, a gimmick match is a way to finish a program, especially if the babyface goes over, as Torito had in our WeeLC match. Despite that, we were told we'd still be working together, which I took as a vote of confidence from the office. If they thought the audience wanted to see more of the little guys wrestling, that was fine by me. I felt confident we could deliver again, so I found Brian and asked if there was a spot for us on the next pay-per-view, *Payback*. Brian said he wasn't sure because that would be like doing things in reverse — we couldn't follow the crazy gimmick match with a regular wrestling match, so anything else would need to have something to make it stand out. First, I suggested doing a mini-cage match where the cage would be inside the ropes; instead of being the standard fifteen-foot height, this one would be eight or ten. Then, I pitched him on the idea of doing a hair versus mask match. If Torito lost, he'd have to take his mask off. If I lost, I'd have my head shaved. Brian liked that one. He pitched it to management at the next creative meeting and so did they. We were told we could do the match — but, once again, it would be on the pre-show.

Being put on the pre-show for a second month in a row felt like a slap in the face, partly because we'd already proven we could deliver a pay-per-view quality match and partly because there was something more on the line in this match. I found it frustrating but, in the end, it motivated us both to go out there and prove they'd missed out by not putting us on the main show. I was also happy that because Chicago isn't too far from Oshkosh, my dad was able to drive down and see me wrestle on a big show for the first time.

Torito and I knew we had a challenge ahead. Not only were we going to have to keep the fans entertained without being able to use tables, ladders, or chairs, but *Payback* was going to be held in Chicago, which is one of the only territories more hostile than New Jersey if they don't like what they're seeing. We realized we'd have to do everything we could to keep the crowd interested, so I decided I was going to try something no one had ever seen from me before — a moonsault. When I told Finlay about my plan at rehearsal, he said there was no way I could do it, practically daring me to give it a go. I hopped from the bottom rope to the middle, leapt into a backflip, and landed perfectly on my front. "Jesus, I thought you were going to break your neck," said Fit. We all agreed I could do it but Torito should move out of the way. Even though I'd lost a lot of weight, I didn't think landing on him with the moonsault would be a good idea for his physical well-being.

To make sure we had the best chance of getting the crowd on

our side, the Matadores had arranged for Torito to wear a Chicago Bulls jersey that night. They'd even had "2/3" put on the back of it, instead of Michael Jordan's "23." The crowd popped for it, but just as the bell rang, the referee started shouting at Torito to take the jersey off. "Vince hates it! He hates the jersey!" The problem was that it had been sewn into his outfit so it was there to stay.

Overall, I thought the match we had at *Payback* was even better than our first. We got to wrestle more. I did a flip dive to the outside through the ropes, and my moonsault came off well. The crowd seemed to enjoy the match and they definitely enjoyed the aftermath when, because I'd lost, I had my head shaved. I knew that would be the outcome from the moment I suggested the stipulation, so it didn't bother me at all. What *did* bother me was when they were shaving my head and the referee started yelling, "Get the eyebrows! Get the eyebrows!" Clearly someone backstage thought that would be funny and was telling the ref to make it happen. I screamed back at them all, "Not a chance! It's not happening!" My hair was fine but there was no way I was going to let them take my eyebrows. I couldn't have done much about it if they'd gone ahead but fortunately, I was spared that extra indignity.

When we got to the back, people seemed happy with what we'd done, although there wasn't as much of an overwhelming reaction as there'd been the month before, I guess because it wasn't such a surprise we'd pulled it off this time. Vince was still distracted and muttering to himself, "Bulls don't wear clothes, goddammit . . ."

Since the show had needed to move on, the Matadores and Torito had to take as much hair off me as they could in as short a time as possible. As a result, some of my head was bald and other areas had tufts of hair still sticking out. It looked like I had some kind of disease that had made my hair fall out in patches. Instead of getting rid of the rest on my own, I asked Fit if I should shave it or leave it. He said he'd check with Vince and later came back to tell me they wanted me to leave it patchy, at least until the end of the *Raw* taping the next night. I did as I was told, and we did a segment the next night where everyone got to laugh at my half-shaved head. After that, I asked if I could go shave now but again was told to leave it just a bit longer. Every show I was on, I'd ask if I could shave my head and every show, I'd be told to just wait. I knew they were ribbing me, but I wasn't going to sell it. I started re-shaving patches into my hair for the shows and then wearing a bandana or a baseball cap the rest of the time.

After three weeks, Michael Hayes finally came up to me and said, "All right, the rib's done, go shave your head."

I grinned back at him and said, "Are you sure you don't want me to keep it this way?"

CHAPTER 25

THE COW COSTUME

There was never any resolution to the program between 3MB and Los Matadores and Torito. Everything suddenly stopped when both Jinder and Drew were unexpectedly released from their contracts. There were a bunch of other releases that day but the one that absolutely shocked me was Drew. He was young, good-looking, and could already work a great match in the ring. Vince had initially taken a huge liking to him behind the scenes and seemed determined to make him one of "his guys." Unfortunately for Drew, somewhere along the way Vince lost interest and that was it. Vince can be like that. If something bothers or annoys him, he'll decide he doesn't want anything to do with it anymore.

As for Jinder, he looked great when he first came in but ended up doing the stereotypical evil foreigner gimmick. The fans had moved on from that trope, but I guess WWE hadn't. Both guys went off and worked hard to get more experience, then came back to the WWE in better spots with Jinder even becoming the WWE Champion.

Even though Jinder and Drew getting cut meant 3MB came to a sudden halt, the release that upset me the most was my buddy Curt Hawkins. Even though he hadn't been doing much on the shows and knew it was coming, it still sucked to see him lose his job. He's such a fan of the whole industry that I knew he'd be fine and enjoy himself on the indie circuit but I hated that I wasn't going to be able to see him all the time anymore.

WWE doesn't hold talent meetings to let people know when their co-workers have been cut; we find out at the same time as the rest of the world, when the news gets put up on the internet. After Drew and Jinder got released, I got a text right away from Heath saying, "What now?" I had no idea. Predictably, neither did the writers. When I went to them and asked if I was going to be kept with Heath on TV, they told me they didn't know. I asked what I was going to be doing next and they told me they didn't know that either.

In the end, they put Heath with my former "rookie," Titus O'Neil. Because Titus used to play football for the Florida Gators, and Gator rhymed with Slater, they became "Slater Gator." It wasn't a good fit for either of them. And if that gimmick wasn't dumb enough, they decided to put me with them in a gator outfit. No, not the football gear. A stupid alligator costume. The writers insisted I wear it on TV, and because people who saw it on TV would expect the same wherever I appeared with WWE, I had to wear it at live events, too. After one attempt to actually wrestle in the outfit, I went to the producers and told them I couldn't do anything because it was so big and bulky. The producers told me I could just wear my regular gear the next time but creative decided to play another rib on me, probably because I'd not cooperated with the gator costume. This time, they added me to the Los Matadores act by putting me in a cow outfit and calling me La Vaquita. They even made sure it was a female cow outfit with udders. Torito was the little bull, I was the little cow. For a couple of weeks, at least.

Having to wear the cow outfit really upset me and I came very close to quitting. It felt like it was just the writers amusing themselves at my expense. I can take a joke, but the whole thing just seemed mean-spirited. At that point, I'd been with the company for eight years and I thought I deserved a little more respect. I put the costume on just before I went out and took it off the moment I got to the back. I did the whole thing with a big, fake smile on my face and didn't give anyone the satisfaction of seeing that they got to me. Just like when they wouldn't let me shave my head, this wasn't something I was going to sell. The moment you sell a rib, they're going to keep on coming. If you ignore it, they'll get bored and move on. And, sure enough, after two weeks, creative got bored of the cow thing and I went back to sitting in catering, waiting, and hoping for someone to give me something to do (other than dress up as a cow or an alligator). Of all the places I wanted to be when I was feeling sorry for myself, catering was last on the list because I was still trying to keep my weight down.

After a month of being back on the bench, I'd had enough. I told Carrano not to bring me in unless there were plans to use me. It was costing the company money to fly me out and pay me. It was costing me money in gas, food, and hotels and sometimes all of that combined would actually be more than I'd make on my guarantee if I wasn't working on the shows. Above all else, I didn't have any interest in leaving my son to travel out to wherever they were only to spend the day in catering watching other people work. After my talk with Carrano, I stopped being brought in for TV and was hardly used at all on house shows. Even so, I didn't regret what I said then and don't regret it now, because that was how I truly felt. If they weren't going to use me, I didn't want to be there.

After months of sitting at home, I saw WWE was swinging through Green Bay for a *SmackDown* taping. I figured they might remember I was local and book me on the show, but I figured wrong.

Whether I was booked or not, I was planning to go along to see the boys. A few days before the show, I texted Road Dogg and asked if there was any way I could do the pre-show match. I said a lot of my friends and family would be in attendance and it would mean a lot to me to be able to do that. Brian told me he'd check and then, a while later, came back with the thumbs-up. On the morning of the show, he asked me who I wanted to work with, so I texted Heath Slater. Knowing how much the show meant to me, Heath was more than happy to do the match.

When I got to the arena for the show, I was walking around backstage with Landon when we saw Hunter and Vince heading toward us. The moment he saw Landon, Vince stepped in front of Hunter and asked, "Who's this guy? Who's this guy?" Vince hadn't really seen Landon since he'd been a baby and was so excited to meet him again. They talked for a few minutes, with Vince asking him about how school was going, if he was having fun, who his favorite wrestlers were . . . Vince was so great with him.

Working with Heath was great, too — he told me, "This is your night" and was open to doing whatever I wanted. I was announced as being from Oshkosh and got a great cheer for that. We had a fun match and I went over with my tadpole splash. My music played and I waved to one side of the audience.

Then I turned around.

Landon was right there in the ring with me.

He ran over to give me a huge hug and I started crying my eyes out immediately. When we finally let each other go, I said to him, "Do you want to go up on the buckles?" Landon did. He climbed the corner buckle and the crowd cheered. As I went to leave, Landon climbed *another* buckle and got another cheer. I didn't want to take up too much time with the dark match, so I told him, "Come on, let's go" and started walking up the ramp, figuring we'd get to the top, turn around, and get one more cheer before we went backstage. Halfway up the aisle, I realized Landon wasn't with me. I looked around and saw him going back over the barrier into his seat next to my dad. Later on, when I asked him why he didn't come to the back with me, he just told me, "I wasn't going to miss the rest of the show!"

When I went through the curtain, I noticed Dolph Ziggler standing there with a huge grin on his face. Earlier that day, he'd seen Landon and asked if he was going in the ring later. When I'd said no, Dolph said, "He has to, it's his hometown!" I didn't think anything more of it, but as soon as I saw Dolph's grin, I knew he was behind it. He'd gone to John Laurinaitis and Scott Aycock and arranged the whole thing. That's not the sort of thing everyone would do. I'd always considered Dolph one of my best friends in the business, but this made me realize that Dolph was an even better guy than I'd thought.

That whole night was incredible. I'd felt like the forgotten man for so long and I had a feeling I was on borrowed time with the company, so to be able to have that match and then that moment in the ring with my son in front of our hometown crowd and all our family and friends meant the world to me. It was the perfect end to my WWE career.

CHAPTER 26

THE PHONE CALL

The WWE drug-testing policy is unquestionably one of the strictest. The tests happen regularly and they're random. I was tested every three to four months. The urine test is "fully visualized," which means your underwear is pulled down all the way to the knees and your shirt needs to be lifted all the way up to your nipples while you're producing the sample. A representative of the testing company then watches you urinate. Believe it or not, the reason for this level of caution is because people across an array of sports have been known to use fake penises, bags of drug-free urine, and other methods to avoid providing the authentic sample that would get them caught out.

If you failed once, you would be closely monitored afterward — the company would put you on a schedule to be tested every other week. Failing because of marijuana use meant a fine of $1,000 when I started with the company and that went up to $2,500 some time later, but without suspension. If you tested positive for anything else, you would be suspended for thirty days the first time, sixty days the second, and then immediately terminated on a third offense. All offenses were reported on the WWE website, which just added to the embarrassment.

Most of the time, being tested was a straightforward, if unenjoyable, process but I had difficulties in delivering sometimes because there was no warning, so you might have peed just moments before you were told you had to produce a sample. During one show, I couldn't pee and had to wait and hope the urge would hit me. When it finally came, it wasn't just a pee I needed, so the tester had to watch me take a dump whilst I filled up the receptacle. Carrano got so mad at me for doing that but it was either that or not deliver, so I didn't have a choice.

If you were off the road, you'd get sent the test at home and take it in to a local lab, where you were given a three-hour time window to provide a sample in line with the same rules they observed at the arenas — the test still had to be "fully visualized." The first time I had to do this when I was off the road, I went over to Options Labs in Appleton for the test and still struggled. Even though I knew the test was coming, I couldn't pee on demand. It doesn't help the process when you have to let some guy look at your junk while you're trying to produce the goods. On that first occasion, I drank so much water that my stomach swelled up and made me look like I was pregnant but I made it in time, delivering at the two-and-a-half-hour mark.

A couple of months later, we went through the same process but this time, no matter how much water I drank or how hard I tried, I couldn't pee in the three-hour window. I went in and out of the testing room six times in those three hours and couldn't manage a single drop. I called the WWE's testing company as soon as time ran out and told them I hadn't managed to get them a sample. The guy I was speaking with didn't want to mark it as a failure, so he went to the person in charge of testing, who then called WWE to figure out what to do.

Later on, Carrano called me: "Well, you always wanted to make history in the business, kid. Now you did." The way he put that really annoyed me. "You're the first person in company history to get suspended for *not* pissing."

"Seriously?" I replied. "I'm getting suspended for *this*? I didn't fail the drug test, I failed to produce a sample. That's not the same thing."

He told me that, in their eyes, it *was* the same thing and had to be considered a Wellness Policy failure. I asked if I could at least make a statement because I didn't want people to jump to the conclusion that I was a drug user. The last thing I wanted was for that to go up all over the internet where my son would see it one day. Mark told me it was "highly recommended" that I didn't put out a statement. After we hung up, I sent long texts to both Hunter and talent relations, begging them that if they were going to report it online, they report it as a failure to provide a sample. I said I would take a hair follicle test if they wanted and pointed out that approach was far more accurate than a urine test and would pick up any substance usage over a longer period. That would definitely prove I hadn't violated their Wellness Policy.

Mark came back to me and said they were going to have to announce I was suspended and they would be wording it the same as if I had actually failed the drug test. I was angry. All I wanted them to do was say that I had "failed to produce a sample which, in accordance with the Wellness Policy, is a violation." I even went to the hospital on Monday and got the hair follicle test anyway, paying for it out of my own pocket to prove my point. As I knew it would, it came back negative for absolutely everything. I sent a photo of my test results to talent relations and then to Hunter, saying, "Here's the evidence — I'm clean." Nothing changed from their side and, soon enough, the internet was going crazy,

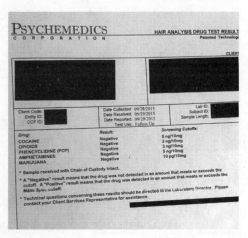

suggesting everything from me being a "recreational weed user" to a "full-blown cokehead."

Even after the court of public opinion had moved onto the next case, the Wellness Policy failure remained a black mark against me that wouldn't go away. I was on a date the next year and she didn't know anything about me or wrestling. When she put my name into Google, the second thing that came up was an article about my suspension and she jumped to the conclusion that I was a big drug user. That's not the only time I've encountered that problem and even after I explain the whole story, there's always an element of suspicion because of how WWE didn't accurately and fairly report what actually happened.

A Short Story: Falling Down

During my suspension, Hawkins got married and asked me to be in his wedding party as one of his groomsmen, alongside Tyson Kidd. One of the other guests that night was CM Punk. As far as I knew, things were fine between us, so I stopped by his table to check in. As I approached, I detected a "What does this guy want?" expression on his face. I was confused but still walked up to him, held out my hand, and said, "Hey man, how are you?" He stared at my hand and just replied, "Fine." I tried, "It's good to see you," which was met with a curt "Yep." I didn't understand what I'd done now, so I just said, "Okay, have a good night," and walked away. It was just weird, especially at a wedding.

Later that night, we'd planned a grand march down the stairs for the men in the wedding party, joining our partners at the bottom, then continuing the procession into the hall. Given my stature and the fact that alcohol was flowing freely, everyone thought I'd be hammered by that point, so I thought I'd play it up and pretend to fall down the stairs. I'd actually only had one glass of wine during the entire evening, and I can definitely handle plenty more than that. I told Hawkins, Tyson, and a couple of the other groomsmen before I did my trick, so that they wouldn't freak out when I fell.

Punk was filming the procession on his phone and after I did my fall, he posted it on Twitter. Before long, it became "public knowledge" that I was wasted and falling down stairs at a wedding. Shortly after that, thanks to Punk putting something that should have stayed private on a public forum, I got a call from WWE HQ, asking how I could embarrass the company like that.

WrestleMania 32 was going to be held in Dallas, Texas, and even though I thought it was unlikely I'd be used on the show, I was excited to take Landon to *'Mania* now he was old enough to really appreciate it. I sent a text to the travel department to see if they had my bookings, but was disappointed to get a message back saying, "As of now, you're not on the list." I texted Carrano directly moments later to ask what was going on and got nothing back. I left it a week, then sent another text but again there was no reply. After another week, I texted Mark, saying "Hey bud, I still haven't heard from you. I need to see if I'm taking Landon out of school. As a dad, I'd really like to bring him to *'Mania*." All I got back was "Currently, you're not on the list." I wrote back, asking if he was joking and he replied, "There are plenty of others who won't be there either." I couldn't believe what I was reading. I texted one more time, saying I just wanted to be able to give my son his first true *WrestleMania* experience. No reply.

The week after that, I wrote a long message to Mark, saying I'd do whatever Axxess sessions or Be a STAR appearances they wanted, even offering to pay for my own flight as long I could stay at the *'Mania* hotel and take Landon to the show. Still no reply.

Two weeks before *WrestleMania*, I sent another text to Carrano that simply said, "Can I come?"

I got a reply this time.

"You're still not on the list. I'm working on it though." I didn't understand it. I'd been with WWE for almost a decade and I wasn't allowed to go to the biggest show of the year, even though everyone in developmental was always brought in for it? What made it worse was that I knew Mark was *in charge* of the list. With one week to go before 'Mania, I sent Mark one more plea and, once again, he ignored me. I wasn't just pissed off because I wasn't getting to take Landon to *WrestleMania*, I was pissed off because of how Mark was behaving. He and I had traveled together back when he was John Laurinaitis's assistant and we'd had some great times. As he'd got more senior in the company, he'd become more removed and I understood that — he was the one telling the boys they were doing a 4 a.m. media day, or that they were suspended or fired. It's a tough job and you can't still be one of the boys when you're doing it. Even so, I found it upsetting that he was ignoring me.

That ended up being the first *WrestleMania* I didn't attend since I'd joined WWE. To be honest, I probably had more fun watching it from home than I would have had in Dallas. I had a bunch of friends over and we had a great time, Landon included. Still, I knew the fact I hadn't been brought in for 'Mania was a bad sign for my future with the company. I knew *the call* would come sooner than later.

On May 6, as I was getting Landon ready for school, I got a text from Binder. It read,

Today 6:56 AM

Binder

> Rumor mill says today is the big "cleaning" day at wwe. No matter what happens stay positive and know that we all are so extremely proud of you and what you have accomplished. Love you buddy

At 9:15 a.m., my phone rang. Usually, calls from WWE offices come from a blocked number but, this time, my screen read "Mark Carrano." This was it. I picked up.

"Hey Dylan. I hate to make this call . . ." he began. "There are a bunch of releases being made today, and you're on the list. I'm sorry."

I told him I'd been sitting home for a year and a half, so it wasn't unexpected.

"I know," he said. "But it still sucks."

That's when I started crying. I thought of everything I'd done for the last ten years, the travel, the hard work, the successes, and the missed opportunities. Above all else, I was hit by the worry that I wouldn't be able to provide for my son. It was overwhelming.

Mark told me I'd be paid for ninety days and I could work any independent show I wanted in that time, providing I didn't make any PPV or TV appearances. He also told me the door wasn't shut and he was sure I'd be back someday.

When I thanked him, he replied, "No, thank *you*, Dylan. Thank you for all the time you spent hanging out with me and thank you for everything you've done for the company. You've touched so many people's lives here and meant so much to so many fans. The company doesn't forget things like that. When I saw your name on the list, it hurt me to know I'd have to make this call. You're one of the good guys and everyone here knows it."

At the beginning of the call, it felt like he was just going through the motions but, by the end, he did sound genuinely upset to have to let me go. It was like I had my friend back for thirty seconds. We said our goodbyes and I sat on the floor of my living room, slumped against my couch, bawling my eyes out. Even though I'd known it was coming, part of me was still surprised it had actually happened. Truth be told, I'd thought I would be with WWE in some form for the rest of my career, since I didn't think they'd fire a midget. I've never wanted to be treated differently than any normal-sized person, but this was one of those situations where I'd secretly hoped my condition might end up being to my advantage.

Who knows — maybe it was part of the reason they'd kept me around for so long in the first place. In the end, they treated me the same as everyone else — I knew it was just business but that didn't make it hurt any less.

I was still crying when I called Hawkins to let him know I'd been released. He told me everything was going to be fine. He said, "There's life after this," and there was no reason to feel sorry for myself. He'd been having a great time and making good money on the indie scene. He told me to give him an hour — he'd help me set things up and we'd be back together on the road, having a great time.

I wasn't looking forward to calling my dad with the news. I felt like, somehow, I'd let him down. I put it off by calling Weimer and Lori first, both of whom were sympathetic and supportive but told me I needed to call my dad. I knew they were right, so I picked up the phone again — still crying — and dialed his number. Dad was supportive as always. When I told him that I was worried about providing for Landon, he told me to get out there and do some independent shows to see if doing it by myself would work out. If it did, great. If not, I could always find another way to make money. When we finished the call, he told me he loved me and was proud to be my dad. I really needed to hear that right then. He told me that he'd never imagined I'd have a ten-year run with WWE and he was so proud that I'd lived out the dreams I had as a kid.

I told Dad I loved him, too, and we got off the phone. I'd finished crying by then.

Later, I texted Stephanie McMahon and said, "I just want to let you know how much I appreciate what you and your family has given me over the past ten years. You've let a four-year-old kid live his dream and made his son incredibly proud of his dad." I got a reply from her saying, "That means a lot to me, Dylan — I don't ever get this kind of text. You're always welcome here, you are part of our family and so is your son."

True to his word, Hawkins called me back less than an hour after we'd spoken and told me he'd already got me booked for thirteen dates. That's not just a *good* friend — that's a *best* friend. I knew then that he'd been right. I was going to be fine.

A Short Story: The Winner

I can't say enough about Curt Hawkins. As an in-ring performer, he's one of the best. He's made a career out of making other people look better, so I don't think most fans realize just how fantastic he is between the ropes. He cares so much about being as good as he can be. I still smile when I remember *The Great American Bash 2008*, when Hawkins and Ryder won the Tag Team Title in a four-way match that also involved me and Finlay. That was such a special night for them both because it was so near Long Island, so all their family and friends — including Mikey Whipwreck, who trained them both — got to see them achieve their dream of becoming champions in WWE.

Although Hawkins is a great wrestler, he's an even better human being. Along with Kofi, he's been the best support system imaginable throughout my wrestling career, whether I was dealing with personal or professional issues. He was the first person I thought to call after I got released. Even now, he'll be the first person I go to when I need career advice. He brings me in regularly for his Create A Pro Wrestling shows, and he and his wife always make me feel welcome at their house.

Back when I was with WWE, whenever Kofi, Hawkins, and I went to a restaurant, we'd order, then Kofi and I would slide out from the table to go call home and check in with our kids. They were our "Team Dad" calls and Hawkins would be stuck at the table by himself, waiting for the order to come or for us to get back.

In late 2016, Kofi and I both got a text from him saying, "Hey guys — I just want you to know soon there's going to be a new member of Team Dad." It was one of the best texts I've ever got. Hawkins is a natural and he loves being a dad. I'll get photos and videos of his daughter, Mackenzie, all the time. He even took some inspiration from me when it came to his WWE Elite action figure. Knowing that I'd had a figure come out which had my tattoos of Landon's name and handprints, he asked the guys at Mattel if they could include the tattoo of his daughter's name that he has on his arm. They did — and, for that reason, it's one of my favorite figures. I'm so happy he has a beautiful family. He deserves every piece of his happiness and more.

The new and improved Team Dad.

CHAPTER 27

THE RESURRECTION

The thought of going back on the independent wrestling scene was intimidating, but I quickly realized the upside could be considerable. I would have much more control over my own schedule as well as how I was presented and what I did on shows. It also meant I was going to be more prominent on the shows I was on, instead of being in a one-minute backstage segment — and I definitely wouldn't ever be brought in to sit around in catering again. Since hitting the indies, I've found that my stature has turned out to be a huge advantage, since there has only really been one well-known midget wrestler on the U.S. wrestling scene in the last couple of decades other than me and Torito. Because Dink didn't make much sense without Doink the Clown (plus it would have been tough for him to get around WWE trademark issues because the costume and face paint was so iconic), he didn't get a huge amount of indie bookings from what I gather. When WWE released Torito, he went back to doing a lot of work in Mexico, so I ended up as the big fish of little guys in the little American pond, so to speak.

The first thing I had to decide was what I was going to call myself. Hornswoggle or Little (or L'il) Bastard weren't options because WWE owns the trademarks, meaning I couldn't promote myself using any of the names by which I was most widely known. They didn't copyright "Swoggle" though and, since a lot of the boys call me that anyway, it seemed an obvious choice. After that came merchandise. Unless you're an ultra-hot indie act, you're not going to sell as much merch on the independents as you would when you've got the global platform of WWE behind you, but you're going to get a higher percentage on profits and you get full control over what gets made, allowing you to avoid shirts featuring a picture of you clutching a huge penis, for instance. (Although Joey Ryan might well be able to make that work.)

Starting out on the indies gave me a great chance to update my look. One of Hawkins's first questions to me about working indie shows was "You're not going to wear your shitty nurse pants, are you?" I called Robert Adams at Main Event Gear, the guy who had made my second and third pairs of pants for my 3MB run and is still making great stuff for WWE superstars today. I told Robert I needed some new stuff within two weeks and he got me three pairs of pants in less than a week. I work in those and one of the T-shirts I've designed and sell at merchandise stands (and on ProWrestlingTees.com).

The first shirt design I came up with was one that said King of Small Style, playing on Shinsuke Nakamura's King of Strong Style moniker. After that, I wanted to use some lyrics from a New Found Glory song, so I asked Weimer to make some suggestions. An hour later, he came back to me with "Watch My Resurrection" — since I was trying to reinvent myself on the indie scene, I thought that was perfect. My buddies from WWE were less enthusiastic, and Zack Ryder went out of his way to ask me if I was trying to market myself as the midget Jesus. I've also had a Muppet-style shirt, Swogplex City, and an eight-bit NES-style shirt.

That's what I will wear. What I won't wear anymore, unless a promoter *really* pushes for it, is the old leprechaun outfit. First, it doesn't fit me comfortably anymore (as Corey Graves kindly observed at the *Greatest Royal Rumble*); second, if the show ends up on TV or online, I could end up in hot water for looking too much like a WWE-trademarked character; and, third, I don't want my WWE gimmicks to be all I'm remembered for. I'd like to show *some* wrestling fans that there's more to me than Hornswoggle.

Right after my WWE release, I couldn't wait to get back on the road because I was going to be doing everything with Hawkins. Joey Ryan and Candice LeRae were having a great run on the indies as a mixed gender team and we figured doing a one-and-a-half men gimmick could make us a similar offbeat attraction. People seemed to like the idea and, before long, we had bookings lined up across the country for months. Everything since my WWE release had been almost too easy, so I knew something had to go wrong. The morning after our second indie show as a team, Hawkins's phone rang as we were ordering breakfast. He took the call outside while I waited for our food and, once he came back in, it was clear there was something on his mind. He was like that all day until we got to the show, when he finally said, "I've got to talk to you." I knew exactly what was coming and said, "You got hired, didn't you?"

He told me WWE had called him and offered him a deal. They were just about to do another brand split and they brought back several guys to fill out the two separate rosters. It didn't make sense to me that if they were about to split the brands, they'd released so many people (including me) just a couple of months earlier, but I guess they were using it as an opportunity to freshen up the roster. I heard that Vince specifically asked for Hawkins. That's a hell of a compliment. No one else in the company had brought Hawkins up as a potential re-hire but Vince remembered him and insisted they go get him because he's such a good hand. He was doing a losing-streak gimmick for a long time after he went back, and I've heard a lot of people saying he would have been better staying on the indies but that's just stupid. He's being used on every show, getting on TV and making a great living for his family. Working for WWE is the best money you can make in wrestling and anyone who says they wouldn't go back is lying.

When Hawkins told me he was going back, I was genuinely happy for him, especially since he had a kid on the way but, selfishly, I was disappointed because it meant I wouldn't get to travel the country with my best friend. It made me nervous, too, because I didn't know if I'd be able to manage without him. He'd been so instrumental in helping me get booked, setting my prices, and getting me started. Fortunately, I was worrying for no reason. Even though the son of a bitch left me on my own, I've worked for and with some great people on the indie scene.

For instance, I worked for Jeff Jarrett's Global Force Wrestling group when they were doing shows at minor league baseball stadiums. Their shows were fun and Jeff and Karen Jarrett took great care of me, making sure I had whatever I needed and putting me up in good hotels.

The first company I worked for after my WWE release was AIW out of Cleveland. Hawkins got in touch with Chandler Biggins and John Thorne, who ran the company, and found out they were interested in bringing us in for their tournament weekend. Since then, AIW has become a second home for me, and John has become a good friend. Biggins was a great guy who always went to bat for me, bringing me in for every show, and I was devastated when he passed away in 2017.

Another guy I've become great friends with and always look forward to working for is Pat Buck. Pat's WrestlePro promotion has become one of my priorities. He also runs Create A Pro Wrestling schools with Hawkins out of New Jersey and Hicksville, NY, and I've learned so much from him about putting shows together and running my own wrestling school.

I even had a brief run in TNA when I was brought in for the *Total Nonstop Deletion* event. Even though their attempt to compete with

WWE hadn't worked out, TNA was still around at the end of 2016, getting some positive buzz around Matt Hardy. Matt had come up with the gimmick that he was insane, and this was built up to a segment with his brother Jeff that was shot at their home. It was presented more as a short film than a wrestling match. I thought it was going to be awful. But Weimer forced me to watch and I actually enjoyed it. It was different enough and good enough to get a lot of attention and led to a full TV episode. During this show, the main event was a Tag Team Apocalypto match, and I was invited to come in as Rockstar Spud's surprise partner.

On the day we filmed the match, I flew out to the Hardy compound in North Carolina. It was a long, strange day. I got there at 12:30 p.m. but didn't shoot my first segment until 8 p.m. and didn't wrap my part until 2 a.m. I enjoyed the shoot, but it reminded me a lot of WWE TV tapings in that you'd wait around for hours to be on camera for only a few minutes. Because I'd started getting used to the indie scene, sitting around for hours to tape a segment seemed like something I'd done in another lifetime.

I'd met Rockstar Spud a year before at an independent show in Milwaukee and we'd hit it off immediately. For *Total Nonstop Deletion*, we shot a scene with Abyss and Crazzy Steve where Spud introduced me, then later I did some comedy stuff with Bobby Lashley and, finally, an in-ring segment where I turned on Spud for patting me on the head. The most difficult part of the shoot was when I went to the top rope for my tadpole splash and realized I couldn't get up there because the six-sided ring had corners with angles that were too wide for me. It was weird *filming* a wrestling match rather than *having* a wrestling match — the directors would keep stopping things and saying, "We'll do that again from a different angle" or "We're just going to change cameras."

That was supposed to be the end of my involvement with TNA but when I was traveling back from that taping, I sent Jeremy Borash at the TNA office a text to thank him for the opportunity and say I'd work with Spud any time they wanted me to. He texted me back later that week, saying that they wanted to bring me in for another set of tapings. They flew me down to Orlando for three days and we filmed several weeks of TV. On the final day, Spud ran out to attack me and caught me right above my eyebrow with one of his dress shoes.

Immediately, I felt my face get warm and put my hand up against my forehead. When I pulled it away, it was covered in blood. I looked down and saw that I was dripping on the ground, then looked up at Spud who just froze and said, "Oh no, mate . . . I'm sorry" right on camera. I wouldn't have minded apart from two things — first, I was going on a Disney vacation three days later and was now going to have a big ugly cut in all the pictures, and second, it meant I was going to have to have stitches and I *hate* needles. That was the first time I'd ever needed stitches and I did not enjoy it. As I was heading to my car to leave, my cut started dripping again, so I had to find the doctor, have him take the stitches out, and start over. Spud and Karen Jarrett stayed with me the whole time.

This was all supposed to lead up to a street fight between me and Spud at *Slammiversary*, but there ended up being a problem with Spud's work visa, so we had to delay the match and do it at a TNA taping in India. That was an awful trip. The flights were thirty hours, the food was terrible, everything was dirty, there were wild dogs running around everywhere, and the tapings were in a studio with three or four hundred actors they'd hired to be the audience rather than in front of wrestling fans. I'm glad I got to tick "go to India" off my bucket list, but it wasn't fun at all.

Traveling overseas as an independent wrestler was a big deal for me. It ended up being an amazing experience and the promoter, Ben Auld of Southside Wrestling in the U.K., took great care of me. Everyone had told me that he was a good guy and they were right. He used me in tag matches, which is definitely the best thing to do with me if there isn't another little person on the show. As much as I love working with normal-sized guys, it's tough to keep it looking believable. Tag matches work best because I can come in, do some actual wrestling, and get out before things start looking too far-fetched. Ironically, after being dead set against them my whole career, I find myself doing a lot of midget comedy spots now because they get such a great reaction from the audience. In the end, you've got to give the crowd what they want to see. I'll make sure to do as much actual wrestling as I can do though, and I can do most things, although I still can't take hip tosses or vertical suplexes.

Like Ben, most of the indie promoters understand what to do with me — they know I'm going to get some attention for their show, sell some tickets, and make some money for them at meet-and-greets or doing photos, and give their fans a chance to see a former WWE superstar up close at a fraction of the price of a WWE ticket. I feel conflicted sometimes because, as a promoter myself, I want people to come in and work hard for me to impress our fans. But, at the same time, I know that fans don't come to see me work the regular indie high-spot match — they come to see my great ass bite and decent splash. They know they're not going to get a five-star match from me. That said, a lot of people have been pleasantly surprised with what I can do in the ring — especially when I'm in there with someone of a similar stature.

Robbie the Giant, the guy who played JB-Elf during my WeeLC match, was the first little person I worked with after my release. We were both worried about it because we didn't know what to expect from each other, but we both wanted to wrestle instead of do comedy, and we tore it down, doing things you wouldn't expect from your run-of-the-mill midget match. I've pushed to wrestle him as much as I can since then because he's so much fun to work with.

Even though Hawkins and I never got to do a one-and-a-half men gimmick versus Joey Ryan and Candice LeRae, I did get to work one singles match with Joey and it was a blast. He's one of the best-known independent wrestlers because of what has come to be known as "the dick spot," a move where his opponent ends up grabbing Joey's groinal area (through his trunks — not under them.

Even wrestling has boundaries . . .) and then he uses his apparently powerful penis to flip them over. When we were talking through what we were going to do, I thought it was funny that he didn't say "Do you want to do the dick spot?" but instead said, "So, how are we getting into the dick spot?" Just like people want to see the midget bite an ass, it's become expected that Joey will do the dick spot. We took it one step further and did an old-school Hogan/Warrior test of strength — with our dicks. The crowd wasn't expecting that, so it got a great reaction. Of course, Joey won.

(And for anyone reading that last paragraph who hasn't seen what I'm talking about, please go find it on YouTube. It's definitely weird but nowhere near as bad as you're probably thinking . . .)

The two guys at the very top of my post-WWE wish list were Kikutaro and Grado, and I've managed to wrestle them both now. I never wanted the typical dream match with Kota Ibushi or that sort of wrestler, because I know a match with me wouldn't really work. The guys who can mix wrestling with comedy — those are the people I'm going to work best with. Kikutaro, a fun Japanese guy who is one of the best known comedy wrestlers in the world, is just awesome to work with. Grado is a wildman from Glasgow who loves to have a few drinks. I can barely understand him because of his accent (Drew McIntyre's got nothing on Grado for a thick Scottish accent) but he's so funny, and great to work with — my match with him was one of those times where I got to the back and I couldn't stop grinning about what we'd just done.

There are a few guys who I was around a little when I was with WWE, but I've got to know them much better on the indie scene. Bob Holly is one of them and now that know him properly, I can definitely say he's a great guy. On one of the tours I did in the U.K., he and I were picked up by a promoter to go to a show. The car wasn't big at all and two of the promoter's students were going to be sitting in the back with me, all of us with our bags on our laps, for six hours. Bob flipped out at this guy for putting me in that situation and really stood up for me. I thought that was very cool of him.

Billy Gunn is another guy I've got to know very well on the indie scene. We played gin a few times when we were in WWE and this led to some smack-talk. That kept escalating to the point where, now, I make it one of my purposes in life to annoy him as much as possible. It started out when I was on an AIW show with him and saw they had Billy Gunn action figures on the merch table. I got one of them and put it in his bag without him seeing. When I got to the back after the show had finished, I found him vaping, sitting directly across from the figure as if they were having a conversation. He looked up at me and said, "I know you did this . . ." Since then, I make sure to hide an action figure in his bag whenever I see him. It's so easy to get him wound up. Sometimes I'll call him Monty (which he *hates*); other times, if I'm tagging with him, I'll stand on the apron and do the Rockabilly dance the whole time or make little gun noises to remind him of his Smoking Gunns days. In a battle royal we were in, I saw him on the mat, so I pounced on him like a lion and stuck my fingers up his nose. I have no idea why I did it, but he wasn't pleased. On another show, I set it up so that after he won his match, the "Ass Man" music he likes to use stopped abruptly and was replaced with the "You Look So Good to Me" music that he used when he was in an "are they/aren't they?" gimmick with Chuck Palumbo. He chased me around the building for pulling that stunt. I love that guy but it's hard to stop ribbing him because it's *so* much fun.

The indies can be humbling. I was on a show in Indiana a while back where the whole thing had been organized and marketed so badly that it drew seven people. Seven. That's not a typo. That's two less than the crowd that made me almost call it a career just before I got that call from Ken, inviting me in to WWE. After a decade in WWE, performing to houses of thousands and, sometimes, tens of thousands, I was back to single digit crowds. There were more wrestlers in the locker room than there were paying customers. It's just something that happens for whatever reason and you can't overthink it or let it get to you. Whenever a show turns out like that, I'll take a picture and send it to Binder and Weimer, saying, "Remember when I was on *WrestleMania*?"

The most nervous I've been since hitting the indie scene was the week before *WrestleMania 33*. I was booked to appear on several shows around Orlando during the time when WWE was running events there, too. For the first time, I'd be in the same place as all of the WWE crew but I wouldn't be at any of the shows. I would be working in front of 125 people at a nightclub while the guys still in WWE would be working in front of 75,000 people in a stadium. I don't often open up about my feelings to my friends in wrestling,

With Hawkins, Ryder, and the Ringside Collectibles crew after the Major Wrestling Figure Podcast *holiday charity toy drive.*

but I did tell Hawkins that I was worried it was going to be the most upsetting week of my life. Hawkins had done a similar thing during *WrestleMania* week for the two years he'd been away from WWE and he was very reassuring, telling me, "It's not like Axxess where people will say, 'Seth Rollins has got an hour-long line for autographs but Hornswoggle's only got a five-minute line — let's go see *him*.' The WrestleCon events might have more than 100 wrestlers there, so the fans only come to your table because they specifically want to meet *you*." He assured me that '*Mania* week is the biggest and best week of the year for an indie wrestler and he was right. It turned out to be one of the most enjoyable weeks I've had since leaving WWE. I wrestled four times in three days (including matches with Joey and Grado), won a title twice (the DDT Ironman Heavymetalweight Championship), held it for about thirty-six seconds total, went to two huge signings (where I got to plant another action figure in Billy Gunn's bag), and got to see a bunch of my friends from WWE at Zack Ryder's place.

A Short Story: Zack Doesn't Party

Zack insisted that the gathering at his house was a "get together among friends" and definitely not a party. Whatever he wants to call it, I had a blast. There were people there I hadn't seen in three years and we picked up as if we'd never been apart. Hawkins was there, obviously, along with Dolph, Miz, Rusev, and Tyson and Natalya. Kofi no-showed but that was understandable since his wife and baby boy had flown in that evening, so he couldn't exactly blow them off just so he could come out to a ~~party~~ get-together.

Zack's place is a beautiful, newly built house in Orlando and he enjoyed showing us around rooms with no furniture and no pictures on the walls — but a $10,000 Ghostbusters pinball machine, a "real" proton pack, and a life-sized Han Solo frozen in carbonite. I think Zack's greatest fear is having kids because then he'll have to share his toys.

At that party, Hawkins and I found Zack's Internet Championship belt and decided it would be a good idea to take a picture of me, naked, with the belt strategically positioned à la Shawn Michaels's *Playgirl* photo shoot. Zack knew nothing about this until the picture was texted to him the next day.

Even now, hardly a day goes by where I don't get some form of insulting text from him, but after I got released, he laid off the insults for the day and messaged me to say he was sorry it happened and felt really bad because I was one of the best guys in the locker room. That text meant a lot, even if he did go back to calling me a fat midget within twenty-four hours.

CHAPTER 28

THE PROMOTER

About a year after I'd been released, I was invited to a WWE show, so they could film a "Where are they now?" piece for WWE.com. I was of two minds about doing it. I knew it would be great to see all my friends, but I didn't want to be one of those guys that shows up and makes everyone think, "He just showed up looking for a job." In the end, I went and everyone I saw that day was awesome.

I don't know if it was caused by being at a WWE show when I wasn't part of the company, but I went through a down time around then. I had a lull in bookings and I just didn't want to leave my house. I called up Hawkins and he told me that everyone goes through it. He said I needed to remember the positives — I wasn't dealing with the behind-the-scenes bullshit, I was setting my own schedule and having fun in the ring, and *that's* what I got into the business for. I kicked out and got back on with it, and I've come to accept there are going to be ups and downs. I still enjoy wrestling very much but when the booking lull comes in December and January, I find myself thinking, "Maybe it's time for a real job." And then it passes.

I also have my own wrestling company to run.

I don't think many people know that I've been the owner of a wrestling company for over a decade now, although I've only promoted it for half that time. I bought ACW back in 2008 and ran it while I was on the road with WWE. I found it was difficult to break even in the early days because even though we were drawing decent houses, three to four hundred people, everyone had their hand in the till. This guy wanted money for photos and that guy to film the show and another to design the cases for the DVDs . . . because I was in WWE, everyone assumed they could get a quick payday. In their minds, it wasn't ACW footing the bill, it was Hornswoggle. We were making $4,000 on a show and spending at least $5,000. I probably lost $20,000 of my own money during that run. The truth is I didn't buy the company as a business investment; I bought it as something fun to do for me and my friends.

When Landon came along, I realized I couldn't afford to throw money away any longer, so I told the others I had to stop. Binder was *pissed* and we didn't talk for a couple of months after ACW closed. I didn't like falling out with one of my best friends, but I had to do what I thought was right for my family. He came around in the end.

In late 2013, when I wasn't getting booked regularly by WWE, it occurred to me that the guy who used to run independent shows in Oshkosh had given up. It seemed like a good time to start ACW back up, so I called a meeting of "the suits" and we put an event together that ended up drawing 250 people. I'd expected to get no more than 100 for that return show, so I was pleasantly surprised. After that, we started running every three months and being careful with the business side of things, so we would at least cover our costs. It was great to be able to give everyone in Oshkosh something to do other than go to bars, and also put on a form of family-friendly entertainment that parents could share with their kids.

When I came off the road in 2015, I started thinking about opening an ACW wrestling school. Even though I knew some people would say, "Why would I want a midget training me?" I knew there would be people who understood that I could pass on everything I'd learned from working for so long with Finlay and with all-time top ten wrestlers like the Undertaker and Shawn Michaels. There's only so much I'd be able to do in the ring, but I could teach holds and psychology, and Binder could do everything between the ropes. We found a pole barn near Fond du Lac and that was great to start with, until it got to winter. Wisconsin winters aren't much fun, especially if you're trying to learn how to wrestle in a barn. We looked around and found the perfect site — a warehouse in Oshkosh that used to be a boat factory. We moved there, and everything was going great until I got a text saying, "There's a huge fire by your camp." It turns out that it *was* our training academy and that it had been completely burned to the ground. When we got there, it was just like I was a kid again, looking at what used to be my family home. We couldn't even get anywhere near the building. This time, instead of my toy wrestling federation being inside, my real wrestling promotion had burned to the ground. This was just five days before we were bringing in Tommy Dreamer for our second anniversary show. Three months later, we'd managed to get a new ring and found another place, an old auto body shop, and started up the school again. It's still going now and it's great when you get people coming through who really want to succeed and are willing to do the work to make it happen. Helping them along is so rewarding.

The best part of being a promoter is when things go better than anticipated. I always imagine the worst-case scenario, at least that way I'll be happy if we overachieve. We ran our first WrestlingCon megashow in 2017 that drew more than 1,000 people, which was considerably more than I thought we'd get. I worked with Torito, and we had Carlito, Ken Kennedy, Kevin Thorn, and Vickie Guerrero on the show, with Bret Hart as the headliner. Even eighteen years after his in-ring career ended, the queue for his meet-and-greet was more than three hours long.

That led to what I hope will be a yearly event for us. In 2018, we moved the event to a newly built basketball arena in Oshkosh. The owners had heard a lot of buzz about ACW and approached us about using their facility. We brought in Ryback, MVP, Scott Steiner, Jeff Jarrett, Joey Ryan, Hurricane, and the Sandman. I worked in an eight-man tag with Binder, Hurricane, and one of my best friends-turned-student, "Big Cat" Chris Baugher against four of our other students. That event went better than I ever could have imagined — we ended up drawing 2,500 people (which was more than *SmackDown* drew when they were in Green Bay earlier that year) and the show was great. Ryback even told me the match he had that night was in his best three matches on the indie scene.

The business keeps growing. The year after we started back up, we began running shows once every two months and, more recently, one each month. Personally, I'd like to go back to running every two months because I don't want to oversaturate the market, but maybe I'm being overly cautious. So long as our audience is coming back for more, I'm happy.

I still hear from WWE now and then. I was asked to come in for *WrestleMania 34* and be one of the little people dressed as pancakes for the New Day's entrance — an offer I declined. Kofi was pissed — well, as pissed as Kofi ever gets — telling me, "The one time I pushed for you, you big-leagued us!" I was going to be in the area anyway, because I was on a couple of shows and a couple of signings in the few days before 'Mania, but I chose not to do it because, well, I didn't want to be a pancake. I also didn't want to come back to WWE TV as one of a bunch of midgets, especially if I was the only recognizable one. And, finally, it actually would have *cost me* money. I would have had to change my flight, which would have cost me $800 and WWE was only going to pay me $500 for the appearance, so I would have been $300 out of pocket. I might have done that if I was ten years younger, but as a single dad I had to make a grown-up decision.

Before I was asked to be a human *WrestleMania* pancake, I'd been asked to fly to Saudi Arabia to appear on the WWE *Greatest Royal Rumble* event, which was a huge deal, literally and figuratively, for the company. I was told they wanted a match between me and Torito, but Torito was already booked elsewhere, so I was asked to recommend another little person wrestler. I told them to book Robbie the Giant, which they did.

Shortly after I was asked to do the Saudi show, I let Hawkins know the news. One of the first things he said was "You're going to have to cut and bleach your hair." I really didn't want to do that again but the more Hawkins pointed out that WWE didn't want Indie-Dylan, they wanted Hornswoggle, the more I realized he was right. As always, he was being logical and looking out for me. He knew this would be a big opportunity and didn't want me to blow it by being stubborn.

Even though it was a great chance to get my face back on WWE TV and a hell of a payday, I nearly canceled at the last minute. Unexpectedly, my dad had to go in to hospital for a heart surgery that he hadn't told me about because he knew that if he did, I would refuse to go to Saudi Arabia. Instead, Dorothy called to let me know, and I'm glad she did because I would have been so angry if Dad had gone in for surgery without me knowing. My immediate reaction was exactly what he'd expected — "I'm not going anywhere." However, after I'd talked it through with Dorothy, I agreed to fly to Detroit and find out how things were — if they were fine, I'd go on the rest of the way, but if there were any complications, I'd turn around and come right back home.

He came through the surgery fine, so I flew the eight hours from Detroit to Paris, had a two-hour layover, and then five-hour flight to Saudi. When I landed, there was a car waiting for me that took me straight to the hotel where I met up with a bunch of the boys. The next morning, I was told a car had been arranged to take me to the show, but I said I'd prefer to go on the bus with the boys just like the old days.

When we got to the arena, after going through all the security checks, Finlay came over and told me, "I think your match has been canceled." When I asked why, he told me they were worried about the show running long. I couldn't help pointing out that it was a six-hour show with another hour for the pre-show! I was furious that I'd left home — with my dad in the hospital — and done all that travel for nothing. Finlay told me he'd try to get me something else and, an hour later, he told me I was in the fifty-man Rumble match. That was better, but I felt terrible for Robbie, who didn't get to be on the show.

A few weeks before the event, I'd been told, "Bring your leprechaun gear." On the day of the show, I was told they wanted me to do my tadpole splash. My weight caused problems with both of those requests. At the beginning of my run with WWE, I could eat and drink what I wanted, never go to the gym, and the scales wouldn't go above 130. Now, I go to the gym four days a week and I can't remember the last time I saw 150-something staring back when I weigh myself. I guess it must be age catching up with me (combined with my enjoyment of the occasional adult beverage).

The last time I'd worn the leprechaun gear was about five years and thirty pounds ago, so I had to get it altered to fit. I definitely didn't want to wear the nurse pants, and I wasn't about to go pay for new gear for a one-off gig, so I took my indie Swoggle pants with me and didn't put them on until ten minutes before I went out there. It was live TV and it's not like they could fire me if they didn't like it. As it happened, no one cared. The pants were green at least, so they went with the gimmick.

I was more worried about the splash. I hadn't been able to do it on indie shows for a while because I was just too big. Again, knowing that when I got out there, it was live and all on me, I didn't say anything to Michael Hayes when he asked for the splash, but I did find Dolph just before he went to the ring. I said that I was going to go to the top but when I got there, if I didn't think I could do the splash, I'd nod to him and he should cut me off. I told Kofi about this as well, since he was the person who I could potentially be killing with my splash if I did it. No one else knew.

When the buzzer went for the twelfth entrant into the match, my music hit, and I ran out from the back. I was totally blown away by the reaction I got because I was worried the crowd might not remember me or know who I was. I'm not saying it was a megastar level reaction, but it was definitely a healthy pop. My first job was to get Dash Wilder out of the ring. Backstage, I'd suggested to him that he could be up on the ropes attacking someone else and I could push him over the top to the floor. He was already wearing the boo-boo face because he was being eliminated by the midget, and his reply was "I don't do the ten-punch spot." I couldn't be bothered to argue with him, so we did it the way he wanted, where he was already mostly out of the ring and I pulled him the rest of the way. I thought his way made him look worse because he was already in trouble before I got there. At least my way, he would have been on the offense before I caught him unaware.

I did something with Kofi where I kicked him in the shin and hit a Samoan drop (that was supposed to be a Celtic Cross), then went to the top. As I climbed, I realized there was no way I was going to be able to nail the splash without killing my friend so I nodded to Dolph, who just stared blankly back at me. I nodded again, and he sprang into action, cutting me off with a superkick. Just like all those years ago on *SmackDown*, he missed by a mile although this was *all* my fault because I didn't lean into it properly. Fortunately, the camera angle masked it and it looked fine for TV. I slid down the ropes to the apron and bit Dolph's fingers, and Tony Nese, a great guy I've become friends with through Hawkins, eliminated me. Although, as Seth Rollins pointed out on Twitter later, I'm not sure I was eliminated. I never actually went over the top rope. I was supposed to, after I had done the splash, but once I realized *that* wasn't going to happen, I didn't think much about

the mechanics of being eliminated. If you want to justify the elimination, my foot went on the top rope, and my head leaned into the
ring. If you don't want to justify it, Braun Strowman, the eventual
winner, probably stepped over the ropes as he left, so *technically* I
won the match . . .

I was upset when I got to the back because I hadn't been able
to do my trademark spot. It was easy to ignore gaining back all the
weight when I'd been working indie shows but going out there on
a huge stage like that and being too heavy to do my splash really
brought it home to me. I went through the side curtain so I wouldn't
have to go through Gorilla. I had my head in my hands and I was
chewing myself out for being too fat. Hawkins must have known
that would be what I'd do, because he found me there and told me
to turn around, go into Gorilla, and thank everyone. I tried to beg
off for a couple of minutes to compose myself, but Hawkins told
me, "No, now."

The first person I saw was Michael Hayes, who said, "Hey kid,
what happened?" I told him I'd felt my knee wasn't good when I
was climbing the ropes, so I called an audible. He said, "That's fine,
it looked great." I thanked Hunter, who told me "great job," and
then I waited for Vince to be done talking on his headset to Kevin
Dunn. When he turned to me, I thanked him for involving me, and
Vince said, "You did great out there, thank you — it's good to see
you again." Everyone seemed more than happy with what I'd done,
but I was still angry at myself that I couldn't do everything asked
of me.

As I was flying back home, I realized I'd been the only person
they brought back for that show who hadn't been on TV in more
than a year. They could have called anyone, and they called me. That
felt pretty good and I really appreciated it. I don't kid myself that
I'm going to get another run though. You never say never in wrestling, but I don't think they'll use me in a proper spot again. If they
use me at all, it'll be as a now-and-then comedy spot. I've come to
terms with that, too. When they did the twenty-fifth anniversary

show for *Raw* and I wasn't brought in, I realized I really was done and the best run of my career was behind me. I wasn't sad, because I got to have a WWE run when so many don't, but it did leave me wondering, "Now what?"

I think I can do this at least until I'm thirty-five. After that, who knows? As long as there's still demand for me and for as long as I can go out there without making an idiot of myself, I'll keep going. I've always said I'll stop wrestling when I can't throw a ball around with my boy. When I was a kid, I never paid too much attention to the longer-term implications of dwarfism but, as I get older, I think about it more because I feel it more. All of those bumps over the years have started to catch up with me. My back and hips hurt, but that's a combination of my condition, the bumps, natural aging, and being overweight. And my knees don't hurt, but they get tired quickly and I have to rest more than I used to. Looking back though, I wouldn't change any of the bumps I took or trade in my frog splash for something less impactful on my joints.

In the last couple of years, I've also developed a fear of standing on the apron during tag matches. Whenever I'm working with Binder, he hits the ropes *hard* so if I happen to be standing on the side of the ring he runs into and I'm not paying attention, I'm going to get launched into the fifth row. I explicitly tell anyone I'm working with on the indie circuit to not physically attack me while I'm on the apron, explaining that the fall to the floor is a lot tougher for a guy of my stature than it is for them. If they want to cuss at me or spit on me, that's fine — just don't bump me to the floor.

It's not just the in-ring stuff that is difficult for me — people wouldn't think about it but flying is a lot more difficult for me than most. It takes me at least twice as long to walk around the airport, I have to ask someone to help me with bags in the overhead bins, and my knees lock up on the plane because I can't put my feet on the floor. If I can't rest my legs on the back of the chair in front, my knees hurt like hell by the time we touch down. Sitting in the exit row is the worst thing for me. Anywhere else is better.

Best friends, partners, champions. With Binder at ACW's *fifth year anniversary show in 2018.*

After I've stopped wrestling for good, maybe I'll get my real estate license or go back to college to become a chef. Not a lot of people know this, but cooking is probably my only passion other than wrestling, plus the short-order cook joke always works. Whatever I do when it's time to step away from the ring, I know I'll be able to look back and say I did my best as a wrestler and realized the biggest dreams I had as a kid.

CHAPTER 29

THE FAMILY

Working for WWE was amazing, but I knew my time there would end someday. As everyone at WWE told me, from the boys to management, "All of this won't last but your family will always be there for you." That's why your family should always be the priority. The reality is hard to see when you're just starting out and working to catch a break, but it's something you learn along the way.

And though Binder and Weimer might not be related to me, they're part of my family.

I would have understood it if Binder had been resentful because his midget friend got a chance to "live the dream" and he didn't, but he's been nothing but supportive. The truth is that because of my condition, I didn't have to be half as good as him to get noticed. And it's a shame he hasn't had more opportunities because he's so good, both in the ring and out of it. He has a great mind for the industry and has been incredible as the head trainer of our school. He almost quit

One of my favorite parts of local shows is being side by side with Landon at the merchandise table.

wrestling for good at the end of 2016 but I talked him into sticking around a while. We started tagging and doing more local shows and now he's working more regularly and enjoying it. It's great being on the road with him and funny to think that when we started out, we would work shows and then go out drinking. These days, when we work a show together, we'll be back in our hotel rooms by 10:15 p.m., in bed and calling home to check in. And it's awesome when we're able to bring our kids to shows. We both remember one specific ACW show where we hung back and watched our boys, Ayden and Landon, standing by the ring at intermission, selling merchandise. They do that regularly now whenever they're at shows with us, but that ACW show was the first time they did it, and it's was one of those moments neither of us will forget. Binder has since married his long-time girl-friend Jess and they have another kid, August (Auggie).

Weimer's a family man, too, now. He ended up marrying Kayla, Lori's daughter and Kim's cousin, and they have a daughter, Savannah. I knew he'd be a great dad because of how he's always been around Landon. Weimer *glows* whenever he's around his girl and works his butt off to do whatever he can for his family. He works his butt off for ACW as well, handling the funds, setting up meetings, and just generally getting every little thing done. We call ourselves the "suits" of ACW and he's definitely the business suit, whereas Binder is more like a tracksuit and I'm more of a Canadian tuxedo. If ever I need life advice from anyone, he's the first guy I go to. He's got an amazing mom-in-law, too. Lori's like a second mom to me — I talk to her most days and we have dinner at least every few weeks.

When I say Lori's like a second mom to me, I'm not putting her after my biological mom on that list — I'm putting her after Dorothy. Dorothy *is* my mom. She's been Mom from the moment she came in to my life. From day one, she never treated me any differently from how she treats her two biological sons, Tim and Ben. I never once felt there was any preferential treatment. Whenever I'd be up in my room, grounded, and Dad would be pacing around downstairs, frustrated, it was Dorothy who came to talk things out. She never took sides, and even when I was acting like a difficult teenager, she saw my potential and believed in me. She still plays go-between now — not that Dad's tried to ground me in a while. If he's concerned about or affected by something I'm doing, she'll wait until he's playing with Landon, then pull me aside and say, "Hey, your dad's worried about this, what's going on?"

Both of Dorothy's biological kids are my brothers. I started getting along better with Tim and Ben during my teens, and by the time I turned eighteen, I'd figured out they were actually really great human beings. They've both gone on to have families: Tim married Julia and they have a son, Ezra, with another on the way, while Ben married Laura and they have two kids, Averie and Elias. Of Dorothy's grandchildren, Landon was the first and the lack of a biological link doesn't mean anything. Landon knows I've got a "real mom" who I don't speak to but all he's ever known is that Dorothy is my mom and his nana. When he's with his grandparents, he'll go to Papa for the more action-based pursuits, like wrestling, Nerf guns, and throwing or shooting things up in the air. For everything else, he'll go to Nana, especially when he's not feeling well. He'll just go and sit by her and that'll give him the most comfort. She's amazing with him and I'm so lucky she's my mom.

Then there's Grandpa. The man who always believed in me, even when my dad (justifiably) had his concerns. The man who would drive to Minnesota for every one of my surgeries, every one of my doctor's appointments. He was always there for me. Apart from moving out of Dad's house without telling him, my biggest regret in life is that I got too busy to make time for Grandpa Postl. After Grandma died in 2002, he still had regular visits from Dad, his other son Keith, me, and, in time, Landon but once he moved into his apartment, I didn't visit as much as I should have, so he didn't see Landon much either. Before he moved, I saw him maybe three or four times a year and then around Christmas. But once he moved into the apartment, I saw him less and less. I justified it to myself by saying I was on the road so much, but I really wasn't that busy at all. I just didn't like seeing him as his health worsened with age. I could easily have dropped by once a month and brought Landon along. It would have made him so happy. Whenever I was on the road, Dad took Landon and Grandpa to the park to feed the ducks at least once a month. Grandpa was moved into a nursing home later in the year and by the time I visited him on

Christmas Eve 2015, his memory was fading fast. He kept looking at Landon and asking, "Who's this?" I found that so upsetting but Landon handled it amazingly well. He'd calmly reply, "My name is Landon," and then point at me and say, "I'm his son."

After that Christmas, I didn't visit Grandpa at all, not even when Dad told me he wasn't doing well. I was told that he still told everyone at the nursing home about me and what I was doing, so I didn't want to upset him by telling him about my WWE release. By the time I finally got around to visiting, it was Christmas 2016 and he wasn't in good shape. He was sitting in a chair with an oxygen tank, refusing his dentures because they didn't fit him anymore. He'd aged so much since I'd seen him just one year earlier. Every year since Landon was born, we'd taken four-generation photos of all the Postl men and this year in particular, there was as much deterioration in Grandpa as there was growth in Landon. It was heartbreaking to see. As I left the nursing home that Christmas, I decided that I was going to make it a priority to visit at least once a month.

On New Year's Day 2017, I was at a belated Christmas party when Dad called me. I took my phone into the bathroom, so I could hear him.

"I'm calling to let you know your Grandpa went down this morning, and he's not going to wake up."

I couldn't comprehend what Dad was saying and asked him what he meant.

"It could be days, weeks, or months, but he could go at any time."

Dad just doesn't cry. On this call, he did. That's when everything hit home. I told him I'd be right over.

The moment I got out of the bathroom, I broke down. Moments later, my son came cheerfully bounding around the corner only to see me squatting against the wall, crying uncontrollably.

"What's wrong, Dad?" said Landon, trying to comfort me by rubbing my back.

"It's Great-Grandpa," I told him. "He's very, very sick."

After I'd arranged for someone to look after Landon, I got myself together enough to drive and headed off to the nursing home. Five minutes later, my phone rang, and Dorothy's name came up on the screen. My eyes started welling up immediately. I knew what she was going to say.

"Grandpa just passed away," she told me. "I wanted to call because your dad is dealing with it right now." She was starting to cry, too. I was in tears for the rest of that journey. When I got to the nursing home, I composed myself before going in. The lady at the front desk directed me down the hallway to a room where Grandpa's ninety-three-year-old body was still on the bed. I walked straight over to my dad, buried my head in his side, and we both cried together.

I found the funeral even harder to cope with. As soon as I saw Grandpa in his casket, it hit me that this would be the last time I would ever see him. Despite the grief, there was some laughter as Dad and I had, entirely coincidentally, worn the exact same shirt and everyone commented on it. As the viewing was finishing, I was standing by the casket when Landon wandered over. We stood there side by side, just looking at Grandpa one last time. It was a very emotional moment. Suddenly, Landon broke the silence.

"When people die, do they cut their legs off?," he asked.

It took me a moment to understand why he'd ask that. Then I got it. "No, they're under the closed part of the casket," I told him.

"Oh." He thought about that for a moment, then continued, "So, he gets to keep his legs?"

I couldn't stop myself from laughing. I laughed, and I cried, and I didn't know which was which. We went to say a prayer for Grandpa in the next room and, all the while, I was still laughing and crying. As more people came in to pray, it was everything I could do to stifle my laughter.

Grandpa would have found it funny, too. He was my number-one supporter in everything I did, and the only real grandfather I ever had. He was so amazing that I never felt like I needed another one. Coming to terms with his death was the hardest thing I've ever done.

One of my most personal tattoos is the "4Gs" I have on my wrist, which stands for four generations of Postl men. Around the outside, I now have a tattoo of Grandpa's ever-present black coffee mug, as well as the letters F, E, D, and L, for Forrest, Eric, Dylan, and Landon.

If I was close to *my* grandpa, Landon is even closer with his. Dad couldn't be a better grandpa. And their relationship is beautiful. They usually see each other at least once a week. Dad is Landon's escape — there've been a couple of times where Landon has got mad at me, grabbed his coat, put his shoes on, and said, "I'm leaving. I'm walking to Papa's." I'll watch him from my front window as he walks down the block and across the road, then he'll stop and kick at the ground awhile, walk back, come in the side door, say, "I'm not talking to you," and head for his room. I'll say "Okay, I love you, bud," and he'll yell, "I *don't* mean that back!" He'll come out later and apologize once he's calmed down. I don't need the apology, because knowing that he feels he can turn to Papa is enough for me.

Throughout my life, Dad's always been there for me. I was definitely a difficult teenager. I didn't care about school, I moved out before I was ready, I quit college for a career in wrestling, I had a child while I was so young, and I had no stability in my life. Despite my awful attitude and questionable decisions, Dad never stopped supporting me. Even now, he still makes sure I'm paying my bills and my taxes. He shows up at my house to help with the gardening or to shovel snow. He's always at the other end of the phone whenever I have a problem with my car or something breaks at my house. I honestly don't know what I'd do without him.

Not one person in Oshkosh has ever had a bad thing to say about my dad. Dad's the kind of guy who would agree to work late so he could build up more vacation time at the end of the year to take Dorothy on motorcycle trips. Now that their knees are making it more difficult to ride motorcycles, Dad has "spent his grandkids' inheritance" on a Mustang. After the way Dad and Dorothy raised their children, they deserve everything they could ever want from a long, happy retirement and I want them to have that.

Having my own child has only multiplied the amount of respect I have for him. My main ambition in life is to be the father to Landon that my dad was to me. As far as I'm concerned, he's the greatest human being on the planet.

Everyone says their children change them for the better and I'm no exception. Every day, my son is teaching me something. I sincerely don't believe anyone on this planet has a stronger father-son bond than Landon and me. We seem to know what the other is thinking and feeling at all times, even when we try to disguise it. He is the nicest, most well-behaved child I know (to other people, at least!). I hear so often how respectful he is and that he's great a listener. He never holds a grudge. If something upsets him and you bring it up the next day, he'll say, "That was yesterday; this is today." The best moments in my life are always when it's just the two of us together. Those moments are filled with constant laughter.

As he's gotten older, he's realized more and more than I'm not built quite the same way as most other dads but my stature's all he's ever known. Whenever he is at the playground and another kid notices me and comments on my height, Landon will just casually reply, "Yeah, he's small, but that's my dad."

He's also grown up knowing that Dad has to go away for work and never shows any resentment about it but if he ever told me he was upset because I was leaving him to go wrestle, I'd quit in a heartbeat. He knows I love what I do. I just hope he knows that all the traveling I've done and all of the things I've missed in his life, including his first steps and first words, have been so he can have a better life.

In 2017, I got to surprise Landon with a trip. I got back from a show in the morning, rushed home to collect the bags I'd packed for us both before I'd left, and drove to Landon's school at lunch hour. I told him that I had to fly to Florida and his mom was going to drop me off at the airport, then asked if he wanted to come along for the ride. When we got to the car, he looked in the back and saw the MagicBands. "Dad, are we going to Disney World?" When I told him that I wasn't really going to work, he said, "This is the greatest day ever. You don't have to go to work, I get out of school, and we're going to Disney World." The whole trip was the perfect vacation. We got the VIP treatment at Disney and each day, at some point and out of nowhere, Landon would just say, "Dad, thank you for this." I texted my dad to tell him about that and he replied, "You're doing all right, kid."

The first thing I do whenever I go to a Disney park is get a picture in front of the castle. When I arranged this trip, I figured it would be the last time I'd get a Disney photo with Landon where I was taller than him, but he had a growth spurt right before we went and he's clearly taller than me in the picture. He's not just growing up physically either. My favorite part of that whole vacation was right as we were leaving Disney World, Landon noticed a piece of garbage on the ground. He went out of his way to go over, pick it up, and put it in the trash. One of the park employees saw that, came over to thank him for being so thoughtful, and offered him a choice of free ice cream bars or two fast passes to any rides in the park. He chose the ice creams, but the employee gave him the passes as well. After we'd finished our ice creams, he looked at me and said, "Dad, I think we should give these passes to someone else." He told me he'd had a great day and he was ready to leave, so we picked out a mom and daughter and Landon made their day by giving them those passes. That's just the sort of great kid he is.

He glows whenever he watches me wrestle and, right now, he wants to follow in my footsteps. He practices at home every day and even comes to our training school to practice in the ring. I would never push him into anything and I will support him in whatever he chooses to do with his life, but if he decides to go into wrestling, I'll be on cloud nine. As far as I know, that would make me the first midget to produce a second-generation wrestler. Whatever he does though, I know he'll make me proud. He already does, every day.

To him, I'm not Hornswoggle, or Swoggle, or Shortstack. I'm just Dad.

That's part of who I am for sure, a huge part now. Just like everyone, I'm a lot of things to a lot of different people. I'm a dad, a son, a brother. I'm a promoter, a wrestler, and, yes, a midget. I've had huge ups and downs. I've had some amazing opportunities, but I've had my share of heartache, too. I've had professional and personal disappointments, I've loved and lost, I've been lied to, let down, and betrayed — just like any normal-sized person. Things don't always work out the way you hope, and sometimes life doesn't seem fair — I could have spent my whole life pissing and moaning about the fact that I was born different than most people. But I didn't let those circumstances determine how I was going to live my life and I didn't let them determine the level of my happiness. Accepting and embracing who I am gave me the chance to live my childhood dream and do so many things I can look back at and smile about.

I choose to make my own happiness each day because life is short — and so am I.

ACKNOWLEDGMENTS

Dylan, Ross and Ian would like to thank Michael Holmes, Jen Albert, Jessica Albert, Susannah Ames, Aymen Saidane, David Caron, and everyone else within ECW Press for making this book a reality, as well as Connor Eck of Lucinda Literary for bringing everyone in this project together and WWE for the usage of several photographs.

Dylan Postl is a promoter and wrestler who spent a decade working for WWE. He currently wrestles for a number of independent promotions worldwide and runs the Wisconsin-based company All-Star Championship Wrestling. He lives in Oshkosh, Wisconsin.

Ross Owen Williams is a business consultant, actor, and writer whose work includes multi-award-winning feature film *Winter Ridge* and books *The Hardcore Truth: The Bob Holly Story* and *Self Help: Life Lessons from the Bizarre Wrestling Career of Al Snow*. Ross lives in Somerset, England